Praise for the French edition
Irène Némirovsky: Biographie

"Weiss's historically rigorous and deftly woven account of the author's complexities is an equally timely contribution to the public's understanding of her life and writings. The biography illuminates most poignantly the drama of Némirovsky's final work."
　　　　—*The Bulletin for Holocaust Studies*

"How is it that this author [Irène Némirovsky], a Ukrainian Jew, deported to Auschwitz in 1942, never to return, has been unrecognized for so long? The biography of the American professor Jonathan Weiss gives us some keys to explain this literary lapse."
　　　　—*Marianne* (weekly newsmagazine, France)

"This biography, extremely well documented, will allow you to discover the world of Jewish Russian émigrés in the period between World War I and World War II."
　　　　—*Horizon étudiant* (France)

"A clear and intelligent work that also brings to light the author's internal contradictions about her Jewishness."
　　　　—*Psychologies Magazine* (France)

"A meticulous biography, neither indulgent nor acrimonious."
　　　　—*France Soir* (Paris)

"Without indulgence, Jonathan Weiss paints a finely-shaded portrait based on [the author's] life and works along with major first-hand documents."
　　　　—*24 Heures* (Lausanne, Switzerland)

"Jonathan Weiss consulted the writer's archives . . . her unpublished correspondence as well as the press of the 1930s and 1940s, and he met some people who had known her. His perceptiveness leads him to unearth in Némirovsky's work (more than 15 novels and 30 short stories) aspects of her life that do not appear elsewhere."
　　　　—*Le Temps* (Lausanne, Switzerland)

"Jonathan Weiss gives us a penetrating, finely-shaded portrait of a particularly complex personality."
　　　　—*La Libre Belgique*

Irène Némirovsky

Her Life and Works

Jonathan Weiss

Stanford University Press

Stanford, California 2007

Stanford University Press
Stanford, California

Irène Némirovsky: Her Life and Works was originally published in French in 2005 under the title *Irène Némirovsky*, © Éditions du Félin, 2005.

Printed in the United States of America on acid-free, archival-quality paper

Library of Congress Cataloging-in-Publication Data

Weiss, Jonathan M.

[Irène Némirovsky. English]

Irène Némirovsky : her life and works / Jonathan Weiss.

p. cm.

Includes bibliographical references.

ISBN-13: 978-0-8047-5481-1 (cloth : alk. paper)

1. Némirovsky, Irène, 1903-1942. 2. Authors, French—20th century—Biography. 3. Jewish authors—France—Biography. 4. Authors, Russian—20th century—Biography. 5. Antisemitism—France. I. Title.

PQ2627.E4Z9513 2007

843'.912—dc22

[B]

2006017052

Photographs courtesy of Denise Epstein
Designed by Bruce Lundquist
Typeset at Stanford University Press in 11/15 Bell MT

Contents

Acknowledgments

First and foremost, I owe the English translation of this book to my wife Dace, whose precision and clarity made for a seamless transition from the French original to this version.

Special thanks are due to my editor at Stanford University Press, Norris Pope, who believed in this book from the beginning, and to Judith Hibbard, who saw the manuscript through to publication; to my agent, Eric Myers, for his help and encouragement; and to the following people in France who read and commented on my manuscript: Jean Marie Goulemot, Régis Meney, Pierre Samson, Jacques Bonnet, Jean-Louis Jacques, Monique Nemer, Bruno Curatolo, and Bernard Condominas.

The research that went into this book would have been impossible without the wisdom and help of Olivier Corpet of the Institut Mémoire de l'Édition Contemporaine. Gratitude also goes to my son Gabriel, for his research at the Bibliothèque Nationale de France, and to Blandine Bricka, who also lent a hand. Numerous other people, in France and in the United States, helped in a variety of ways: Marinette Lacombre, Yvonne Comesse, M. and Mme Jean Laudet, Natacha Duché, Iulia Komska, Cristina Jaleru, Eva Sartori, and Yves Desrichard.

Finally, I would not have been able to write this book without the generosity of Irène Némirovsky's two daughters. Élisabeth Gille encouraged and helped me before her untimely death in 1996. Denise Epstein opened her files and photo albums to me, and spent hours telling me about her mother and father. I hope that this book contributes to the tireless efforts of these two women to keep alive the memory of their mother and of all victims of Nazi barbarism . . .

J.W.
Sidney, Maine
June 2006

Preface to the English Edition

Irène Némirovsky was virtually unknown in the English-speaking world until the spring of 2006, when her posthumous novel, *Suite française*, appeared in an English version. A prolific French author of seventeen novels and dozens of short stories, Némirovsky was already known in Germany, Italy, Spain, and Scandinavia, where much of her work had been translated during her lifetime. Only two of her novels had been translated into English, however. The most popular of these, *David Golder*, was published in New York in 1930, shortly after it appeared in Paris. The novel was hailed as "a stirring and powerful piece of work," and its young (27-year-old) author as "a woman who has the strength of one of the masters like Balzac or Dostoievsky."[1] The film version of this novel did not fare so well in the United States; Julien Duvivier's first sound film was criticized for having poor studio acoustics and generally poor acting.[2] A second novel was translated into English in 1937 under the title *A Modern Jezabel*. Hailed as a "brilliantly sophisticated novel," it nonetheless met with less critical enthusiasm than *David Golder*.[3] In 1940, the *New York Times*'s Paris correspondent reported on Némirovsky's novel *Les Chiens et les loups*, which had just appeared. Although the article hailed Némirovsky's skill in creating "a vividness in the descriptions and an intensity of emotion, which impart to the story great force and appeal,"[4] the novel was never translated into English. From 1937 until 2006 (with the exception of a biography of Anton Chekhov, translated in 1950), no works by Irène Némirovsky have appeared in English.

Némirovsky's fate as a writer in her adopted France was, as *Le Monde* characterized it in 1992, that of a "comet."[5] One of France's most popular novelists and short story writers of the 1930s, her works virtually disappeared from view after World War II. Some of them were re-published in Paris in the 1980s; her youngest daughter wrote an imagined biography in 1992; and a collection of her short stories was released in 2000. But until the appearance of *Suite française*, Némirovsky was usually included with authors such as Raymond Guérin, Emmanuel Bove, or Henri Calet—writers who had achieved a certain celebrity between the world wars but were now read only by scholars intent on their revival.[6]

In the summer of 2004, Irène Némirovsky's only surviving daughter, Denise Epstein, was persuaded to give a French publisher the manuscript of the novel her mother was writing at the time of her deportation. Using a first-generation word processor, Epstein had lovingly transcribed her mother's tiny handwriting. She had resisted trying to have the manuscript published, partly because its very existence reminded her of the painful loss of her parents and partly because her mother had neither finished the five-volume work nor had she been able to revise and edit it.

Suite française appeared in October 2004. It was an immediate sensation at the Frankfurt Book Fair of that month; within a few days, the translation rights were sold in more than twenty languages, and Random House bought the English language rights for an undisclosed sum. By December, more than 260,000 copies of Némirovsky's novel had been sold in France, and it stayed on the bestseller list into the next spring. In a gesture that was controversial and without precedent, Irène Némirovsky was awarded the prestigious Renaudot prize posthumously. But even those who believed that literary prizes should encourage living authors rather than make up for past wrongs recognized the incisiveness of Némirovsky's portrayal of France on the brink of collapse and the humanity of her depiction of life during the occupation.

Random House had projected publication of the English translation of *Suite française* for September 2006, but the translator, Sandra Smith, had her work ready for the press six months early. The book first appeared in London in March and in New York in April. It earned immediate praise and climbed almost instantly onto the best-seller lists (reaching number four on the London *Times* list, twelve on the *Washington Post* list, and number one on the *Toronto Globe and Mail* list). What impressed English speaking readers was what had fascinated the French: this is, as the critic of the *New York Times* wrote, "the first work of fiction about what we now call World War II."[7] For the first time, an author writes about the defeat of France and the German occupation from the inside, as an observer in a small French town. "In Némirovsky's *Suite Française* we have the perfect mixture: a gifted novelist's account of a foreign occupation, written while it was taking place, with history and imagination jointly evoking a bitter time, correcting and enriching our memory," wrote the reviewer of the *Washington Post*.[8]

The fact that the author of *Suite française* was deported to Auschwitz gave the book an Anne Frank type of urgency.[9] "It is . . . tempting to ask what the fate of *Suite française* might have been had Némirovsky died a natural death during the war," asked Alice Kaplan in *The Nation*. "Would her daughter have found a publisher in 2004? How would *Suite française* have been received without the tragic backstory?"[10] Undoubtedly Irène Némirovsky's arrest by the French police put her novel into a polemical context that she could never have predicted. "Némirovsky's magnum opus is almost certainly more acceptable now, two generations down the line, than it would have been had she been trying to place her finished book in the Fifties," wrote Jane Stevenson in *The Observer.* "The postwar French preferred to remember that they had barely tolerated the Vichy government and had resisted the Germans. Némirovsky saw something different."[11] What Némirovsky saw was the behavior of the French during the occupation, and it is her description of individuals of many socioeconomic levels and political loyalties that is so compelling today. What she shows us is a country in which fear and the desire for self-preservation take precedence over patriotism or the will to resist oppression. Unwittingly, Némirovsky has entered the debate about France's reaction to its June 1940 defeat. But beyond this historical controversy, Némirovsky's novel can be seen as a metaphor for France's current problems. In a country still beset by anti-Semitism and racism, where the question of national identity is still debated, *Suite française* reminds people of how easily the values of the republic can be lost.[12]

Irène Némirovsky began to fascinate me in the mid 1990s. At the time, her two daughters, Denise (the eldest) and Élisabeth, were alive; Élisabeth has since passed on. These two women had just given all of what remained of their mother's papers (notes, drafts, letters) to the Institut Mémoire de l'Édition Contemporaine (IMEC), a repository for the archives of a great many French writers. Albin Michel, Némirovsky's publisher after 1936, had kept all their correspondence. Élisabeth, who was six years old when her mother was killed, had few memories, but Denise, who was thirteen, recalled a great deal.

My research took me to the IMEC, to Albin Michel, to the Bibliothèque Nationale de France, and to Denise's apartment. One day, Denise and I borrowed a small photocopier and made copies of her mother's personal documents that were not in the IMEC archives. Denise let me look through her photo albums, which had miraculously survived the war. A letter written to Élisabeth put me on the track of an elderly lady who knew Irène in her youth, but most of Irène's contemporaries had long since passed away. I had few of the kind of documents that allow a biographer to give a depth and richness to the account of someone's life.

Irène Némirovsky was above all an author, and I decided to emphasize her literary work in my account of her life. Denise had unearthed and transcribed numerous short stories that her mother had written under pseudonyms. More remained to be discovered, however, as I learned when my son, doing research for me at the Bibliothèque Nationale, came across a short novel that neither Denise nor I had heard of, but that was very definitely written by her mother. As I read through Némirovsky's considerable work, patterns emerged that would later explain various episodes in her life. In the absence of intimate, personal correspondence or notes, it was the fiction itself and the author's notebooks that gave me insights into the ambiguities that characterized her public persona. Now that *Suite française* has brought Irène Némirovsky back into the literary limelight that was hers in the 1930s, it is entirely possible that personal correspondence and other documentation will be unearthed and that this documentation will allow us to see more clearly what Irène was like in her private life.

A Brief Note on *Suite française*

The manuscript is remarkable, as is the popularity this book has enjoyed in and outside France. The first part of the manuscript—that which details the effect of France's defeat in June 1940 and is titled *Storm in*

June—is in two versions. The first of these was written longhand by the author herself, in very tiny handwriting (ink was a scarce commodity, as was paper). The second was typewritten, very likely by Irène's husband Michel. It contains major differences from the first; some chapters are eliminated, some are entirely rewritten. There are handwritten corrections in the margins, in both Irène's and her husband's handwriting. When Denoël decided to publish *Suite française*, it used, on the advice of Némirovsky's daughter Denise Epstein, the first manuscript; despite mistakes and inconsistencies, Denise believed that this manuscript better reflected her mother's intent than the second. In this book, I quote both from the published version (in the Sandra Smith translation) and (briefly) from the manuscripts that were not published.

Suite française would have been, in its final form, one of the most important works of literature produced in twentieth-century France. Critics in both France and the English-speaking world have remarked on the resemblances of this work to that of Russian authors (Turgenev and Tolstoy) and of French authors, particularly Flaubert (for the author's cold lucidity) and Balzac (for the precision of her descriptions a wide variety of characters).[13]

Némirovsky's original concept for the structure of the five projected volumes—a musical framework, loosely based on Bach's "French Suites"—has also come in for praise;[14] the author herself (in notes attached to the manuscript) called the work a symphony and was particularly preoccupied with issues of rhythm. The care that Némirovsky took in composing *Suite française* allowed her to escape, briefly, the anguish and hardship of her existence in occupied France. This is no memoir; it is self-consciously a work of fiction. In this respect, it is one of the works that least reveals the author's life and thoughts. There are no Jews in the novel, and yet Jews were a subject Némirovsky wrote about frequently. There are no Russians in the novel, indeed, there are none of the immigrants and misfits who populate many of her other novels and short stories. If Némirovsky is to finally take her place among the pantheon of French fiction writers of the 20th century, it is important that she be recognized in all her complexity as a French-Jewish-Russian author with deep-seated ambiguities. This is the purpose of the biographical study that follows.

Irène Némirovsky

Introduction

On Monday, July 13, 1942, two French gendarmes knocked on the front door of a large stone house in the little Burgundy village of Issy-L'Évêque, nestled in the hills of the Morvan. The house had been recently rented by a family from Paris. Like many villages, Issy-L'Évêque had become a refuge for Parisians fleeing the city. It was easy to get food here and to live relatively well on homegrown vegetables, eggs, and chickens. When it got cold, as it often did on the Morvan plateau, wood was readily available for the stove. But Issy-L'Évêque, though close to the "free" (Vichy) zone, was in occupied territory. A contingent of German soldiers had been stationed there and had recently left, called to battle on the Eastern Front.

The large house was near the middle of the village, just opposite the monument to the war dead erected after the Great War of 1914–1918. In July 1942, it had been rented to a family of refugees from Paris, the Epsteins. Everyone in Issy-L'Évêque knew them. Michel Epstein was a former banker who had left his position in Paris for health reasons; he was gregarious and spent hours chatting with neighbors at the *bureau de tabac.* His knowledge of German had enabled him to help translate for the Wehrmacht troops when they had been billeted in the village. His two daughters, Denise and Élisabeth, were at the village school. A local woman, Cécile Michaud, was employed as their governess.

Michel Epstein's wife was called Irène, and most people knew her by the name Irène Némirovsky. She was a highly successful novelist and short story writer who had chosen to keep her maiden name for her literary work. Two of her novels had been made into films and her stories appeared often in the popular weekly newspaper *Gringoire*. Irène was less sociable than her husband. When she left the house out it was usually to visit the local priest or to climb up into the woods close to town with her note pad and, occasionally, her two daughters in tow.

Everybody in Issy-L'Évêque had seen the Epsteins at Sunday mass and had noticed Denise's white gown when she had her first communion. Yet they knew that this family was different from most of the inhabitants of the village, and they were not surprised when Michel and Irène appeared, in May 1942, with a yellow Star of David sewn to their clothes. It was not as though the Epsteins wanted to keep their origins a secret. People knew through their governess that Michel and Irène had been born in Russia and that they had applied for French citizenship. Everyone in the village who had read Irène's most popular novel, *David Golder*, or who had seen the movie, knew that she had an insider's view of the community of Jewish businessmen in Paris. The Epsteins were not hiding; they were simply trying to survive in a country at war.

The gendarmes who came to the big house on the Route de Grury on that July day were looking for Irène, not Michel or the children. They politely asked her to come with them; she prepared a little suitcase with some clothes, toiletries, and a book. The manuscript of the novel she was working on, an epic of the war and occupation, remained behind her; it would stay hidden for more than half a century before being published and hailed as a masterpiece.[1] She kissed her husband goodbye; she was certain she would be home again soon. The gendarmes took Irène to the police station and from there to the village of Toulon sur Arroux, about thirteen kilometers from Issy-L'Évêque.

Three days later, on Thursday, July 16, Irène was sent to a detention camp at Pithiviers, in the department of the Loiret, north of Orléans. A day later—on Friday, July 17, in the early morning hours—she was awakened and told to get dressed and packed. Along with 118 other women and 809 men, she was herded into a waiting train. For two days this train traversed France, Germany, and Poland. Its prisoners had no water, no food, and no toilets. The heat was stifling.

On July 19, 1942, Irène and the others arrived at Auschwitz concentration camp in Poland. She passed her first inspection and was assigned to a barracks. For almost a month she managed to survive in almost unimaginable conditions. But in mid-August an epidemic of typhus raged through the camp. Irène, who drank the polluted water like everyone else, fell ill. On August 19, 1942, she died.

More than sixty years after Irène Némirovsky's death, it is tempting to see her as a martyr, and surely she was that. The country she loved, and whose literature she so enriched, arrested her and gave her over to the enemies of humanity. Tragically, she never attained in her lifetime the status she has been awarded posthumously, that of one of the twentieth century's most important French authors.

Yet, when the life and work of Irène Némirovsky are closely examined, the results are troubling, even disconcerting. When one looks for consistency, one finds contradictions.

Irène was born in Kiev and emigrated to France in 1919, when she was sixteen years old. Yet she had little to do with Russian émigré circles and never wrote in Russian. Although she was Jewish, her friends and acquaintances were often on the political right, even on the extreme right, at a time when virulent anti-Semitism was the bread and butter of these circles. She could count as friends anti-Semites such as the writers Paul Morand and Jacques Chardonne, or political figures such as Jacques Benoist-Méchin and Joseph Caillaux. She often published her works (which include more than a dozen novels and more than thirty short stories) in reviews and weeklies that also published vitriolic articles against Jews.

Even more troubling than Irène's choice of friends and colleagues were the caricatures of Jews she inserted into some of her novels and short stories. At times, these caricatures seem almost to mirror those that we can find in the right-wing publications where her work appeared. How can we explain the harsh cruelty of these portraits?

And how can we explain the fact that Irène Némirovsky, along with her husband and children, was baptized in the Catholic faith in 1938, at the very time that she seemed to have made her peace with the Jewish people and had written some of her most sympathetic portraits of Jews? Was this conversion the result of profound religious conviction or was it a futile effort to avoid racial and religious persecution? What was Irène's relationship to the Jewish people?

We find ourselves faced with an enigma: who was Irène Némirovsky?

A French author? She wrote in French, and her name is engraved on the Pantheon in Paris, but she was never able to acquire French nationality, in spite of a request made in 1938. A Russian author? She certainly spoke and read Russian, and she is the author of a biography of Chekhov, but she never wrote in the language of her country of origin.

Was Irène Némirovsky a Jewish writer? This is the most problematic aspect of her work. Her first major novel was about a Jewish businessman and it earned her a reputation as a Jewish writer. But certain aspects of her portrayal of Jews offended the Jewish community in Paris. For Léon Poliakov, the French historian of anti-Semitism, Irène Némirovsky was simply an anti-Semite.[2] But the situation is more complex. Her attitude toward Judaism is at once critical and sympathetic. During the nightmare of the occupation, she never denied that she belonged to the Jewish people. Baptized as a Catholic, perhaps even believing in Christianity, Irène nonetheless died as a Jew.

To properly grasp the multifaceted persona of this author, it would be tempting to delve closely into her life. But a biography of Irène Némirovsky, in the strict sense of the term, comes up against an understandable—though tragic—lack of pertinent documentation. The Nazi occupation of France, Irène's arrest, the fate of her husband (who was also deported to Auschwitz), as well as that of her children (who were hidden from the Nazis)—all these factors combined mean that most of the private documents that allow the historian to give shape and color to a life have been forever lost. The family's Paris apartment, abandoned of necessity in 1940, was ransacked and its contents stolen or destroyed. A childhood friend kept some personal letters; the children carefully preserved, even in their flight from the Nazis, family photos, several notebooks, and the unedited manuscript of *Suite française*. That, and the memories of Irène's eldest daughter (who was thirteen years old when her mother was deported), is all that remains.

We nevertheless have inherited the wealth of the literary work of Irène Némirovsky, and it is here that one can search for keys to the puzzle that is her life. From the first of her works—her severe depiction of Jewish life in Czarist Russia—to the texts penned just before her deportation, we see a woman caught in all her ambiguity, rejecting her past and then assuming it, admiring a France she seemed to believe eternal and then conscious that it was losing its soul. By studying the way in which her works inform the choices she made in her life, we can attempt to make sense of her faith in her adopted country and its people, even as this country, and many of her friends, abandoned her.

If our approach to Irène Némirovsky is critical and if we pose the questions that her daughter, Élisabeth Gille, dared not ask in her loosely imagined biography *Le Mirador*,[3] it is not because we wish to sully the memory, dear to so many, of this courageous woman who made a career as a writer while remaining a devoted mother and who did her best to protect her offspring from the barbarism looming over France. It is essential that Irène's tragic end not eclipse her multifaceted life. For Irène Némirovsky to be recognized as an important figure in twentieth-century French letters, we must first clear the air that surrounds her. Our study of her life and work will reveal a complex individual, torn by a desire to escape the materialism of her parents' Jewish circles but sympathetic to the fate of her people, enamored of France and its culture yet conscious of her own Slavic background. In short, Irène Némirovsky was an author in search of an identity.

1   *From Kiev to Paris*

To understand the intricacy and contradictions in the life of Irène Némirovsky, we must first understand her past. This is not an easy task. Irène left behind very little biographical data: no passport or other official document prior to her immigration to France; no auto-biography; just a few scant photos taken in Russia before the family's departure. Rarely forthcoming with regard to her Russian origins, she did, after the success of her third novel in 1930, consent to speak freely to the chronicler of *Nouvelles littéraires*, Frédéric Lefèvre. She granted him an interview in which she traced the steps that brought her from her native Russia to France. But of her childhood before the flight from Russia she revealed little.

Despite the dearth of any precise information, we can reconstruct the general atmosphere in which Irène spent her early childhood. The context is that of the upper middle-class Jewish community in Kiev which, before the Russian revolution, moved in imperial governmental circles. This context goes a long way to explain her linguistic, cultural, and ethnic affinities.

She was born in Kiev to Léon and Fanny (Margoulis) Némirovsky on February 24, 1903.[1] The registry of the inhabitants of Kiev in 1909[2] lists several Nemirovskys, including Léon and Boris (Léon's father). Boris Solomonovitch is identified as a businessman, living at 9 Niko-laievskaya Street.[3] This is the Ginsburg House, a sumptuous villa in the classic Italianate style; it still exists today. As for Léon Borisovitch, the registry identifies his address as 11 Pushkin Street. This house also still exists. Three stories high, it boasts an arched entryway headed by an

escutcheon and flanked by two lions. It is a spacious house, richly ap-
pointed and comfortable. Like the Ginsburg house it is situated in the
upper city, above the poorer neighborhoods, in a street bordered by linden trees. It is in this house that Irène Némirovsky was raised.

Of her mother we know very little. We can only infer from Irène's
writings and from the anecdotes of her granddaughters that Fanny
Némirovsky was a beautiful but vain woman who happily spent her
husband's money and enjoyed the company of slick Latin-American men.
Although Irène never characterized her novels as strictly autobiographical, the mother-figures in the works containing some biographical value
(such as *Le Vin de solitude* [The Wine of Solitude], which describes a
young girl in a family in Kiev that closely resembles Irène's family) are
repulsively selfish individuals who have no love or even sympathy for
their offspring. Irène's daughter Élisabeth recounts that Irène's mother
slammed the door in the face of her granddaughters when, orphaned after
the war, they sought refuge with her.[4] We know that, after her father's
death in 1932, Irène became increasingly estranged from her mother.
Fanny Némirovsky seems largely irrelevant to Irène's youth.

On the other hand, Irène took great pleasure in talking about her
father. He was, she says proudly, "an important Russian banker." Business often called him to Moscow where he had "a *pied à terre*, lodgings
that he sub-let, furnished, from an officer of the guard who had been
posted to London."[5] This relationship with an officer of the imperial
guard is one of the indicators of the privileges the Némirovsky family
enjoyed. There are others. In 1913, the Némirovskys won the right to
move to Saint-Petersburg (later Petrograd), a city that, like other cen-
ters in the empire, only permitted admission to a small number of Jews
(approximately three percent of the population at the beginning of the
century). Important Jewish financiers such as the banker Ginsburg or
the railway magnate Polyakov lived here, alongside assimilated (and
sometimes converted) artists such as the painter Isaac Levitan or the
musician Anton Rubinstein.[6]

In a country where the majority of the population never traveled,
and where it was necessary to obtain a passport for any trip outside the
city in which one lived, the Némirovsky family enjoyed the privilege
of taking vacations far from Kiev. "During my childhood," stated Irène,

"we sometimes went to the seaside in the Crimea; at that time there was no train linking Simferopol and Yalta, our Nice. It was a twelve-hour trip by horse-drawn carriage, and we slept over at Simferopol." The Némirovskys seem to have easily obtained visas for travel abroad, even in foreign countries; they regularly spent vacations in France, notably on the Côte d'Azur.

In every respect the Némirovsky family lived an exceptional life. Although Jewish, the family's social position brought them much closer to Orthodox Christian high society than to the Jewish commercial classes. Léon's world of business was far from the small artisanry and commercial shops and pushcarts of the majority of Russian Jews. His closeness to the economic system of the Russian Empire put him clearly on the side of those Russians who hated Bolshevism and often blamed the Jews for fomenting the Revolution. Finally, the family's linguistic situation was typical of the highest strata of Russian society, for French was spoken at home almost exclusively. For Irène, French would become her linguistic home; if it was not strictly speaking her mother tongue, it would become the language of her cultural identity.

An Uneasy Jewishness

Long after having left Russia, Irène looked back on her native city of Kiev and the position of Jews there: "The Ukrainian city ... was, in the eyes of the Jews living there, formed of three distinct regions, as one sees in old pictures: the damned down below caught between the shades and flames of Hades; mortals in the center, illuminated by a pale and tranquil light; and up above, the realm of the chosen."[7] The upper regions of this Dantesque portrait were those of Irène's family:

At the summit of these hills festooned with linden trees, one found, between the homes of high Russian civil servants and those of Polish nobles, several beautiful residences belonging to rich Jews. They had chosen this neighborhood because of its pure air to breathe, but also because in Russia at the beginning of this century under the reign of Nicholas II, Jews were only tolerated in certain areas, in certain districts, in certain streets, and even sometimes on only one side of a street, while the opposite would be forbidden to them.[8]

The "chosen" Némirovskys lived in the neighborhood that was reserved for them but that bordered Christian communities and kept them quite separate from the majority of other Jews in the city.

Were Irène's parents practicing Jews?[9] Nothing would lead us to believe this, even if in her works Irène displays a certain familiarity with the rituals and customs of Judaism. The Jewish middle class sought to dissociate itself from the more observant, poorer Jews of the lower quarters. Thus, notes Irène, "[Jewish] traditions were really too complex and too primitive to be followed strictly; one picked and one chose. One fasted one day a year, and for Passover one ate unleavened bread along with standard Russian bread, which, naturally, was a great sin."[10]

From her perch high in the city, Irène observed the Jews of the *podol*, the neighborhood on the banks of the river Dnieper, with its narrow streets, small shops, and modest homes.[11] She found this community of small shopkeepers strange and, in all, repugnant. "A group of people with children who rolled in the mud, who spoke only Yiddish, who wore tattered shirts and enormous caps on narrow necks with long black forelocks,"[12] she wrote. Is it class superiority that led her to say these children "were . . . like swarming vermin," and that their parents were "garrulous and obsequious"?[13] More likely, Irène—like most of the assimilated Jews of Kiev[14]—wanted to set herself apart from other Jews by adopting wholeheartedly the culture and even the prejudices of the country in which she was born. Social acceptability and religious observance could not coexist.

But Irène's attitude implies more than social class. Judaism, in her view, is not only inimical to life in the beautiful neighborhoods of Kiev, it is detrimental to literary creation. To become an author, Irène would try to put a distance between herself and her Jewish heritage. Nothing reveals this attitude more clearly than a novella she wrote when she was twenty years old—in 1923—and that was published in 1928. It is a work that encapsulates in a parable all the anguish of a writer whose Jewish heritage condemns him to live in a milieu hostile to artistic endeavor.

L'Énfant genial[15] (The Brilliant Child) is the story of a Jewish poet, Ismaël Baruch, born in a "large commercial, coastal city in the south of Russia on the banks of the Black Sea"—without a doubt, Odessa. His father, "a dealer in old clothing and tin" dresses in the traditional fashion (caftan, Turkish slippers, and forelocks, or *peyes* in Yiddish). His mother had her head shaved the day of her marriage and, according to Jewish orthodox custom, wears a black wig "that gave her the vague appearance of a Negro woman, washed by the snows and rains of the North." But rather than continue in his father's path or follow any customs of his parents, Ismaël spends his time composing and reciting poetry in the taverns of the port city. One day he is "discovered" by a young man and a woman, who in the eyes of young Ismaël are a baron and a princess; in reality they are nothing but a bohemian poet and his mistress. The pair proposes that Ismaël come to live with them, and he thus becomes the fount of inspiration for the "baron" and the "princess." The three of them become bound together by sympathy and an affinity that the young Jew's parents cannot comprehend. But one day, at the peak of his self-styled glory, Ismaël loses his confidence and stops writing. No longer able to eulogize the beauty of the "princess," he is forced to return to his own people. His father finds him a position in a tailor's shop and Ismaël becomes what he would have been had he never met the "baron." But the soul of the young poet remains tormented. One evening he chances upon the "baron" and pours out to his friend his despair at no longer being a poet. Hopelessly despondent, Ismaël takes his own life.

Significantly, Ismaël's problem as a writer has nothing to do with the persecution suffered by Jews at the hands of Russians. For Irène, it is the Russian bohemian who encourages Ismaël's poetic imagination, while the boy's parents and the Jewish community keep him from composing his verse, preferring to have him work in their grimy shops. Descending from, in Irène's words, "the impoverished race, weakened by books, and fearing the light of day,"[16] Ismaël, in his native Jewish milieu, no longer finds the strength necessary for artistic creation. He is struck by "an invincible laziness . . . a sensation of emptiness . . . a sort of dreadful fatigue, disgust . . . a feeling of emptiness that is almost physical."[17] And his family, of course, understands nothing of this: "They were all there, bent over him, around him, clinging to him like beings trying to force open a flower bud with their sacrilegious fingers."[18] From a youthful poet Ismaël becomes an ordinary young Jew once again: "Previously he had been a child prodigy; now he is nothing more than a gauche youth, as stupid as all the others."[19]

If Ismaël's family does not understand the reason for his suicide, the "baron" does, for he, like Ismaël, has the soul of a poet. The "princess" brings flowers to his grave in the Jewish cemetery, a gesture abhorrent to his traditional Jewish family: "His parents . . . found on the stone a bouquet of roses still quite fresh; they recognized this as the last respects of the princess. They cast them far away: Jewish law forbids the offering of flowers to the dead."[20]

The bitterness of this early work is remarkable. Irène seems oblivious to the artistic and literary richness of the Jews of Eastern Europe, and she ignores the generosity of a culture that, even as it feared for its very existence, created a literature rich in hope and full of humor. It is as if she were peering at the *podol* from the balcony of her Pushkin Street home. The disdain she seems to have for the Jewish community also translates a fear of being identified with it. Only by breaking with that community and by assimilating into Christian Russian society, she seems to say, can a poet (or a novelist) be free to create. As a more mature writer, Irène seems to have realized how scornful her novella was of her fellow Jews in Russia. "Don't speak to me of [*L'Enfant génial*]" she said in an interview in 1930, "I just took a look at it and closed the book back up tight. I find it so awful."[21]

But despite this disavowal, Irène's work—even that written after 1930—shows a great deal more sympathy for the plight of non-Jewish Russians and Ukrainians than for Jews. In *Le Vin de solitude* (The Wine of Solitude), published in 1936, she paints a comforting portrait of a Russian Orthodox church: surrounded by "two poor candles lit under the image of the virgin," listening to "the gentle sputtering of tears of wax flowing down onto the flagstones, in the interval between responses," Hélène, the young Jewish protagonist of the novel, "feared nothing . . . allowed herself to be rocked by a soothing dream." The contrast between the warmth of the church and the cold of the Jewish quarter is striking: "as soon as [Hélène] found herself in the black street, as soon as she moved along the dark and fetid canal . . . her heart tightened in mortal anguish."[22]

Similarly, Irène's portrayals of Ukrainians show a clear admiration for a way of life that seems, from the outside, to offer imaginative possibilities well beyond those of her native Judaism. In a "childhood memory" published in 1940 she tells a story she claims happened in her youth, when,

accompanied by her French governess, she would visit a Ukrainian family in the countryside, not far from Kiev. Even if the story[23] is not strictly
autobiographical, it nonetheless confirms a preference for the Ukrainians
over "the Jewish rabble with which one cannot associate."[24] Titled "Le
Sortilege" (The Magic Spell), the story evokes magic and forbidden love.
The young narrator (Irène) is at first attracted to the physical beauty
of the Ukrainians, particularly to the mother of the household, "strong,
blonde, faded, mellow and white as cream." She is intrigued by the sense
of magic and mystery in a family where "one sleeps in the living room,
one eats in the bedroom, one washes on the front stoop." Children run
freely on wet grass, go out in the evening during a storm, give free rein
to their instincts—in contrast to the regulated life of the narrator (and,
by all accounts, of the author). Accustomed to conversations about money
and business, kept on a short leash by conservative parents, "Irène" is
seduced by these Ukrainians, in whose home one could do such things
as draw cards and play at magic; the "disorder, negligence and decay" of
this Ukrainian home made it the "the warmest and most lively of dwellings that I have ever had the pleasure of experiencing," she writes.[25]

Irène Némirovsky's admiration of Russians and Ukrainians does
not, however, make her entirely oblivious to the persecutions suffered
by Jews at the hands of these people. Two deadly pogroms—in July and
October of 1905—killed hundreds of Jews in Ukraine. Indeed, pogroms
make up the background of the first part of a novel Irène had published
in 1940, and which she titled *Les Chiens et les loups* (The Dogs and the
Wolves.[26]) "There were," writes Irène, "two dangers that were not spar-
ing of the rest of humanity, but were directed more specifically against
the inhabitants of [Kiev], of this quarter . . . These two dangers were
pogroms and cholera."[27] This is the context in which Ada, the young
artist and protagonist of this novel, passes her childhood: "The entire
lower city breathed with fear, crouched behind double windows, in dark
and close little rooms."[28] Hidden in a shelter, she survives days of destruction and massacre. The "patriotic hymns" and the "prayers of the
Russian church"—which in a previous novel gave comfort to the narrator—here become the background sounds of the pogrom, and the "deep
and rhythmic swell" is the chanting of the crowd that throws rocks at
the Jewish stores, that pillages and massacres.[29]

Did Irène personally know Jewish children who would have suffered in this way? Neither her notebooks nor literary works give any indication of her having had direct dealings with Jewish victims of pogroms. It is highly unlikely that the Némirovsky family, living far from the Jewish quarter, would themselves been the victims of pogroms. But it is clear that commiseration with the fate of the Jews of Kiev could coexist, in Irène's mind, with disdain for their way of life. These images of Kiev and Russia—of their beauty and violence—are the fruit of a mature writer's memory and imagination. It is significant that it is not until 1940, when Irène was 37 years old, that she was able to give this more balanced picture of the world of her youth.

Pictures tell their own story. The world of Irène's youth was photographed and the photographs lovingly kept by her daughters. There are no narrow streets here, no forelocks or caftans. We see Irène dressed for a masked costume ball; we see her mother adorned with rings and necklaces in a casino between her husband and another man. We also see a well-dressed, mustachioed Léon photographed in Nice and Kiev. The childhood world of Irène Némirovsky seems to have been composed of society dinners, fancy-dress balls, and vacations at the seaside. Jews did not enter the picture. The *podol* was far away indeed.

A Passion for France

"From the age of four up until the war, I came to France regularly once a year. The first time, I stayed there a year. I was raised by a French governess, and with my mother I always spoke French."[30] This is how Irène described her linguistic situation in Kiev and later in St. Petersburg and Moscow. She lived in Russia almost as one lives in Paris. It was the custom then in Russian high society to employ foreign governesses, either French or English, for the children. But for young Irène, French was more than a language used to distinguish oneself from the less advantaged classes. Well before she emigrated to France, French language and culture were part of her life.

Her French governess seems to have played a fundamental role in young Irène's life. This woman enters Irène's literary work both in the short story "Le Sortilège" and—more significantly—in the novel *Le Vin de solitude*. In the former, she is called simply "Mademoiselle" and she accompanies Irène on her visits to the Ukrainian family. She is portrayed as "very straight in her armchair, with her strict black dress, small white collar and golden chain crosswise on her narrow chest."[31] She displays a certain sobriety and wisdom, which contrast sharply with the excesses and magical conjurations of the Ukrainians. In *Le Vin de solitude* she is called "Mademoiselle Rose," a fictitious name, Irène admits, but she is nonetheless "as faithful a portrait as possible of my old teacher."[32]

If we take Irène at her word, *Le Vin de solitude* can provide a good description of the French governess. Hired by Irène's parents to serve as a teacher, her role seems to have expanded into that of a friend and sometimes even a surrogate mother. In the novel, Irène takes care to note that it is Mademoiselle Rose and not the mother who tucks the young Hélène in at night, who accompanies her outside the home, and who, most importantly, understands the anxieties of her adolescence.

Beyond the personal relationship of the governess and her pupil, Irène presents a portrait of a woman who incarnates a certain Mediterranean beauty, sorely tested by the frigid Russian winter:

Mademoiselle Rose was slim, soft figured and delicate of features, features which must have been beautiful, graceful and gay, in her youth, but which now were wrinkled, faded and thin; her small mouth was a tight fold of bitterness and suffering, as one sees in the lips of women over thirty; she had the beautiful lively black eyes of the Mediterranean, brown frizzed hair, light and frothy, arranged according to the fashion of the time, in an airy halo around her smooth brow, the skin of which was soft and scented with fine soap and the essence of violets. She was calm and wise, always maintaining a just measure in all matters; for some years a certain innocent gaiety had remained in her in spite of the apprehension and sadness inflicted on her by this disjointed home of hers, this country beyond bounds . . . [33]

In her physical appearance and nature, "Mademoiselle Rose" is opposite to the Slavic character. "She was orderly, exact, meticulous, French to the tips of her fingers, somewhat reserved, and a little sarcastic. No grand words . . . No preaching; only the simplest, most ordinary suggestions."[34] She was the incarnation of France in all the simplicity of a young girl's imagination. She sang patriotic songs ("*Vous avez pris l'Alsace et la Lorraine mais malgré vous nous resterons français*"),[35] and love songs

("*Plaisir d'amour ne dure qu'un instant*")[36]; she spoke of France as "the most beautiful country in the world."[37]

It is with her French governess that the young Irène Némirovsky returned to France each year[38] and it is from this governess that she seems to draw her immense love of French language and culture. Hélène's cry from the heart in *Le Vin de solitude*, "Oh! How I would love to be French,"[39] as well as the narrator's characterization of Russia as "a barbarous country where [Hélène] never felt completely at home,"[40] echo Irène's own discomfort with her birthplace and a rather naïve identification with the culture of her governess. "Mademoiselle Rose" has another incarnation in Irène's later prose; she becomes "Mademoiselle Blanche"—an aging French music teacher who had formerly been a governess in a wealthy Russian family—in a short story published in 1938 ("La Confidence" [The Secret]). Of the memories of the persons who peopled Irène's world in Russia, the French governess was the most indelible.

French was the preferred language of the Némirovsky family, but Irène's youthful readings were more widely European. At the home of an officer of the guard in Moscow, a friend of her father, Irène discovered Huysmans and Maupassant as well as Oscar Wilde and Plato. It was Huysmans and Wilde that she read with the greatest of passion: "Of Huysmans I read *À rebours* [Against the Grain]. I didn't understand it all, but the book was a revelation to me. It introduced me to the heart of the best contemporary French literature; almost all of Des Esseintes's preferences would become mine. I would even admit that I tried to learn Latin in order to delve into the decadent authors so adored by Huysmans. It is from this period that dates my attachment to Oscar Wilde, whose *Picture of Dorian Gray* is the book I prefer."[41] This enthusiasm doubtless stemmed from a reaction against the moderation and rigor advocated by the French governess; yet the decadent aestheticism of Huysmans or Wilde would not leave its mark on Irène's work to come. Other readings would prove to have more influence on her art. In notes on her readings, inserted in her writer's notebook, Irène quotes Turgeniev (whose biography by André Maurois she had read), James M. Cain (she wrote the preface to the French edition of *The Postman Always Rings Twice*), and Pearl Buck (she appreciated the stylistic simplicity of *The Mother*).

Irène was a precocious writer. "Quite young," she recounted, "I was intrigued by all those who lived around me, and I began to scribble at around 15 or 16 for the pleasure of understanding lives other than my own, and better still, for the pleasure of creating lives."[42] But at that time she destroyed all she wrote; "It was not very original: fairy stories, prose poems, imitations of Wilde."[43] She began to keep a writer's notebook at the age of 15; first she copied quotes and adages (primarily from *The Picture of Dorian Gray*, but also from Chamfort, and La Rochefoucauld). Later she included in her notebook ideas and projects for novels and short stories. Her first writings date from her arrival in France in 1919.

Like everything else she wrote, Irène's first literary efforts were in French. She was not unconscious of the inherent contradiction between her Russian origins and her language of adoption. "I try," she said in an interview, "to pour into a French mold—as clear, ordered and simple as possible—a foundation that is still somewhat Slavic."[44] This is what the author Jean Jacques Bernard called "being able to think Russian in French."[45] Irène is certainly not the only Russian author to adopt the French language; Lev Tarassov became Henri Troyat and wrote in French, as did Nathalie Tcherniak, who became Nathalie Sarraute. But what distinguishes Irène Némirovsky from other Russian writers who immigrated to Paris at the same time is the coexistence of Slavic and French influences. Troyat, who immigrated from Russia to France in the same year as Irène and was later admitted to the French Academy, devoted his life to making Russian subjects available to the general French public; he wrote great cycles of novels about Russia as well as ten biographies of Russian figures. For Sarraute, with the exception of *'Enfance*, the fictional world, when it can be defined, is that of France. Irène's situation is more ambiguous. In one novel she plunges the reader into the world of pre-Revolutionary Russia; in the next, we are in a middle-class French family in the 1920s. In her biography of Chekhov she takes a decidedly Russian point of view and comments in her notebook that André Maurois, as a Frenchman, is incapable of understanding Turgeniev. At the same time as she was working on a manuscript that would be titled *La Vie amoureuse de Pouchkine* (The Love Life of Pushkin), she was working on novels describing traditional French families in Paris and in the provinces. A third of the fifteen novels she wrote concern Russia, and these are interspersed throughout her life, rather than forming any specific period. It is as if her Russian and French selves were inseparable.

From Russia to France

If the young Irène dreamed of living permanently in France, history would grant her that wish, although not under the circumstances she would have desired. Contrary to the vast majority of Russian Jews, for whom the Soviet revolution offered a glimmer of hope for social justice, the Némirovskys were in the camp of the "white" refugees who fled the new Russian regime to settle elsewhere—in Western Europe, and most importantly in France.

In the summer of 1917 the Némirovsky family found itself in St. Petersburg. For Léon Némirovsky, a banker, this city—the cradle of the revolution—was becoming a hostile environment. The czar had abdicated and the provisional government under Kerensky was not able to control the situation. Lenin's return from exile in Switzerland and the workers' strikes of July 1917 rendered the situation critical for those who had financed the imperial government. Léon decided to move his family temporarily to Moscow. "My father, who was often called to Moscow on business, had a *pied-à-terre* there, a lodging that he sublet, furnished, from an officer of the guard, who had been named to London, no doubt at the embassy. Believing we would be left alone there, my father brought us to Moscow,"[46] recounted Irène. For the young girl of thirteen, this refuge became a sort of enchanted castle. "There are in Moscow old homes that are so close together they are interlocked. We lived in the innermost house, which would be the keep in an old French chateau. It was surrounded by a courtyard to which I escaped to pick up spent cartridge shells when no one could see me."[47] Largely unaware of what was going on in the outside world, Irène continued to delve into the officer's library. "It is in Moscow that the revolution exploded with the most violence. The bombings were so terrible that soldiers who had been involved in the fighting noted that it was more terrifying there than at the front. Luckily for the young girl I was, the officer was a well-read man . . . Curled up on a couch, I was proud to be reading *The Banquet* while a fusillade raged outside. My mother was outraged by my indif-

ference, and each time she passed by she never failed to chastise me."[48]
The circumstances in Moscow became intolerable, and Léon preferred
to bring his family back to Petrograd. However, the situation there in
October 1917 was hardly less dangerous for the banker.

On the November 7, 1917, workers occupied the Winter Palace and a
Bolshevik government was installed. All hopes for a liberal government
were shattered, and Léon Némirovsky was obliged to hide. It is then
that the Némirovsky family took the same route as many other Russian
anti-revolutionaries—that of Finland. "We were saved by going to Finland disguised as peasants. It was in December, 1917. We stayed there
a year, in a village with hardly more than a traffic light, always hoping
to be able to return home."[49]

The stay in Finland left its mark on Irène, for, far from being the
peaceful refuge expected by the family, this country was also in the throes
of a civil war. Red Guards and conservative forces under the command of
General Mannerheim fought over the whole southern half of the country.
Memories of this war would later give rise to two short stories. One of
these, titled "Aïno," is an autobiographical account of Irène's stay in Finland: "I was 15 years old. I was the child of Russian immigrants. I lived
in Finland in a hamlet lost in the woods . . . it was winter and there was
a civil war,"[50] the story begins. Although Irène never identifies the town
in which her family lived, it is quite probably a village close to Terijoki,
a "red" town that the "white" conservatives under General Mannerheim
tried to take in April 1918. Thus the Némirovskys, as anti-Bolshevik as
they were, found refuge "amongst these woodcutters and Bolshevik hunt-
ers"[51] who had occupied the village since December of 1917.

In this village the Némirovskys suffered no privation. Along with
other Russian refugee families they lived in a hotel and were served by
Finnish peasants: "The daughters and wives of these peasants served us
in the hotel in which we took refuge. Imagine a one-story house, with
small windows, icy halls, walls of fresh wood, still scented and sticky
with resin. All about us in the summer season was a garden, with paths
and grass."[52] In fact this Finnish sojourn resembles a country vacation
more than an exile: "We breathed deeply in health and happiness on
these bright mornings when we ran about the forest or rode the fast
and light sleighs."[53] While the adults played whist, the children romped

in the snow. For the young Irène, the only drawback to this haven was a diminished wardrobe ("We had fled Russia so quickly that my only possessions were some underwear and two dresses")[54] and the lack of electricity ("We had no electricity; gasoline was rare").[55]

Without much to do and without friends in this circle of refugees ("At the hotel there lived grown-ups, very young children and a group of young people aged 20 to 22 who did not deign to socialize with me"),[56] Irène, along with a young Finnish girl, discovered an abandoned house in which they uncovered a well-stocked library rich in French and English books: "I was in love with books. I had eyes only for them, French books, English books, Russian books. I remained there immobile, ruining my eyes in the cold white light given off by the snow. The books were unique, enchanting: Maeterlinck, Oscar Wilde, Henri de Régnier . . ."[57] To the young Irène, Finland was a place of visual as well as imaginary enchantment.

War, actually quite close, seemed decidedly far away: "There was fighting at a short distance from the village . . . The forest was aflame . . . Servants with lowered eyelids continued to prepare meals and serve them . . . and certainly no one could guess that the fate of their husbands, brothers and sons was played out there."[58] The war does, however, enter into a short story called "Les Fumées du vin" (The Fumes of the Wine), published in 1934. "Fifteen years ago, neighboring countries were in turmoil, and peaceful Finland also became enflamed," she begins the story.[59] The turmoil that interests Irène is less that of politics or ideology than of passion: the strict Protestant ethic of the Finns becomes destabilized by the war, and the consequence is chaos. The Red Guard, invading a peaceful village, unleashes an outburst of violence and drunkenness among the inhabitants. The cellars are emptied of their wine as enemies shoot at each other; "the orgy ended in a bloodbath."[60]

At the end of the Finnish civil war, in May 1918, the entire country passed under the control of the Whites with General Mannerheim named as regent. But the situation in Russia was hardly favorable to a return for the Némirovsky family. Lenin had consolidated his power in Moscow and St. Petersburg, and the intervention of allied forces on the side of the Whites had not achieved success in destabilizing the Bolshevik regime. Léon Némirovsky decided to move his family west, and to find a way to emigrate to France. "When we saw that the situation was only growing worse, we got to Stockholm and stayed three months. It was an enchanting city, of which I have excellent memories."[61] These recollections, however, gave rise to no literary texts; Sweden was only a stopping-point in the family's pursuit of its final objective. It is Finland, not Sweden that would remain for Irène "the most mysterious country in the world."[62]

"When we left Stockholm we came to France by way of a small cargo ship, ten days on the seas with no stopping in a frightful storm."[63] In the spring of 1919, Irène arrived in France with her family. Like other Russian émigrés, Léon Némirovsky came to France not entirely without means. He had enough money to be able to rent an apartment in a wealthy neighborhood and he had sufficient connections to begin negotiating business deals again. His flight west was a question of political choice as well as economic necessity.

For Irène arrival in France turned out to be the fulfillment of a dream. It was a heady time for this adolescent of sixteen. Fifteen years later, in *Le Vin de solitude*, Irène would express this emotion through the eyes of her young Russian protagonist, Hélène, who also arrives in France in the spring of 1919:

Hélène went to hide in her favorite spot at the front of the boat . . . For a long time she watched the shores of France wavering in front of her in the night. Never, in returning to Russia, had her heart beat so joyously . . . As she approached, she seemed to recognize the perfume of the breeze; she closed her eyes . . . The sea shimmered, illuminated faintly by the lights of the ship. Gently she stretched forth her lips as though to kiss the sea air. She felt light and uplifted with joy, transported by a force stronger than herself.[64]

The freedom that France offered Irène was not political or economic; it was personal. It was a freedom to write in the language she preferred and, finally, to become a published author. As soon as she arrived in Paris she began to write in French: "I had sent comic dialogues to *Fantasio*; they published them."[65] *Fantasio*, whose first volume dates from 1906, was a monthly publication of a somewhat racy nature, which contained erotic sketches of unclothed women, comic drawings, short stories and light dialogues, all aimed at "gentlemen." For Irène the nature of this publication mattered little; it was a matter of getting published in France. "You can be sure I was proud!" she exclaimed in an interview.[66]

There is a certain degree of naivete in Irène's attitude to her adopted country. Neither her fiction nor her notebooks give any evidence that she was preoccupied with the problems encountered by other immigrants or the scandals—such as the Stavisky affair—which increased public hostility to central European Jews. Throughout the 1920s and 1930s, and even as anti-Semitism rose in France, Irène would keep a blind faith in the essential goodness and justice of this country. She thus makes a point of ending *Le Vin de solitude* with an idealized portrait of the protagonist, Hélène, in front of the Arc de Triomphe:

> Hélène listened to the wind; she pricked up her ears as though hearing the voice of a friend. The wind rose up from the Arc de Triomphe, rippling along the tips of the bent trees, whistling and surrounding Hélène, burning her eyes . . . "I am not afraid of life," thought she . . . She rose up, and at this moment, the clouds parted; between the pillars of the Arc de Triomphe blue sky appeared and illuminated her path.[67]

Like Hélène, Irène saw her future, in 1919, illuminated by the skies of France. Her honeymoon with her beloved country was about to begin.

Paris

The France that the Némirovsky family found when they arrived in 1919 corresponded completely to the image Irène already had in her mind. Immigrants were welcome in a country recovering from its victory in a war that cost the lives of 1,300,000 men. Immigrants did not arouse the suspicion that they later would, in the 1930s. Furthermore, the Némirovskys spoke French and were already familiar with French culture and customs. There was also considerable empathy in France for victims of persecution in Eastern Europe, whether as the result of revolution or of religious hatred. The 1926 acquittal in Paris of the Yiddish poet Scholem Schwartzbard, who had killed a Ukranian soldier he held responsible for pogroms, is indicative of a sympathy that was to soon wear thin.[1] For the Némirovskys and other refugees of the Bolshevik regime, France also offered a panoply of economic opportunities that would allow them to quickly resume the life of luxury they had left behind.

Russian Jews had begun to emigrate to France from 1881 onward, and lived almost exclusively in Paris. The Némivoskys were part of a second wave that arrived after the First World War. These immigrants took root in different neighborhoods according to their social class and their occupations; intellectuals usually lived on the left bank of the Seine, workers on the right. Those fleeing the Tsarist regime also gravitated toward the Left Bank while rich Russian Jews, running from Bolshevism, flocked to the Champ-de-Mars neighborhood, where they lived among the White Russians.[2] The number of Jews as a whole in Paris rose considerably: from 75,000 before 1914 to approximately 150,000 in the 1930s; as for Russian immigrants, they numbered approximately 400,000 in the same period, the vast majority of them in Paris.[3]

Just as the Némirovskys lived quite differently from most of the Jews in Kiev, they also had little in common with the majority of Jewish immigrants in Paris. These were for the most part workers whose political leanings were decidedly leftist; Socialists and Communists indulged in violent verbal disputes in Yiddish newspapers. France, the country of human rights and, even more important, the country that gave Jews their emancipation in 1791 represented for them "a model of inspiration on which the hopes of new revolutionaries could be based."[4] Léon Némirovsky, obviously, shared none of these sentiments. For him, as for most of the White Russians, Paris was a refuge to the extent that France allowed them to resume their commercial activities. These refugees kept out of politics and had no interest in the creation of a new, just society. Most of them wanted only to continue living as they had in Russia (with whatever luxuries they could afford) and spent a great deal of time mourning over the loss of their beloved country, believing that, someday soon, they would return to their former state of privilege.[5]

Irène's personal situation fits neither that of Jewish immigrants nor of White Russians. Hers was a case apart; indeed, she was hardly an immigrant at all. "I had already lived in Paris as a child," she explained. "When I returned, all the old memories came back to me."[6] Nor did Irène or her family share the state of poverty that refugees—even some White Russians—experienced upon arrival in France. All of Irène's family— her mother, father, and her maternal grandparents—moved into one of the most elegant neighborhoods of Paris, at 115 rue de la Pompe, in the 16th arrondissement. By 1921, they had a telephone (PASsy 32-79)[7] and had engaged an English governess (Miss Matthews) to be in charge of Irène's education. They had a cook. For them, life in Paris was much like life in Kiev.

"Having barely settled in France . . . my father was fortunate enough to find a branch of one of his banks, and he was able to rebuild a fortune that had been reduced to zero," explained Irène.[8] But it is doubtful that Léon Némirosky's fortune had been reduced to zero; living in the 16th arrondissement does not come cheap. Two years after his arrival in Paris, the telephone directory identified Léon as a "banker," and his visiting card stated that he was "President of the Board of Directors of the Bank of Commerce of Voronezh, Administrator of the Bank of the Union of Moscow, and Member of the Board of the Private Bank of Commerce of Petrograd." In addition to his activities as a banker, Léon had (as his last will and testament confirms) acquired a considerable number of shares in the International Match Corporation.

The economic climate of the time certainly helped Léon Némirovsky become a wealthy man. Investment was the motor force behind France's prosperity in the 1920s. Banks such as those for which Léon Némirovsky worked speculated in everything from oil fields in Eastern Europe to armament factories in France. This is a world Irène knew well and that she would later depict in her most celebrated novel, *David Golder.*

Quite apart from the world of business, Irène herself, as she tentatively began her career as a writer, profited from the new Russian "mode" that had won over Paris. Russian émigrés—especially those who could contribute to the world of art and entertainment—were all the rage: in music (Igor Stravinsky); in dance (the Ballets Russes and its choreographer, Serge Diaghilev); in theater (Georges and Ludmilla Pitoëff). After performances, Parisians gathered at the "Caveau caucasien," a Russian cabaret whose success spawned other restaurants, cabarets, and tea houses with Russian themes, particularly in Pigalle.[9] Everywhere one spoke of Russians, and while some of the popular press took them to task for having given up the fight against Germany in 1917, others focused on the difficulties of the lives of these émigrés and pointed out, for example, that some aristocrats were reduced to driving taxicabs. In literature, too, Russians figured prominently; according to Ralph Schor, "one quarter of the literary works devoted to foreigners featured Russians as main characters; no other nationality achieved this level of attention."[10] One of the most popular novels of the early 1920s was called *Nicky, roman de l'émigration russe* (Nicky, A Novel of the Russian Emigration). It was written by Jean Vignaud,[11] who would later befriend Irène Némirovsky and sponsor her to be a member of the the Société des Gens de Lettres de France (The Society of French Men and Women of Letters).

Madeleine

The Némirovsky residence in Paris was far from the neighborhoods of most Russian immigrants, Jewish and non-Jewish. This geographical distance was also a cultural one. Irène's relationship with the Russian émigré community was limited to participation in the occasional benefit ball; she had no association with Jewish groups. It is, rather, within the Catholic French bourgeoisie that she sought to find her place.

When Irène arrived in Paris at the age of thirteen, she quickly became part of a community of young people. On January 14, 1921, for example, she appears to have invited to her home friends or acquaintances called Olga, Soria, and Mademoiselle Aïtoff—all Russian surnames. In February of the same year (perhaps to celebrate her eighteenth birthday), one finds on her invitation list, in addition to distinctly Russian names, those of Mademoiselle Renaud and Mademoiselle Jouarre, and young men named Suchard and Albert.[12] Her friendships were diverse and showed evidence of a growing attachment to members of the French upper middle class. It is in this context that she met the girl who was to become her closest friend, Madeleine Avot.

Nothing is more revealing of Irène's desire to meld completely into the French landscape than correspondence she carried on with Madeleine. Daughter of a prosperous paper manufacturer from Lumbres (in the northern department of Pas-de-Calais), Madeleine Avot was about the same age as Irène. Although she lived in the provinces, she often came to Paris to visit her brother René, who was studying engineering. It is through René (whom Irène must have met at a social gathering) that she met Irène.

What could have motivated this unlikely friendship between a Russian Jewish girl, an aspiring author and student of literature (for Irène had enrolled at the Sorbonne), and a Catholic girl from the provinces, whose horizons seem to have been limited to her family and her community? This situation, like so many others in Irène's life, can only be understood in the light of Irène's profound desire to become something she was not. Her fascination with Madeleine and the entire Avot family, far from being a transitory whim of adolescence, would have a lasting effect on her values and her literary sensibility.

Irène's letters to Madeleine also give us a good picture of the life

Irène led in the Paris of the 1920s. Soon after her arrival in France, Irène began to study literature and formed friendships with other students who attended the Sorbonne. She had passed her baccalaureate shortly after her arrival in 1919 (her French lessons with Mademoiselle Rose having stood her in good stead). In a letter dated December 1921, she wrote to Madeleine: "I am working assiduously at my Sorbonne."[13] Yet it took Irène five years to pass her "licence" (equivalent of the BA degree).[14] For her, studying was less important than pursuing an active social life in the company of a whole group of rather frivolous and easygoing young people.

In fact, Irène's life seems to have consisted less of endless nights poring over books than of endless parties and social gatherings, interspersed with lengthy vacations. On one occasion she describes settling in to the luxurious Negresco Hotel in Nice for several weeks; although accompanied by her parents and under the close watch of her English governess, she manages to meet many young men, to participate in outdoor activities, and to become a proficient dancer.

I have spent three delightful weeks here. I have met several young Englishmen, who dance well and are charming. Unfortunately they are not going to Paris. I am making the most of their company while I can. Last night we went together to the Cercle. That brought back memories of good times at the Paris-Plage bar, because I came home in the wee small hours. Since during the day I had been on an outing, climbing rocks, etc., you can imagine how exhausted I am, and this evening I'm going to a dance again.[15]

At times, Irène enters into great detail about her activities, and seems to take pleasure in showing off her conquests to her rather staid friend:

First we dance, every evening until one o'clock, and twice a week all night long. We're a band of six . . . all aged 21, 20 and 18, with lovely names such as Fink, a tall blonde whom we tease and is also called Sphinx, . . . Victor Aumont, called Totoche, as funny as can be, and the one I flirt with—the 20 year old—Henry La Rochelle. If you saw the crazy things we did! I'll tell you the latest one. The day before I was to leave we went to have our afternoon snack at a farm. When we got there we discovered an immense barn full of hay. We decided right away to eat our chocolate up in the hayloft. You can imagine the look on the maid's face! We all used ladders to get up into the hay, which smelled of mint, and had our food brought up. The chocolate was all over the bread and the butter was in the hay. I have never eaten with such a good appetite. Then the boys made sleds out of bundles of hay and we rolled down from up there like little kids. At the end of the afternoon the three couples dispersed into different corners in the hay and we spent our time . . . flirting, and for so long that we totally forgot the time and saw when we were leaving that it had already long been dark.[16]

Another vacation spot favored by Irène and her parents was Plombières, in the eastern Vosges Mountains. Plombières and Vittel were, at the time, watering places often frequented by Parisians who took the *train des eaux*, the "watering train," to get there. These spas offered cures to treat intestinal problems and to address a variety of other maladies. The morning was always spent in the same fashion; baths, showers, massage. After lunch, people napped and then had the afternoon free. They went to the Stanislas fountain (a pretty walk in the woods at the end of which there was a restaurant where they took tea), or they took excursions to interesting sites. They dined in the hotel, and gathered in the salon afterwards for companionship and discussion.

In July 1922, Irène was at the Grand Hôtel of Plombières. She writes that she made the acquaintance of "the family of a factory owner from the Vosges." This was the Comesse family, whose daugher Yvonne, 76 years later, would keep vivid in her memory Irène's presence.

She amused the adults, she amused the children, she organized outings, and she had, above all, an extraordinary infectious liveliness, which really created a quite special ambiance in the hotel. We would have been bored had it not been for Irène . . . She was kind to everyone, and she had this talent for organization that struck me . . . parlor games, lively ones such as hide and seek, or trying to catch people with your eyes blindfolded. She was always there in bad weather when we couldn't go out; she really animated things. She was what we call now a leader.[17]

Irène's own version of her stay in Plombières puts the emphasis elsewhere. Animating games with children took a back seat to finding handsome young men:

The casino is vile, the dancers awful . . . Hardly amusing at all. But there you have it. God, who always manages to put the good alongside the bad, has sent to our hotel a family of mill-owners from the Vosges. Mother, daughter, and two sons aged 25 and 18. Both are very nice. They have a great automobile, take me out in it every day, and try to surpass each other flirting with me. I have a soft spot for the younger one. You know I have a grown-up taste for boys. Anyway, he is beautiful enough to paint, the face of a page at court, and every bit as cheeky. In the evening I got the idea of bringing all the children in the hotel into a big room and playing with them. The parents were touched, the children overjoyed, you can picture the scene . . . In fact the kids made a terrible racket without paying any attention to us. The din sent the parents off to escape, and my page and I were left to flirt to our hearts' content; we had wangled just what we wanted. I'm planning to stay here until August 15 and then to leave for Saint-Jean.[18]

Whether in Nice, Paris Plage on the north coast, or in the Vosges, Irène continued her romantic escapades. Sometimes these adventures fizzled out comically ("romantic distress or a stomach upset after eating lobster? I'm not sure");[19] sometimes, when Irène went too far, the results were serious:

Choura[20] came to see me and lectured me for two hours: it appears I'm too flirtatious, that it's very bad to stir boys up, etc. You know I have dropped Henry, who came to see me the other day, pale and staring, with a very nasty look and a revolver in his pocket? I was not very much at ease I can assure you. With this hothead I was as much at risk of getting a bullet in my head as of seeing him put a hole in his own. Fortunately, in the end, his friends came and he left. However I'm beginning to think that you should not trifle with love . . . the love of others![21]

Irène's boasting of amorous conquests to a conservative young girl, living with her parents, far from Paris and the fashionable watering places, reveals more than the desire to shock. It is also an attempt to give herself an identity and to hide, as we shall see later, the more serious thoughts that were going through her head and that would lead to her first literary efforts. Her letters to Madeleine sometimes create a persona that resembles more the mature but shallow women that will populate the pages of her novels than the intellectual adolescent she really is.

> Can you imagine, dear Madeleine, that I have again found the gigolo I told you about? He is a professional dancer from Nice . . . He has suddenly fallen for me and wants to dance with me all the time. When I tried to pay him he grew red with anger and now holds me tight while dancing and keeps showering me with compliments. So I've got my dancer, Madeleine, and a good dancer at that! Next year in Paris, I'll have to put him to use. . . . If you knew how great he was! I would really have a crush on him if he were of my class, that's for sure . . . But I don't want to keep shocking you any longer, my dearest.[22]

If she occasionally gives Madeleine advice in matters of the heart, it is because she can pose as the woman of experience, for whom love can be commanded or denied: "Wisdom has it that there are more fish in the sea, and that's right, and anyway who cares? You have to treat love like a sickness. Keep walking and try to flirt with others. An excellent cure. I also could be sad. One of my male friends left me, but I have too much will power to cry over it and too much pride, too. You have to 'make' yourself not think of him any longer. It's crazy. You have to be proud."[23] As if to reinforce her position of authority, she recounts scenes intended to shock the moral sensibilities of her provincial friend. She writes, for example, of her friend Choura, who came to her room "at ten o'clock when I was undressed and ready for bed,"[24] or she brings up Madeleine's brother, René, whom she can't introduce to her promiscuous Russian friends: "Yesterday I saw friends, some Russians and others, young Tania and a few gigolos. It was amusing and I would have liked to have you there if only to scandalize you a little. Our 'innocent' games were so much fun that my friends were still there at nine in the evening (they had arrived at four). And you, Madeleine? What are you up to? Always behaving properly in that home I remember so fondly? I'm not seeing René. I am so busy I don't dare invite him when I have the Russians here for fear of shocking him and leading him into perdition. Really."[25]

All things considered, however, Irène's behavior was not as scandalous or as mature as she would have had her friend believe. The "gigolos" she saw were dancers, not prostitutes,[26] and even though Irène may have enjoyed exploits of a sexual nature in country barns, she nevertheless kept quite a conventional attitude toward marriage and relationships between couples. In fact the tone of her letters changes considerably after she meets the man who would become her husband, Michel Epstein. He was Russian, Jewish, the son of a banker, and in the end he prevailed over Irène's frivolous life. This is how Irène describes him to Madeleine: "And there is something, or rather someone, which keeps me in Paris. I don't know if you remember Michel Epstein, a short dark-haired and dark-complexioned type, who came back with Choura and me in the taxi that miserable night or rather that memorable morning of January 1. He is pursuing me, and my heavens, I find him to my liking . . . So since my crush on him is so strong at the moment, you can't ask me to leave, you understand."[27]

Despite the frivolous tone of her letters to Madeleine, Irène seems to have continued her literary studies with a measure of application. On one occasion, she admits to being somewhat nonchalant with regard to her work ("No exam for me this year. In the end I haven't cracked a book and I don't want to expose myself to sure failure. So I continue to do nothing"),[28] but more often she shows evidence of a more responsible attitude: "I have started up more seriously this year at the Sorbonne. More and more. I'm taking Spanish lessons. As much as I can, I avoid dances and parties."[29] At the age of 23, she passed the exams for her degree:

> I have made up for all my sins, that of laziness above all, by working like a dog. I've put my nose to the grindstone like never before. I finished my exams just yesterday and I've passed "cum laude." My composition got 19 out of 20, and I'm first in literature, which really pleased me, but also fairly wore me out. I'm sorry it has all come to an end. We were such a good group, splitting our time between the Sorbonne, dancing and picnics on the lawn.[30]

In addition to revealing some important elements of Irène's life during the early years in Paris, the letters to Madeleine also give strong evidence of a gradual pulling away from the family and its influence, and an increasing appreciation—even infatuation—with the life of a Catholic French family. Irène was certainly an apt pupil for this sort of acculturation. She seems to have had little interest in spending time with Russian émigré circles, and although well aware of the tribulations of Russians who did not assimilate, she shows little inclination to identify with them. While her friend Mila goes out with "Prince Gagarine,"[31] Irène finds herself less than at home in the company of her compatriots: "Saturday evening I had a good time. It was the Russian 1st of January. There was a dance at the Russian Club. I found all the people I usually flirt with, but can you imagine that, already at the beginning of the evening, I felt completely out of place, almost a stranger in their midst."[32] The feeling of being estranged from her origins was only reinforced by the visits she makes to Madeleine's family.

In many ways, the Avot family's life was the antithesis of that of Irène's family. They did not have balls or evenings out in the theater; the father was not often abroad on business trips; the mother was not preoccupied with young dancers and jewelry. Quite the contrary. In 1921, Irène, aged 17, paid two visits to the Avots in Lumbres. Returning from her first trip, in November, she wrote to her friend: "You can't imagine how empty I felt leaving the station. The house seemed sad and gloomy to me, and I felt alone."[33] Her Christmas visit served only to accentuate the alienation from her own family. On December 22, 1921, accompanied by her governess (who was headed for a visit to her own family in England), she took the train to Boulogne, where Madeleine came to meet her. It was a Christmas she would never forget. When she finally returned to Paris, she wrote to her friend:

Here I am back in the Paris hell. I assure you that I will never forget that it is at Lumbres that I was able to get to know and love family life. I will always remember you all fondly. I found Paris gloomy, cold, rainy, and sad, and I am horribly down in the dumps. The first few days I felt so alone, if you only knew. It's your fault too! You spoiled me too much in Lumbres![34]

Normally circumspect with regard to her parents, Irène, after living with the Avots, seems to have put in doubt the quality of her own life at home. Whether it is her father's repeated absences or her mother's coldness (all of which are alluded to without being made specific), the home atmosphere became one of disorder and discontinuity. The contrast between this description of her family's return from vacation and the homey atmosphere of the Avot household is striking:

> I arrived in Paris soaked, and all I have kept as a souvenir of this exquisite excursion is a head cold which decidedly lacks charm. We arrived at two in the morning, much to the great bewilderment of the concierge; we found the house empty, the beds unmade, and the sheets locked in a trunk that we had to break open with fireplace tongs, since my father couldn't find the keys, which incidentally the next day we found in his pocket. The apartment is pretty and I hope soon to be able to show you around.[35]

When Irène invited her friend to Paris, it was not with a view to having Madeleine meet her parents, but rather for the two girls to spend some intimate time together. There was no family life to experience during the visit, but rather, as Irène writes, "our little life of two."[36] Her friendship with Madeleine allowed her to regain, even for a few days, the familial warmth of the Avot family. "About your trip to Paris, I want to tell you something that gives me great pleasure. I saw René yesterday; he is going back to Lumbres for All Saints Day and is more than willing to bring you back with him. So I am again inviting you to come and stay with me in my apartment made for an old bachelor. Surely at last I'll succeed in getting you to come, my dear."[37]

The experience of having known Madeleine and her family are the first building blocks of an ideal of French life that would characterize Irène's literary work. It is an ideal not unlike that of Maurice Barrès's *chant profond* (profound chant), expressed in novels such as *Les Déracinés* (The Uprooted); the true essence of France is to be found not in the dehumanized, cacophonic capital but rather in the provinces, respectful of tradition and resistant to change. This is the gist of Irène's novel *Les Biens de ce monde* (The Wealth of the Earth), written in 1940.[38] The area around Lumbres serves as a model for the background of the novel,[39] which features a family, the Hardelots, that bears an uncanny resemblance to the Avots (Pierre Hardelot, like Madeleine's father, owns a paper factory). It is a family characterized by "an extraordinary feeling of stability"[40] with strong ties to the land. Pierre Hardelot and his wife live through the First World War, the social upheavals of the postwar period, and the French defeat of 1940 without ever leaving their ancestral home, even when their city is bombed. It is by no means fortuitous that Irène, immediately after the defeat of June 1940, wrote to Madeleine, "I find that your father shows incredible courage staying in Lumbres. Besides, it doesn't surprise me: he personifies the good decent Frenchman."[41] This faithfulness to the land, not to mention a conjugal fidelity Irène never found in her parents' home, would come to constitute a model to be contrasted with the world of international business depicted in *David Golder*.

The intensity of the relationship between Irène and Madeleine would gradually wane as the two friends found husbands and had children. Irène married in 1926, but Madeleine married earlier, in 1924. In April 1924 she wrote to Irène to announce her engagement. The announcement surprised Irène; evidently the two young women had been growing apart:

Your letter with its happy news and the announcements only arrived yesterday, because it was forwarded to me here in Nice where I have been for a few days. This explains why I couldn't congratulate you earlier. I am very happy for you, dear Madeleine. I send you sincerest wishes for your happiness. I am eager to meet your fiancé. As you describe him, he must be charming and I am sure you will have a blissful existence.[42]

Irène's literary ambitions and projects, of which she never wrote to her friend, would also take their toll on the friendship. The intimacy of their relationship as adolescents could not withstand the demands of matrimony and professional life. From 1924 to 1930 they did not correspond, and when, in 1929, *David Golder* propelled Irène into the spotlight, Madeleine would be reduced to asking for an autographed copy of the book. Irène, caught off guard, answered:

How could you imagine that I could forget my old friends because of a book people have been talking about for two weeks but will be soon forgotten like everything else in Paris . . . It is with great pleasure that I am sending you a copy, and I would have done so earlier had I thought it would entertain you.[43]

After 1931 they no longer wrote one another. The war, however, moved Irène to resume their correspondence and to rekindle their friendship. In April 1940, Irène wrote: "You will perhaps be surprised to see my signature, for we have been out of touch for a long time now . . . But in these trying times one remembers old friends and wonders if they are all in good health."[44] War and the occupation would bring Irène and Madeleine back together. Their friendship would have an influence even beyond Irène's death at Auschwitz; Madeleine's brother René took it upon himself to care for Irène's youngest daughter, Élisabeth.

Michel

When Irène met her future husband, she was living at 18, Avenue du Président Wilson in a luxurious (though in her view cold) apartment with a spectacular view of the Eiffel Tower. Michel Epstein was living with his parents at 29, Avenue Victor-Emmanuel III (today called Avenue Franklin-Roosevelt) in the 8th arrondissement. These details are not without importance; not only was Michel Russian and Jewish, his family was of the same social class as the Némirovskys and the fathers of the bride and groom shared the same profession.

Michel Epstein was born in 1896 in Moscow, where his father, Efime, was an administrator with the Commercial Bank of Azov-on-Don and vice-president of the Central Committee of commercial banks of Russia. In 1916 the family moved to Petrograd where Michel studied physics and chemistry. In 1918 he left Petrograd with his family to go to Kiev and enroll in the Graduate School of Business Studies. In 1919, while still in Kiev (where a nationalist government opposed to the Communists was in power until 1920), he took a job as an attaché at the Ministry of Finance. With the Treaty of Riga, Kiev became part of the Soviet Union, and the Epstein family was forced into exile. In Paris, while his father was rebuilding his fortune as a banker, Michel enrolled in the École Spéciale des Travaux Publics (The Public Works Institute), with a view toward a degree in engineering. He fell ill, however, in 1923, gave up his studies, and decided to pursue a career in a financial institution.

When they first met, Irène and Michel were living parallel lives. Like Irène, Michel spoke and wrote perfect French; he had also mastered German and English, albeit less well than French. He was very sociable but not excessively ambitious. A career in business was not a lifetime goal but a measure designed simply to enable him to live in the style his family accustomed him to. At the time he met Irène, he was still in the process of looking for a position. Irène's enthusiasm for this handsome, gregarious young man was not shared by her mother, who undoubtedly imagined a more motivated son-in-law. Irène wrote to Madeleine:

> I'm having a flirtation with a certain Michel Epstein, whom you must know. You also know that I'm rather devil-may-care, that I never hide what I do, and that because other people's business doesn't interest me, I usually think others will leave me alone. Obviously, a big mistake. Yesterday an idiot asked my mother: "is it true what is being said everywhere? Your daughter is marrying Epstein?" You should have seen my mother's face . . . In short, things are not going well at the moment.[45]

Despite her mother's disapproval, Irène, at 23, married Michel. On Friday, July 23, 1926 she and Michel appeared in the office of Maître Goupil, a notary, at 11, rue Louis-le-Grand in Paris, to sign a marriage contract. Significantly, this contract bound the couple to the rule of *separation de biens* (separation of possessions), which stipulates that each partner keeps control of the wealth brought into the marriage and acquired after it. In Irène's case, the marriage contract gave her complete control over her literary property, despite laws inherited from Napoleonic times, which denied women the right to work or open bank accounts without their husband's permission.

The nuptials were celebrated on Saturday, July 31, 1929, at 4:15 P.M. in the *mairie* of the 16th arrondissement. All indications are that Irène and Michel had only the civil ceremony required by French law. Despite assertions of one of Michel's nieces (who was only a few years old at the time) that there was also a religious ceremony in a synagogue,[46] no evidence of such an event can be found in the records of the Jewish *Consistoire* of Paris; in any case, Jewish marriages are never celebrated on Saturday, the Sabbath. Nor is there evidence that either Michel or Irène had any religious education or even that Michel had been *bar-mitzvah*.

Following her marriage to Michel, Irène was finally able to leave her parents' apartment. She and Michel rented a large, five-room flat at 8, avenue Daniel Lesueur. This is a short dead-end street, perpendicular to the Boulevard des Invalides in a less fashionable neighborhood than the Avenue du Président Wilson, but still prosperous. The building had just been completed in 1924. Here, Irène could devote herself freely to the activity she preferred over all others: writing.

Writing

At the time of her marriage, Irène was already in the process of forging for herself a reputation as an author. She had written dialogues for the magazine *Fantasio*; one short novel (*Le Malentendu*) had already appeared, and another had been accepted for publication. While the *Fantasio* dialogues were written under a pseudonym, all her future work would appear under her maiden name.

The dialogues Irène wrote for *Fantasio* cannot be found today, and it is perhaps for the better. The character of this magazine did not lend itself to the publication of good literature, but the experience of having her dialogues accepted brought Irène a certain amount of pride: "I will long remember the expression of Félix Juven when I came to collect my royalties, which amounted to approximately 60 francs. I was truly proud of pocketing my first earnings. But Fantasio's director stared with amazement at this 17 year old writer, who looked more like 15."[47] Had Jouven known the truth about Irène's situation he would have been even more surprised. The English governess, Miss Matthews, accompanied her everywhere, and the hair she had tucked under her hat was long, for her parents had forbidden her to cut it in the boyish style of the time. "I had long hair down to my waist and a respectable English woman who went everywhere with me. I had to find a pretext to get rid of her, which was not too easy, and then in the staircase, I had to push my hair under my hat!"[48]

Quite apart from the satisfaction of earning a bit of money from her writing, Irène had more somber ideas on her mind. She had begun to write *L'Enfant génial*. The fact that she renounced the book in 1930 should not make us forget the circumstances of its beginning. It is while Irène was becoming close to the Avot family that the story of the misunderstood Jewish writer came to mind. In retrospect, we can see that in writing *L'Enfant génial* Irène was exorcizing the demons of her own past and renouncing a cultural heritage that weighed heavily upon her. Immediately after finishing the novel she plunged into another project that turned its back on Jewish subjects and Russia, and dealt exclusively with French subjects. Had not Irène used her own name in submitting her next novel, it would have been impossible to tell that the author was a Russian Jew.

Le Malentendu, begun in 1925, concerns the adulterous love affair of a young married woman and a penniless aristocrat who live in Paris and vacation in Hendaye. For the first time Irène sent a manuscript to a prestigious publisher, Arthème Fayard, who agreed to put it in *Les Œuvres Libres*, a monthly literary anthology that published unedited works of authors well known (André Billy, Henri Bernstein) and aspiring. Founded in 1921, this magazine had acquired a reputation for publishing works of distinction and for discovering new talents; it was thus the ideal vehicle for a young author to make herself noticed. *Le Malentendu* appeared in the February, 1926 issue;[49] subsequently Irène would sign a contract for an edition of the novel in book form.

In writing *Le Malentendu*, Irène turned her attentions to a milieu she knew only from the outside. The Némirovsky family rented a chalet, called Villa Ene Etchea, at Hendaye Plage on the Basque coast, where the family often came to spend their summer vacation. It was one of the grand houses "in a pseudo Basque style"[50] with large verandas facing the beach, constructed at the beginning of the century. The characters Irène depicts in her novel are of the upper French bourgeoisie; these are people she would have observed on the beach, in the restaurants, and in the casino of Hendaye, but who would not have been friends of her family. It was a curious choice of a subject for a young woman who could see so much more drama in the world of her own family; in fact, Irène came to this conclusion when she began writing *David Golder*.

The plot of *Le Malentendu* is disarmingly simple. A young married woman, Denise[51] Jessaint, on vacation in Hendaye, falls in love with a young bachelor, Yves Harteloup, who, in spite of his aristocratic background, lives in poverty in Paris. When they return to the city, the lovers must deal with the complexity of their relationship; to Yves' financial problems are added Denise's transparent lies to her husband. Her affair with Yves becomes an open secret. Faced with their problems (including the "misunderstanding" of a kiss exchanged by Denise and an amorous cousin, witnessed by a greatly distressed Yves) their passion wanes and Yves finally leaves Paris, putting an end to this impossible love.

The novel gives us access to a postwar world where adulterous love affairs are so commonplace that they scarcely elicit a raised eyebrow on the part of friends or relatives. Denise's husband, as well as her mother, accept the situation with a "sigh of resignation," for "the conjugal bond [gives] way imperceptibly, like a knot made of two separate ropes that have quietly worn through."[52] From then on events transpire as though Denise were entirely liberated, and an adulterous affair is transformed into a simple love story, free of all moral or psychological conflict. The result is light reading, for a summer at the beach.

But there are aspects of this book that give a hint of what is to come in *David Golder* and other novels and stories concerning money and finance. While Denise lives out her love affair, Yves tries to find a way of rebuilding his fallen fortunes and getting out from under the burden of debt. He consults a Jewish colleague at work, "the typical young Jew, rich, elegant, with a long pointed nose in a narrow, pale face;"[53] the latter gives him advice on investments "which earned the young Jew several thousands of francs [but] cost him as much."[54] This Jewish stereotype, like that we saw in *Un Enfant genial*, would not have shocked French readers in the 1920s as it would disturb readers today. That the stereotype is penned by a Jewish writer is, however, notable. It is indicative of Irène's preoccupation with Jewish identity, especially that of the rich Jewish banker, which she would soon explore in depth.

In spite of its weaknesses, *Le Malentendu* was well received by the critics. "One of the most powerful 'revelations' of the postwar period," wrote a critic in the weekly *Gringoire*, adding, "one again finds all the qualities of vigor and exactness that are the attributes of the wonderful talent of this author."[55] Frédéric Lefèvre, in *Les Nouvelles littéraires*, found in the work "a sensitive, discreet realism" and added, "in its moderation and good sense, this novel is very French."[56] Irène had clearly won her wager; her novel was hailed as "French" by the press.

The review board of *Les Œuvres libres*, impressed by *Le Malentendu*, agreed to accept *L'Enfant genial*, written—as we have seen—in 1923, well before the first novel they published. In 1927, this "original novella,"[57] as it was called by *Les Œuvres Libres*, came out. It did not make news, however, and, unlike *Le Malentendu*, was not accepted for publication as a book. Was the subject matter considered too narrow, too Jewish? More probably, the editors had some doubt about the publication of such a personal work, and the fundamental ambiguity that inspired it was doubtless too personal to interest the public at large. The novel appeared in book form only in 1992; it was slightly edited for adolescent readers.[58]

Irène had yet a third manuscript to send to Fayard, that of a short novel she named *L'Ennemie* (The Enemy); it would appear in *Les Œuvres Libres* in 1928.[59] But this time she chose to submit the work under a masculine pseudonym, Pierre Nérey. Why the pseudonym? Irène was already known to Fayard and had no need to hide behind another name to get herself published. In fact she never did—and never would—have difficulty getting published as a female author, even in the early 1920s when their number was extremely limited. The pseudonym, however, had another use in her early literary career: it allowed her to inconspicuously publish texts such as *L'Ennemie* that would serve as sketches for novels to come. Later in Irène's career, pseudonyms would prove useful in allowing her to publish her work at a time when Jews were forbidden this occupation.

In fact, *L'Ennemie* is a sketch for a novel Irène was beginning and which would appear in 1935, *Le Vin de solitude*. In *L'Ennemie*, the protagonist is a young, misunderstood girl, whose mother, a "pretty woman, delicate as a porcelain figure,"[60] with a face "always tense in an expression of spite and anger,"[61] is a monstrous egotist who cheerfully cheats on her husband and neglects her children. It is less the young protagonist, Gabri, who interests Irène, than the monstrous mother, her vitriolic temperament, and her devastating effect on her children. Gabri's young sister is killed by boiling water which falls on her when she is left alone at an age too young to be responsible; consumed with guilt and anger, Gabri throws herself from a balcony, after having vengefully seduced her mother's lover.

This short, quite melodramatic novel never appeared in book form and Irène never spoke of it in her interviews. It was as though she wanted it to slip by unnoticed behind her pseudonym. Did she believe the portrait of the mother to be too harsh? Did she think her own mother, with whom relations were strained,[62] would take offence in reading descriptions such as the following: "This bourgeois woman, who had read too many novels, was greedy for money and luxuries; she reproached her husband for not amusing her or spoiling her enough."[63] She does not hesitate in her fiction to draw freely upon her own family situation. Gabri's father is called Léon; the family lives on the Avenue de l'Iéna (close to the Avenue du Président Wilson), they hire an English governess for their daughter and they spend their vacation "in the sad little spa in the Vosges."[64] Later, in *Le Vin de solitude*, Irène uses a dramatic scene borrowed from *L'Ennemie*,[65] and the portrait of the neglectful and vain mother will reappear, with some variation, in *David Golder*, *Le Bal*, and *Jézabel*.

The publication of *L'Ennemie* brought to a close an initial period of literary output that lasted two years, from 1926 to 1928, and saw the appearance of two novels and a short story. It was a period of experimentation and trial. Irène had written, without much success, of her own interior dilemma as a Jewish author; she had done better by almost pretending to be French, but the success of *Le Malentendu* only made her identity as a writer more confused. She still had not found her voice or her style. It is in the midst of this questioning that Irène would decide to turn her attention to the world around her, and write—for the first time—a powerful, authentic novel: *David Golder*.

The Event

At 26 years of age, Irène Némirovsky was projected from the fringes of Parisian literary society onto center stage.

The appearance of *David Golder*, the novel that would make Irène famous, was more than a mere book publication; it was a literary happening. And like other literary happenings, it surrounded itself in legend.

Irène had sent the manuscript of her novel to the publisher of Marcel Proust, the quirky but respected Bernard Grasset. Henry Muller, a close collaborator of Grasset, claimed that the manuscript arrived in an envelope with only "Epstein, General Delivery, Paris-Louvre"[1] for a return address. Muller was assigned to read the manuscript:

> As soon as I finished my report I looked at the author's card in the book of manuscripts; there was a simple name, Epstein, and a general delivery address. The next day Grasset . . . wrote to the author to inform him that he would eagerly publish the work, and he requested that he come by as soon as possible to sign the contract. Then we waited three weeks; so long that at one point, one of us, full of consternation, suggested placing an ad in the newspapers: "seeking author who sent a manuscript to Grasset under the name Epstein." In the end things moved quickly; it took less than one half-hour for the young woman who appeared (petite, dark-haired, of Russian origin, and ostensibly quite intimidated) to sign her contract.[2]

In sending Grasset an unsigned manuscript, Irène was not trying to be coy. She had already experienced a rejection after attempting to have *David Golder* published with Fayard, and she was fearful of a similar experience happening again:

> When my last draft was ready, I quite naturally sent it to the *Œuvres Libres*, which had been quite receptive to my work. The reader, Mr. André Foucault, told me he liked the book but that for the *Œuvres Libres* it was somewhat long, and that it would be advisable to shorten it by 50 pages. The book was only 200 pages long. This radical cut was painfully difficult for me. I was, however, resigned to it when I fell sick. I no longer had the strength or energy to undertake a long revision of my manuscript. It occurred to me that what had worked already at *Fantasio* . . . and at *Les Oeuvres Libres*, could work for me once again, and I sent the manuscript to Grasset. I gave a General Delivery address in order to be able, in the event of a rejection, to keep my action a secret.[3]

In writing "Mr. Epstein" on the manuscript, Irène undoubtedly hoped to avoid any prejudice against a female author; at the same time she made it unlikely that Grasset would make a connection between the manuscript at hand and other works that Irène had published in *Les Oeuvres Libres*. Hence Henry Muller knew nothing at all of the author when he saw the manuscript: "it has only happened once in my career that I have opened the pages of a manuscript signed by an unknown author and experienced the deep joy of discovery."[4] Muller's enthusiasm was shared by Grasset, who chose to publish the text in his personal collection entitled "Pour mon plaisir" (for my pleasure) that he had launched in 1929 when he published three of his favorite authors: Jacques Chardonne, Jean Cocteau, and Jean Giono. To these works he added, as the fourth volume of the collection, Irène Némirovsky's *David Golder*. Irène signed a contract with Grasset on October 25, 1929, agreeing to give him an option on the next three of her works.

This story of the publication of *David Golder*, which has several variants,[5] is indicative of the importance of the event. "In just a few days," wrote Marcel Thiébault, director of the prestigious *Revue de Paris*, "*David Golder* was elevated to the rank of a subject for conversation in salons . . . One spoke everywhere of the 'torrential power,' of the 'exceptional power,' of this work which 'recalled Balzac' and was 'a masterpiece.'"[6] Grasset did all he could to create a stir about the publication of the novel. First, he made Irène appear younger than she actually was;

he encouraged the press to state that the author was only 23 years old (while actually she was 26), and Irène did nothing to correct the misrepresentation.[7] In addition, Grasset did not hesitate to lavish praise on the novel, maintaining that *"David Golder,* by its power and by its very subject, was reminiscent of *Le Père Goriot."*[8]

If most critics were hesitant to raise Irène Némirovsky to the level of Honoré de Balzac, they did give the novel exceptionally favorable attention. "There is no doubt about it," wrote André Thérive in *Le Temps,* "*David Golder* is a masterpiece."[9] Other critics took up the chorus, and a little more than a month after the publication of the book (in December 1929), Grasset was able to describe it as "an unheard-of success," quoting happily from the highly laudatory commentaries of Henri de Régnier and Gabriel Marcel among others.[10] Marcel Prévost, in his literary chronicle in the weekly *Gringoire,* chose this "prodigious" novel as one of four "formidable" books of the year that "become profoundly inscribed in [one's] memory."[11] For the critic of *La Nouvelle Revue française,* Irène's novel was "at all times moving, and the artistry of the author in the composition of her dialogues gives all the characters an equal intensity."[12] The only dissident note was that of Marcel Thiébault in *La Revue de Paris,* who wondered if the commotion surrounding *David Golder* was justified: "*David Golder* is an excessively uneven book where successful 'pieces' alternate with long passages of a quite artificial inspiration," he wrote.[13]

While *David Golder* certainly benefited from a cleverly orchestrated launching by Bernard Grasset, its success can also be attributed to its subject. For the first time in her career as a young novelist, Irène describes the milieu of her father, that of the Jewish businessmen who had immigrated to France within the past ten years. The idea of situating a novel in this world came to her in 1927 during her vacation in Biarritz, where she beheld the spectacle of "all these idle, unhinged, vice-ridden types . . . this whole world of shady financiers, loose women in search of pleasure and new sensations, of gigolos and courtesans, etc."[14] This is the milieu into which Irène places her character, David Golder, a man raised in the port cities of the Black Sea which Irène and her family knew before the Revolution. She chose the city of Simferopol, "in reality teeming with life and movement, brilliant with light," but in the novel gave it "a melancholy and funereal atmosphere,"[15] so that her protagonist would have his origins in a dark, mysterious, hostile environment. From this city in the murky confines of central Europe, David Golder first emigrates to New York, where he is a peddler, then to Paris, where, because of his intelligence and ambition, he quickly grows rich by investing in oil wells in the newly formed Soviet Union.

The world of speculative business greatly interested the public of the late 1920's. Authors like Paul Morand, André Maurois, and Jacques Roujon also wrote novels that dealt with, as was said at the time, "the inhumanity brought about by great fortunes."[16] The financial collapse of Wall Street, which occurred just before the appearance of *David Golder*, made the world of high finance all the more fascinating. It was a world where fortunes were made and unmade in the blink of an eye, and where the careers of unscrupulous men "seemed to rise or fall just like international rates of currency."[17]

To capture this "upside-down underworld,"[18] as one critic described it, Irène informed herself by reading *La Revue pétrolière* and *L'Impérialisme du pétrole*,[19] two business magazines for specialists like her father. Curiously, however, she did not speak to her father about her project or the manuscript until after the book was accepted for publication:

> When the book was about to appear, I shared my concerns with my father. "Why didn't you speak to me about it?" he said. "I would have enlightened you. You must have been floundering . . . " I showed him the proofs. After looking at them he returned them with a smile. "Like father like daughter. I don't see too many gross errors."[20]

David Golder concerns a specifically Jewish world of businessmen, clearly identified by the names of the principal characters (Golder, Fischl, Soifer) and by their often caricatured physical traits (hooked nose, greasy complexion, etc.). It was this Jewish context of the novel that fascinated both critics and public, who linked Jews to the world of business. In this context it was less the established French Jewish families—the Rothschilds, the Finalys, the Pereires—than the immigrant financiers from Eastern Europe who held the public's attention. There was something slightly unhealthy about this fascination, which assumed that Jews had specifically racial characteristics that defined their attitude towards money. But there is also a current of philo-Semitism, coming principally from Jewish authors writing for a non-Jewish audience. *Juifs d'aujourd'hui: Les Polacks* (Polish Jews Today) by Jacob Lévy was a popular book in 1925. The film *Le Juif polonais* (The Polish Jew), which presented a Jewish man wrongly accused of a crime, had a long run in the Paris cinemas in 1929. Critics picked up quickly on the specifically Jewish nature of *David Golder*. For some it was a confirmation of what they already suspected: Jews were mercenary and rapacious, bent only on acquiring money. The critic of the weekly *Comœdia* wrote: "Is it not strange to note that today, this role of the perpetual trafficker imposed on Jews by history is described in a Jewish novel that seeks to show the horror of it and to deliver itself of it, as one does with a burdensome garment?"[21] Another critic suggests that "the Jew finds bitter solace in poverty . . . as long as he knows he has millions in a London bank for his children, that the 'Promised Land' awaits him, and that more money is on the way. One wonders if this eternal striving for a future happiness, so strongly expressed by the Jewish race, is not what motivates in some obscure way all of mankind."[22]

In the final analysis, what gave *David Golder* its authenticity was the fact that its author was Jewish and therefore able to describe the milieu from within. Irène herself brought her advantageous position to the critics' attention: "Young Frenchwomen do not ordinarily have the experience my circumstances . . . have allowed me to acquire: a background of Jewish high finance with all its dramas, collapses and catastrophes transpiring daily."[23] One of the literary correspondents imagined that "the Jewish public [would] read *David Golder* with passion; it would be able to say 'touché.'"[24] In fact the Jewish press reeled, as if struck by a bomb. It reacted emotionally to Irène's unflattering portraits of Jews and accused her of providing fodder to anti-Semites. Nina Gourfinkel, a Jewish journalist, herself of Russian extraction, went to interview Irène (whom she found perfectly charming) and protested, "Your work paints a Jewish society so distasteful that Jewish opinion has been aroused."[25] Irène attempted to justify herself by raising two points: first, as a Jew herself she couldn't be charged with anti-Semitism; second, she was merely giving a faithful portrait of characters she knew from her own life: "that is the way I saw them." These words, which Irène repeated three times within the course of the interview, did not sway the journalist. "Why do none of your [Jewish] characters have the least bit of tenderness of softness in them? Why do you refuse to give them even a glimpse of a better life?" Gourfinkel asked. "They are Russian Jews," answered Irène, and she added, "obviously, Jews like money." But, she said, it is above all "pride . . . the outlandish pride of his race" that characterizes David Golder as a Jew. Her response to Gourfinkel only exacerbated the anger of the journalist, for whom a Jewish author had a responsibility "not to give ammunition to those against Jews." Gourfinkel walked away from the interview convinced that, if Irène Némirovsky was "not an anti-Semite," she was "also not very Jewish."[26]

The sales of the book were so successful that the already established filmmaker Julien Duvivier wanted to bring it to the screen. His producers (Delac and Vandal) came to an agreement with Bernard Grasset on August 28, 1930, and the film was shown (at the Pigalle theater) on December 17. It was Duvivier's first talking film; it featured the actor Harry Baur in the role of Golder, Paule Andral as his wife Gloria, and Jackie Monnier as his daughter Joyce. Duvivier was captivated by the novel as soon as he read it; in the course of an interview during the filming he commented, *"David Golder* swept me away, and that's why I'm going to turn it into a film. I picked up the book in the evening and couldn't put it down until I had finished it. That's a recommendation."[27]

Duvivier was faithful to the author's intentions, even though he rearranged some scenes and shortened others. He chose Harry Baur, a non-Jewish actor,[28] for the principal role of David Golder; he thus avoided caricaturing the Jewish businessman, producing what one critic called "a drama of Jewish life treated with respect and conviction. We are far from purely Jewish narrative and other gross exaggerations."[29] In addition to voice, Duvivier uses sound for the first time in his cinematographic work. He includes particularly, as the accompaniment to the scene in which Golder dies, a Hebrew prayer said for the dead ("El Maleh rachamim"); coming at the very end of the film, this deeply religious music sets a decidedly pro-Semitic tone. Critics, unable to distinguish between Russian chants and Hebrew prayers, felt that "Duvivier allows his film to peter out in a superfluous sequence of Slavic choirs."[30] Irène, on the other hand, found nothing to reproach Duvivier in his interpretation of her novel; according to one account, "she left the showing [of the film] totally transported."[31]

Even before Duvivier began filming *David Golder*, the dramatist Fernand Nozière (whose real name was Fernand Weyl) went to Bernard Grasset for the rights to turn the book into a play, which were granted in 1930. Nozière had planned to ask Aurélien Lugné-Poe, creator and director of the Théâtre de l'Œuvre (which produced works of such playwrights as Claudel, Romain Rolland, Strindberg, and Shaw) to direct the play and take on the role of Golder. But Lugné Poe's theater was already closing, so Nozière turned to Harry Baur (who was already rehearsing the film version) and found a new venue (the Théâtre de la Porte Saint-Martin). Nozière, who was at the end of his career (he was to die in 1931), had already adapted novels to the stage.[32] He conceived of a loose adaptation of *David Golder*, focusing less on the Jewish aspects of the work than on the psychological drama, in particular Golder's almost fanatical love for woman he wrongly believes to be his daughter—a relationship which, he says, "should be at the forefront."[33] This interpretation met with mixed reactions. "A vibrant, feverish presentation" wrote the critic for *Comœdia*,[34] while in *Gringoire* Georges Champeaux was more reserved: "the novel is too rich, too episodic to be condensed into three acts."[35] Another critic in *Comœdia* held a similar view: "anyone who has read the novel, and then seen both the Vandal, Delac and Duvivier film and the Nozière play, would come to the same conclusion: neither the film . . . nor the play approach the flavor, the structure or the power of this quasi-Balzacian novel."[36]

The play had its première at the Théâtre de la Porte Saint-Martin on Friday, December 26, 1930, just nine days after the first showing of the film. It was a short run; by January 1931, it was taken off the theater's program. On the other hand, Duvivier's film was still showing at the Verdun Palace cinema in the 10th arrondissement as late as September 1931.

But the rivalry between the director of the Théâtre de la Porte Saint-Martin, Maurice Lehmann, and the filmmaker Julien Duvivier exploded, and gave another episode to the "events" surrounding the publication of *David Golder*. When Duvivier learned that Lehmann had accepted Harry Baur as both actor and director of the play *David Golder*, he was

furious. With his producers (Delac and Vandal), he penned a letter to
Irène in which he shared with her his concern that the play was an illegal copy of his film script. Irène was entirely in the dark concerning
these affairs. She declared that she would take sides with neither party,
and that she found the film (excerpts of which she had seen) equal to
the play whose text she had also read. She refused to be drawn into the
quarrel: "I have never breathed a word of the scenario to Mr. Lehmann
or Mr. Nozière, any more than I would have had the idea of speaking of
the play to Mr. Vandal or Mr. Duvivier."[37] But Lehmann attacked Duvivier publicly, in the weekly *Comœdia*. Lehmann did not like the cinema
in the first place, and he was glad to have almost all the actors from the
film in his play; on the other hand, he was not unaware that the success
of the film would certainly encourage people to see the play. In his published letter, Lehmann claims that it was the playwright Nozière, not
the cinematographer Duvivier, who had first obtained Grasset's autho-
rization to adapt the novel. Furthermore, he asserts, "M. Harry Baur
requested that M. Duvivier be present at [play] rehearsals to prove to
him that he had stolen nothing from his film script."[38] Duvivier reacted
by bringing suit against Lehman for having violated his artistic property rights. The trial itself was an anticlimax to the vitriolic letters in
the press. The affair, which probably heightened public curiosity more
than anything else, ended in an amicable arrangement between the parties. Irène Némirovsky stayed on the sidelines.[39]

The Novel

David Golder is an important novel not only because it was popular or
because it launched Irène's career; it also clearly defines the relationship
of the author to her heritage and opens up a path toward the development of a profoundly ambiguous body of literary achievement.

Basically *David Golder* is the story of a man who says no. He says no
to the supplications of a ruined associate who asks him for help; he says
no to his wife who, even as she embraces her gigolo, demands more and
more money from her husband; he says no to the very idea of wealth,
preferring to live modestly and alone rather than in the company of
rich businessmen and bejeweled women. He would like to cease being
a rich Jewish businessman, but there remains one person to whom he

cannot say no, and this is his daughter, Joyce. This is the situation that determines the denouement of the novel. In order to find more money for Joyce, David Golder undertakes a difficult business trip to the Soviet Union, and, returning to France sick and utterly worn out, dies.

As she herself claimed, Irène makes every attempt to portray faithfully the milieu in which Golder evolves. She does not, however, totally eliminate caricature. Quite to the contrary. Golder's wife, Gloria, is portrayed as a rapacious hawk, so eager to get her claws on her husband's money that all other sentiments seem to be excluded from her character. Her Latin American gigolo, Hoyos, is "dry and refined with his small head and silvery hair brushed very high, his tall frame, his fine features and his big, bold nose, with its open nostrils, palpitating with life and fire."[40] The Jewish businessman Fischl, Golder's associate ("drawn directly from life,"[41] according to the author) is described as

a fat little red haired Jew, with pink cheeks, his figure comical and cheap, but a little sinister, too, his eyes gleaming with intelligence behind his thin eyeglasses with their golden frame . . . His his hands were like a murderer's; he carried a china box, full of fresh caviar that he held close to his chest.[42]

Similarly, Soifer, another of the Jewish characters who "exists in flesh and blood," is a miser without the humanity Molière gave his theatrical Harpagon:

[Soifer] was avaricious to the point of madness. He lived in a squalid furnished apartment, in a gloomy street in Passy. He never took a taxi, even when some friend offered to pay for it . . . On rainy winter days he would wait for a motor bus for hours, letting one after another go past when the second class was full. All his life he had walked on tiptoe to make his shoes last longer. For several years, ever since losing all his teeth, he had eaten nothing but slops, soups, minced vegetables, and such things to save the expense of false teeth.

Even David Golder does not escape being caricatured by the author, who stresses "above all his nose . . . enormous, hooked, like that of an old Jewish usurer . . . and his soft, trembling flesh smelling of fever and sweat."[43] Yet in his complexity, David Golder goes beyond the stereotype of the rapacious Jew; he has a soul and a consciousness that set him apart from all the other characters in the novel, Jews and non-Jews.

Victimized by Christians (Tübingen, a Protestant banker, actually controls the financing Golder is trying to negotiate in Russia) as much as by his family, David Golder, alone in the novel, has an awareness of the forces he cannot control and that will finally crush him.

The contradictions in Golder's character only serve to make him appear more human. He is at once cruel (when he rejects a call for help from an old associate and brings about the man's suicide), benevolent (in his attention to the needs of his daughter, Joyce), astute in business affairs (making a fortune in oil wells in Russia), and naïve with regard to the life around him (not seeing the hypocrisy of his daughter). But he is above all victim of his own destiny. Rejected by his colleagues who see in him an implacable enemy, he is also hated by his wife and daughter, although the latter is capable of feigned sweetness when she needs money. Golder will learn in the end that this daughter is not even his own, but rather the offspring of one of his wife's gigolos.

Deprived of love and human warmth, all that remains to Golder is his intelligence—for he sees clearly the hypocrisy of his family—and his identity as a Jew. It is an identity he had repressed in his attempt to integrate into French society; he had even changed his foreign-sounding first name and that of his wife. But as Golder grows more and more isolated, he reconnects with his origins. Along with Soifer, he goes to eat in "a little restaurant with a sign in Hebrew letters" in the Jewish quarter of the Marais, in the Rue des Rosiers; it is the first time since his arrival in France that he becomes conscious of his origins:

> He half closed his eyes. Now what with the gathering darkness, the sound of a lumbering truck, that drowned the sound of motors in the next street, and the shadows that concealed the true height of the houses, he seemed to be back, in his thoughts, in his own country; it was like a dream of familiar sights . . . [44]

He will once again have a flash of consciousness of his origins, this time after he has negotiated his oil contract in Russia. He suddenly finds himself in the village of his birth, which he recognizes "as if he had left it yesterday."[45] It is here that he embarks on his last voyage, just as in his youth he had embarked on the trip which would bring him to France. Later, after he has suffered a heart attack and is about to die, Golder begins to speak Yiddish, and his last human contact is with a young Russian Jew, who like Golder many years before, is preparing to go and make his fortune in France.[46]

But even as he is dying, Golder keeps a clearness of mind that allows him to find his place in the world. "He felt himself losing his voice, the warmth of life, his consciousness of being the man he had been. But to the very end he kept his sight."[47] It is this awareness that allows him, as he is dying, to imagine the house where he was born ("a street of his childhood, a candle close behind a frosted windowpane, the evening") and to hear the voice of his mother ("the voice was deadened by the snow, by the crowding sky, and the deepening darkness, a faltering voice, which was lost to him all at once, as if it had been cut off by a turn in the road").[48] The wandering Jew has stopped wandering. Golder has finally come home; he has reconciled himself with his origins.

One perceives behind *David Golder* aspects of Irène's own personal dilemma. Even as she rejects the world of small Jewish shopkeepers who are unable to fathom the poetry of Ismaël in *Un Enfant prodige*, she also takes exception to the world of Jewish financiers, who are guilty, in her eyes, of being unaware of human love. But while she only saw Ismaël's world from afar, she lived right inside a world much like that of David Golder. In creating a protagonist who is part and parcel of this world and at the same time critical of it, she reveals her own dichotomy. Firmly rooted in the world of her parents, married to a Russian Jew, Irène is torn between rejection of this world (in the name of an ideal of sacrifice and love which will not be made explicit until later in her career) and the certainty that she will never be able to escape her origins. It is this "incomprehensible destiny of all Jews on earth" that she seems to carry with her all her life and that she tries to understand through her literary works. For the moment, her explanation, implicit in *David Golder*, rests on the notion that sees in all Jews the same desire for gain—not so much to grow rich in the present, but to create a bulwark against future calamities, all too real in a world where political regimes and financial catastrophes drive Jews from country to country. Later, Irène would lend a more psychological character to her notion of Jewish destiny; it will include, as we shall see, a search for the impossible not so much in the realm of wealth as in the realm of art and the intellect.[49]

The right-wing press—*Le Temps, La Revue de Paris, Comœdia*—applauded, for quite understandable reasons, this idea of Jewish destiny because it confirmed their own ideas. Gabriel Boissy in *Comœdia* drew from David Golder's tragic end a lesson for the comportment of all Jews: "Should we see here a sign of the time when all gradually assimilated Jews will acquire a taste . . . for the norms and disciplines of the societies with which they are associated?"[50] The far-right *Gringoire* gave more space to *David Golder* than any other newspaper and began to take a very active interest in Irène's career. Gaston de Pawlowsky (the editor) perhaps best describes what he and his editorial staff thought about the Jewish character, linking it to the Germanic myth of the wandering Jew, transformed from a religious myth (the Jew refused to help Jesus on the way of the cross) to a psychological diagnosis, a neurosis that accentuates the Jew's otherness as much as presumed physical characteristics. "The Jew of today remains what he has been for millennia: the wanderer in the desert seeking the Promised Land," writes Pawlowsky.[51]

The relationship that Irène maintained after 1930 with the right-wing press—*Gringoire* and to a lesser extent *Candide*—is worrisome in more than one respect. Founded in 1928, *Gringoire* was to become the weekly newspaper that, more than any other publication, reviewed Irène's work, and it published most of her short stories and novels from 1933 onward. Its editor, Horace de Carbuccia, who had founded a publishing house (Les Éditions de France) in 1924, had a brief political career as a deputy from Ajaccio, but only made one appearance in the Chamber of Deputies. This man was described in a magazine of the times as, "a very Parisian personality . . . one sees him at all the theatrical and film premieres; at the Opéra balls; he is the dandy of the racetracks . . . in season he is found on the fashionable beaches in close proximity of the casinos."[52] To launch his newspaper, Carbuccia had brought together a heterogeneous group of writers, the majority of whom were politically on the right, among them Sacha Guitry, Georges Suarez, Joseph Kessel, Abel Bonnard, and Colette. Taking a lively interest in the question of immigration and national identity, *Gringoire* defended the right-wing leagues, blaming the Jews, and sometimes attacking them in particularly scathing fashion. Under the pen of Henri Béraud, editorials came

down hard on the *métèques,* the Jews and other foreigners whose caricatures—frizzy hair, an enormous nose, bony hands—often found their
way to the front pages of the newspaper. The Jews of the Popular Front
government drew the very personal hatred of Béraud; it was he who promulgated the lie regarding the origins of Léon Blum, creating for him
the false family name of Karfunkelstein and a fictitious Bulgarian parentage.[53] *Gringoire's* literary critic was Jean-Pierre Maxence. Although
he professed to be completely neutral in politics ("I am in agreement
with *no* party, neither the left nor the right," he said in 1939),[54] his articles evidenced a strong antipathy towards the Popular Front coupled
with virulent anti-Semitism. In 1938, for example he wrote about Louis-
Ferdinand Céline's *Bagatelles pour un massacre* (a diatribe against Jews
and other *métèques* whom Céline believed to be responsible for all the
evils in France):

[Céline's book] is a blood cry, an appeal, a free man's revolt . . . It is not
Céline, but rather Jews, who have placed a Blum at the height of power; Blum,
this sophistical aesthete who reeks of rot! It is not Céline who creates the
abusive intrusions of Jews in the world of high finance. He only points out
what already is evident to even the least perspicacious among us, what Jews
themselves—and I have friends among them—deplore and disavow.[55]

Was Irène Némirovsky one of Maxence's Jewish "friends?" There is
no evidence that the two of them knew each other. Yet Maxence continued, throughout the 1930s, to review most of Irène's literary works
and became one of her greatest admirers.

As for Carbuccia himself, there is no doubt regarding his anti-Semitism.
He held Jews accountable for all the outrages of the Third Republic:
"At the heart of all these scandals one finds cosmopolitan adventurers,
the stateless or the newly naturalized: Cornelius Herz, Reinach, Aaron,
called Arton, for the Panama scandal, and also Joanovici, Stavisky, Lévy,
Sacazan, Marthe Hanau, Lazare Bloch."[56] But Carbuccia, like Maxence,
took great interest in Irène; it is he who, even after other editors had
abandoned her during the German occupation, published her texts in
his newspaper and allowed her to earn enough money for survival.

One finds a similar paradox in the case of another weekly, *Candide,*
which after 1938 published two short stories and a novel by Irène. Founded

in 1924 by Joseph Arthème Fayard (who also published the highly anti-Semitic *Je suis partout*), and under the direction of his son Jean from 1936 on, *Candide* never experienced the success of *Gringoire* (with a record printing of 650,000 copies in 1936, outclassing by far all the other weeklies). In its caricatures and articles it rivaled its competitor in its anti-Semitism. Pierre Gaxotte wrote this diatribe against Léon Blum a few days after the fall of the second government of the Popular Front: "First of all he is ugly. On the ungainly body of a puppet, he carries the sad head of a Palestinian mare . . . he holds it against peasants that they walk on French land with their wooden shoes and that they have not had camel driver ancestors wandering in the Syrian desert."[57]

Why did Irène become, after *David Golder*, the darling of a significant portion of the extreme right-wing press? The fact is that even before the advent of the Front Populaire, which further fanned their hatred, the extreme right, true to its mentors (Barrès, Drumont, Maurras), had reproached Jews for wielding an illegitimate political and economic power. To this anti-Semitism, with its Catholic origins, these publications added a second element, that of the racial separateness of Jews and the impossibility of their integration into French society. This racial separateness rests upon the notion of a supposed eastern origin of all Jews; the trumped-up Bulgarian background of the very Parisian Léon Blum was not a coincidence. Gringoire treated Léon Blum and Jean Zay as "oriental oppressors"[58] and mixed all Jews in with immigrants from Eastern Europe or from the "Levant," and with people coming from any known or unknown country with "doubtful origins."

Irène's deep ambiguity with regard to her own origins must have interested the far right, as it sought confirmation of its theses about Jews. By giving David Golder an Eastern European origin, by painting (but not naming) his birthplace as a dark port, home to ships engaging in "strange traffic,"[59] Irène played into the hands of people like Béraud and Maxence. By saying that she had painted a true-to-life portrait of a character (Soifer), whose description corresponded very well with the caricatures of Jews depicted in *Gringoire*, she gave these caricatures a certain legitimacy. When all that Golder has created—his villa, his family life—tumbles like a deck of cards, Irène seems to confirm the notion that Jews exist only through their money; that they are only transients in France, with no real connections; that their true destiny, like their origin, lies far away, somewhere in the East, in mournful cities that one cannot know.

This is doubtless why Irène believed it necessary in 1935 to respond to the accusations of anti-Semitism which continued to appear in the Jewish press. "I never dreamed of hiding my origins," she stated in *L'Univers israélite*. "Whenever I had the occasion, I protested that I was Jewish, I even proclaimed it!"[60] All the while she maintained that David Golder painted a faithful portrait of a Jewish milieu intimately known to her, she was aware of the effect her novel could produce in anti-Semitic circles. "It is quite true," she said, "that if there had been Hitler [at the time], I would have greatly toned down *David Golder*, and I wouldn't have written it in the same fashion."[61] Four years later, when anti-Semitism raged in France in the wake of right-wing opposition to Léon Blum's Popular Front, Irène had another regret. She declared, in *Les Nouvelles littéraires*: "How could I write such a thing? If I were to write *David Golder* now, I would do it quite differently . . . The climate is quite changed!"[62]

The Ball

In July 1930, Bernard Grasset, conscious of the success of *David Golder*, published a second novel by Irène Némirovsky, *Le Bal* (The Ball). According to the author, this novel of just over 100 pages was written "between two chapters of *David Golder*" in 1928.[63] The novel had already appeared in Fayard's *Les Œuvres libres* in February 1929, under the pseudonym that Irène had used for *L'Ennemie*, Pierre Nérey. *Le Bal* would probably not have seen the light of day under the author's real name had there not already been *David Golder*; it appeared in June 1930.

This novel had its origins in a rather ordinary event that Irène claims she witnessed:

One day on the Alexander III Bridge, I had noticed a young girl leaning on the railing, watching the water flow beneath her, while the person accompanying her, who seemed to be an English governess, waited, visibly agitated, for someone who was not coming. The little girl struck me because of the wretched, hard air she had about her. As I watched her, I imagined all sorts of stories, of which *Le Bal* is one.[64]

From this occurrence Irène conceived a scenario pitting the young girl against her parents in an adolescent revolt. Monsieur and Madame Kampf, the *nouveau riche* parents, are planning to give a grand ball to make an impression on all their friends. They do not wish their fourteen-year-old daughter, Antoinette, to attend. Antoinette, however, dreaming of romance, imagines the ball as an occasion "to dance for once in a beautiful dress like a real young lady, pressed in the arms of a young man."[65] For her mother, however, Antoinette is but a "sniveling child"[66] who must spend the evening relegated to a laundry room, and not even allowed access to her own room, which will be used for guests. Madame Kampf asks her daughter to put the invitations in the mail, but Antoinette, crossing the Alexander III Bridge, tears them up—all but one—and tosses them into the Seine. As a result, on the evening of the ball, only one guest arrives, a cousin normally disdained by the Kampfs. Antoinette observes the entire scene from her hiding place behind the couch. She watches her mother break down in hysterics, her father leave after arguing with her mother, and her mother totally collapse, convinced that the guests have refused to come in order to shame the family. Antoinette does not admit her crime; the English governess, who actually saw what happened on the bridge, could divulge the information, but, seeking to keep secret her own illicit affair, chooses to say nothing. Unaware that her daughter has betrayed her, Madame Kampf says to her, "my poor little girl, I only have you . . ." while behind her back Antoinette smiles, savoring her victory.[67]

Critics were not as captivated by this small work as they were by *David Golder*. While for some *Le Bal* was a "surprisingly powerful and suggestive"[68] book, whose author had succeeded in writing "a poignant poem, inspired by the pain . . . of those who have not known the sweetness of being loved by their parents,"[69] for most, the novel lacked the literary qualities of *David Golder*. "The author, for a thousand excellent reasons, trips up and botches a work, scraping the bottom of the barrel," said Simone Ratel in *Comœdia*;[70] "the subject is more vaudeville than drama," wrote the correspondent in *Le Populaire*.[71] Irène was reproached for having created "a highly unlikely story" and for confusing "brutality with power" in the biting dialogues between mother and daughter.[72] In short, most critics agreed that "*Le Bal* is akin to a brief diversion offered during the tragedy of *David Golder*."[73]

Beyond the melodrama of Antoinette's story, however, this novella describes a Jewish social scene that Irène satirizes just as bitingly as she does the financial one in *David Golder*. Monsieur and Madame Kampf are converted Jews who have become Catholics not through conviction or faith, but with a view to penetrating the Parisian upper bourgeoisie. Their world intersects that of David Golder. Monsieur Kampf is "a dry little Jew with fiery eyes" who, having begun as "an insignificant courier in a blue uniform at the door of the bank," ends up a rich speculator on the stock exchange.[74] Their friends are all the pretentious upstart type of Jews, the Levinstein-Lévys, or the Count and Countess du Poirier (in reality Abraham and Rebecca Birnbaum). But here, as in *David Golder*, the identity of the Jew is transparent, all the more so as these Jewish characters try to hide their past. "My word, you think that people don't know who you are, where you come from!" hurls Madame Kampf at her husband.[75] The more the Kampfs try to imitate the French Catholics around them, the more they reveal themselves to be Jewish.

The press was not oblivious to this aspect of the book. "Madame Némirovsky has keenly observed these types of Jews who earn a lot of money, but who later are at odds with the worldly life it creates" said one critic,[76] while another highlighted the "cruelty" of the author's eye "delineating with an implacable clarity all the imperfections and villainies" of the family.[77] But in general the Jewish aspect of the novel interested critics much less than in *David Golder*, where the destiny of the protagonist took on a much more tragic dimension.

One month after the publication of *Le Bal*, Delac and Vandal asked Bernard Grasset for the cinematographic rights to the film; they signed a contract on August 28, 1930. They entrusted the direction of the film to Wilhelm Thiele, and the film was released one year later, in September 1931.[78]

Thiele was much less faithful to Irène's text than Duvivier had been to *David Golder*. He turned *Le Bal* into a farce, obscuring the mother/daughter conflict and the Jewish aspect of the book. He changed Madame Kampf's first name, Rosine, to Jeanne, and made the couple into a pair of shopkeepers who have recently inherited a fortune. Antoinette (played by Danielle Darrieux in her first screen role) is not the rebellious adolescent of the novel, but rather a well-brought-up young girl who adores her parents. If Antoinette throws away the invitations to the ball, as she does in the novel, it is only partly because she has been forbidden to go by her mother. In the film she has caught her mother planning a romantic rendezvous with a young man—a character that is not in the novel—and it is mainly this that motivates her. Furthermore Thiele throws in a happy ending, which distances the film immeasurably from the cruelty of the novel. In the salon, where not a single guest has arrived, Antoinette rises and explains to her parents what she has done; the parents then "begin to smile and all three go out for a meal, arms about each other, just as before."[79]

The press warmly greeted this "pleasant story of a family of hat makers recently grown rich"[80] and the "witty diversion"[81] it provides. The film had a second version, released late in 1931, this time in German.[82] But the essence of Irène's novel had been lost.

Recognition

The publication of *David Golder* and the success of Julien Duvivier's film brought about immediate recognition of Irène Némirovsky's talent. On June 18, 1930, only six months after the novel appeared in bookstores, the author-journalist Gaston Chéreau nominated Irène to the Société des Gens de Lettres de France (the Society of French Men and Women of Letters, founded in 1838 to protect authors' rights). Citing two novels (*Le Malentendu* and *Le Bal*) that had not yet been published, Chéreau affirmed his belief in the author: "[Irène Némirovsky] is not one of the 'hopes' of French literature, she is a 'certainty' for us." One week later Irène sent in her request for admission, citing all the works she had written to date, including two under the pseudonym Pierre Nérey. Her nomination was sponsored by Chéreau and the novelist Roland Dorgelès (author of the antiwar novel *Les Croix de bois* [The Wooden Crosses]), who wrote, "when one has written *David Golder* does one even need sponsors?"[83]

Irène now considered herself a professional author, or as she would later say, "a woman of letters." Her career, if we compare it to that of a similar Russian-Jewish immigrant "woman of letters," Nathalie Sarraute (née Nathalie Tcherniak), appears remarkably less intellectual, and certainly less innovative. Irène was content to keep to the style of Balzac, where the story would unfold as a reconstruction of reality, either real or imagined. She found her editorial home not with avant-garde publishers such as Denoël or Gallimard but rather with the conservative Bernard Grasset or Albin Michel. Her literary output would be large, some of it of great quality and some of it less memorable. Alongside novels such as *David Golder*, well worth a secure place in the literary history of the twentieth century, she would also produce more conventional texts with anecdotal subjects. What merits attention in the life and work of Irène Némirovsky is not then any experimentation with literary form or the creation of a new style; it is rather the relationship between the act of writing and her search for an identity as an author. These two elements are inseparable in Irène's work; if she chose to write *David Golder* and *Le Bal* it is because she wished to be recognized as a Jewish author who could cast a critical eye on her own community. Later in her career, when she chose to abandon Russian-Jewish subjects and write the conventionally French *Les Feux de l'automne* (Autumn Fires), it is because she then wanted to be identified with certain values that she saw as eternally French. That she was torn between these two identities is the heart of the drama that was her life.

David Golder is important in her career, then, not so much because it launched it as because it gave a certain definition to it. All her life Irène would be known as the author of *David Golder*, and all her work to come would be compared to this novel. But Irène would never be content to rest on the laurels of her precocious start. Her ambition was to build a literary career for herself as a French, rather than Russian or Jewish, author. In 1930, this ambition seemed attainable. She seemed to be on the threshold of a stellar literary career.

"Twenty years in France made Irène into a French author," wrote a critic on rediscovering Irène Némirovsky after the war.[1] In fact recognition came much earlier. Only eleven years after her arrival in France, Irène's name was everywhere in the press, on film posters, and in bookstores. One novel, however, does not make a literary career. Irène was conscious that, to become a "woman of letters," she would have to sustain a regular literary output and continue to find favor among Parisian literary reviewers.[2]

As a woman of letters, Irène would publish novels regularly (at least one a year from 1931 to 1941 with the exception of 1932 and 1937), many of them in serial form. Short stories were another matter. Irène wrote prolifically (at least thirty-three short stories from 1931 to 1942), but unlike novels, whose publication was assured through contracts with editors, short stories had to be sold individually to the types of publications that would take them. In this regard, she found the situation of newspapers and reviews particularly favorable.

In the 1930s there was a burgeoning of reviews and political-literary weeklies in France, in which authors could regularly get their works published and be paid a reasonable sum. Authors such as Colette, Simenon, Stefan Zweig, or Jack London (the latter two in translation) were able to have their novels serialized frequently. When the serialized novel grew out of fashion in the course of the 1930s, authors were able to make a living selling their short stories. In fact the short story was having a virtual renaissance, and Irène took full advantage of this situation.[3]

Monthlies such as *La Revue des Deux Mondes, La Revue de Paris,* or *La Nouvelle Revue Française* were the most sought-after periodicals by young authors. *La Nouvelle Revue Française,* in particular, had played a pivotal role in encouraging both French and foreign authors of talent. Under the aegis of André Gide, and later the direction of Jacques Rivière and Jean Paulhan, the NRF made an effort to welcome authors without regard to their political affiliation—which was not the case with many publications. Most reviews adopted well-defined political orientations. *La Revue de Paris,* where Irène sent two stories for publication in 1933 and 1934, was rather moderate; founded in 1894 by the Éditions Calm-ann-Lévy, it had supported Dreyfus and was open to political diversi-ty.[4] But *La Revue des Deux Mondes,* where Irène had four short stories published between 1935 and 1940, upheld a narrow nationalism in its columns, and attracted numerous military contributors, among whom was the General (then Marshall) Philippe Pétain. This publication did not hesitate, moreover, to exhibit xenophobia, not unlike *Gringoire;* a 1936 article against Léon Blum's Popular Front, for example, reminded readers that "France's mistake . . . was to allow within its borders a foreign rabble that thanked her for her hospitality by working for her downfall."[5]

Weekly newspapers made their appearance in the 1920s and 1930s. They were sponsored by publishers who hoped to offer to a broad public political analyses as well as literary texts and critical articles. Larousse launched *Les Nouvelles littéraires* in 1922; Fayard *Candide* in 1924 and *Je suis partout* in 1930; Les Éditions de France *Gringoire* in 1928; Gallimard *Marianne* in 1932; and Albin Michel *Noir et blanc* in 1934.

These weeklies evolved towards the right of the political spectrum, with the exception of *Marianne,* which, even as it hovered on the left, always kept from offending the right. Some, like *Gringoire* and *Candide,* were founded as right-wing publications; others, like *Je suis partout,* turned conservative in the mid-1930s, during the turmoil of the antisocialist and antidemocratic movements that opposed the Popular Front.

These monthlies and weeklies furnished authors with an income far greater than what they would get by publishing their novels in book form alone. When a book was published in installments before coming out in a single volume, an author could sometimes count on 40,000F

($16,000) or more for a novel, double what was offered by publishers. In fact, *Marianne, Candide,* and *Gringoire* served as "large banks" for their authors,[6] and Irène did not hesitate to use the term *nouvelles alimentaires* (potboilers) to describe many of her short stories. As an example, Irène received 64,000F ($23,000) from *Gringoire* for serializing her novel *Deux* and contributing a short story in 1938, and 34,000F ($12,200) from *Candide* the same year for a novella. In contrast, her contract with Albin Michel in 1936 stipulated monthly payments of 4000F ($2055) for a minimum of one novel per year.

Irène's decision to become a woman of letters did not arise simply from a desire to forge an identity for herself; it was also a very practical decision, for she was able to earn as an author more money than her husband made as director of the Banque des Pays du Nord (a job he held until 1939).[7] In fact, Irène earned enough so that the family could move into a spacious apartment on the seventh floor of an attractive building in the Avenue Constant Coquelin, in the Invalides quarter. She was able to employ a maid, a cook, and a governess. The family took summer vacations in Urrugne, near Hendaye, and winter vacations in Megève or Villars.[8] A tax form filed in 1938 by Irène and her husband shows the disparity of earnings between the two: Michel declared 41,850F ($15,054) for the year, while Irène declared 137,000F ($49,280), of which 107,000F ($38,500) was for short stories and serialized novels published in weekly magazines.[9] Thus we can say that at the end of the 1930s, Irène could live by her pen and that she was one of the rare women who, like Colette, could succeed financially in the literary world.[10]

Irène's success required a great deal of effort. First she had to find the right formula. Should she keep to the subject she had taken up in *David Golder*? In fact Irène dealt with several different subjects in her works. Without completely dropping the business world and the French bourgeoisie, of whom she painted an intimate and incisive portrait, she turned her attention to her own past in Russia and Ukraine. She even dabbled in cinema, and wrote a script titled *La Symphonie de Paris* (Paris Symphony) for a film that was never made.[11] She tried her hand at literary biography and wrote about the life of Chekhov; she began, but never finished a book on the romantic adventures of Pushkin. None of the work she published after *David Golder* achieved that novel's re-sounding success.

Irène had thoroughly captivated Bernard Grasset with *David Golder* and had signed a contract with him in October 1929. Between 1930 and 1932 she signed three more contracts with this same editor, for three novels: *Le Bal* in 1930, *Les Mouches d'automne* (The Flies of Autumn, a brief story about exiled Russians in Paris) in 1931, and *L'Affaire Courilof* (The Courilof Affair, regarding the assassination of a Russian minister in the years preceding the October revolution) in 1933. At the end of 1933, however, she found herself, through this close association with Grasset, in an untenable position. Grasset suffered from depression, and spent a great deal of time away from his publishing house in Paris. He con-sulted the psychologist Jacques Lacan for 23 days; under his influence he checked into the clinic of Doctor Garrant at the Château de Garches (where Jean Cocteau had also had treatment). His sisters brought suit against him, alleging that he had grown incompetent to direct his en-terprise. In 1934, following a small incident (a fainting spell), Grasset was replaced by a provisional administrator. A court hearing to decide Grasset's competence took place on July 11 and 12, 1935. At the order of the court, three doctors examined Grasset and found him perfectly capable of supervising his business. A final verdict was rendered on Janu-ary 3, 1936, and on February 8, at a general meeting of the publishing house, confidence in Grasset was restored.[12]

Irène tried to keep herself discreetly at a distance from this affair, but through the intermediary of her husband, took sides for the man who had launched her literary career. Michel was her mouthpiece. One finds, for example, a letter addressed to him by one of Grasset's employ-ees, pointing out the emotional instability of his employer: "He told me he would name me in the . . . will for three million . . . he took me for a complete idiot . . . he uses language so vulgar I wouldn't dare repeat it to you."[13] Michel and Irène kept information such as this to themselves, and on November 6, 1934, Michel sent Grasset's lawyers a letter protest-ing that the publishing house "keeps doing everything it can to isolate [Grasset] completely" and offering to serve as an intermediary in an eventual meeting between Grasset and the lawyers.[14]

Irène, however, did not wish to remain with a publisher whose future seemed so insecure. She was not alone; Jacques Benoist-Méchin, who had good dealings with Grasset, found himself suddenly, and for no apparent reason, forbidden access to the publishing house. Grasset's literary director, André Sabatier, had also had enough.[15] In the fall of 1933, Benoist-Méchin, Sabatier, and Irène all picked up and moved to Éditions Albin Michel, where Irène signed a three-year contract. At about the same time, she made the acquaintance of two men who were to play a major role in her literary career: the newspaperman Horace de Carbuccia (who, as we have seen, welcomed with great enthusiasm Irène's stories and novels in *Gringoire*)[16] and the author Paul Morand.

In 1933, Morand had just edited a collection of short stories titled "La Renaissance de la nouvelle" (The Renaissance of the Short Story) for the publisher Gaston Gallimard. Morand included texts by his friends and acquaintances (such as Pierre Drieu La Rochelle and Marcel Jouhandeau) alongside those of celebrated foreign writers such as Conrad and Poe. Clearly impressed by the stories Irène had published in *Les Œuvres Libres*, Morand contacted her. "Paul Morand has asked me for a book of short stories for a collection he will direct at the NRF [Gallimard]," wrote Irène to Albin Michel,[17] requesting permission to have some works published elsewhere without submitting them first to the editor with whom she had just signed an exclusive contract. "Our spiritual union is truly too recent and it would be disagreeable to me to allow you infidelities when our first offspring is yet to be born,"[18] Albin Michel answered cutely. Irène responded in the same vein: "A wife owes allegiance to her husband. This is why I bow to your decision and hope you will have the same feelings toward our children after they are born as you have while they are in their embryonic stage."[19] In the end Albin Michel mitigated his position and accorded her the right to publish her short stories elsewhere; Grasset also relieved Irène of the obligations she had with him and Paul Morand was able to publish Irène's stories under the title *Films parlés* (Spoken Films).[20]

Having promised Albin Michel a novel that would be called *La Proie* (The Prey), Gallimard a collection of short stories, and Carbuccia several more short stories for *Gringoire*, Irène devoted herself entirely to her writing. She took a nanny for her daughter Denise, and allowed the little girl to play under her writing table as long as she made no noise.[21] With favorite pen in hand, installed on her glassed-in balcony from which she had a view of the garden,[22] Irène wrote prolifically, devoting only a portion of her day to her family, "for you have to divide your life in two!"[23]

Since her contract with Albin Michel assured her of a small but regular monthly allowance (equivalent to $1900), she was free to bring out her novels in serialized form before having them published. In 1934 she met Emmanuel Berl, who had just become editor in chief of the weekly *Marianne*.[24] He agreed to serialize her novel *Jézabel*, which Irène had not yet given to Albin Michel, for the handsome sum of 35,000F ($17,600). Berl and Carbuccia wrangled over Irène's novels; since Carbuccia's weekly sold twice as many copies as *Marianne*, he could offer twice the money for the serialization of her next novel, *Deux*. Albin Michel grew worried; he feared that the novels in installments would attract so many readers that sales of the books would be affected.[25] He was right; sales for *Jézabel* were much less than expected. When Irène complained about this to Albin Michel, he replied: "Authors can write for the weeklies, which do so much harm to publishers, but publishers, who live only from book sales, do not have this extra source of income!"[26]

Irène maintained an output of a novel and several short stories a year, except in 1932 (when her father died) and in 1937 (when her second daughter was born). She kept close watch on what critics had to say and on the sales of her books, which were never as good as she wished.[27] She complained on several occasions to Albin Michel, who pleaded the stiff competition of the weeklies or the economic situation and politics of the Popular Front (guilty, in his eyes, of not having encouraged workers to buy books!).[28] The overdraft in Irène's account with Albin Michel in 1936 was 73,000F ($37,500) and in 1938, 60,000F ($21,600).[29] But her income was steady, thanks to the weeklies. And Albin Michel never asked her to reimburse the overdraft.

Irène bowed to the wishes of her editor and autographed her works in bookstores. She was observed, for example, at the "Eleventh Afternoon Festival for Servicemen-authors" alongside the American dancer Josephine Baker, actors Michel Simon and Arletty, and authors Jules Romains and Colette. "Colette is promoting *Duo* and Irène Némirovsky is again pushing *David Golder*," noted a journalist,[30] and indeed no work sold as well in the 1930s as *David Golder*. In December 1939, during the "phony war," Irène participated in "patriotic activities," giving lectures on French radio and writing articles for the Dutch press on "France's magnificent morale" and "French simplicity and valor."[31]

Although not as sociable as Colette, Irène occasionally invited other authors and intellectuals to her home. These were often, it would appear, members of right-wing political associations. In interviews made in the 1960s, Cécile Michaud, the governess Irène hired for her daughters, claimed that dinner party guests often included members of the anti-republican league called La Croix de Feu [The Burning Cross]. She recalled one particularly tumultuous evening: "All the windows were open, and it caused a scandal in the Avenue Daniel Lesueur, all that was said! What a battle!"[32] That Irène would have had friends in the Croix de Feu is not surprising. Her anti-revolutionary stance, clearly exposed in *L'Affaire Courilof*, caused her to regard with much skepticism the politics of the French left and the Popular Front; moreover, the Croix de Feu, although it held Léon Blum and other socialists in abomination, was not as anti-Semitic as partisans of Maurras's Action Française or leagues such as the Cagoule. Colonel de la Roque, leader of the Croix de Feu, rejected anti-Semitism as incompatible with French tradition, preferring an ideology based on "social, patriotic and paternalistic Christianity,"[33] allied with a fair amount of opposition to immigration.[34] There was even a Jewish Croix de Feu, founded in 1934.[35]

To what extent do Irène's social gatherings indicate her political leanings? The Croix de Feu's emphasis on family and enterprise as the backbones of French society was certainly not incompatible with Irène's convictions; as for their anti-Republican stance, the circles in which Irène moved may speak louder than the words she never uttered. Could she really have had such a close relationship with Horace de Carbuccia without accepting in some way the political orientation of *Gringoire*?

Irène's literary connections in the 1930s are similarly revealing. From the meager correspondence that survived the war, it seems that Irène maintained relationships above all with Jacques Chardonne and Paul Morand. In 1932, Chardonne sent her a copy of his book *L'Amour du prochain*, an essay dealing with subjects as diverse as love, politics, and country living. Writing to acknowledge receipt of the book, Irène expressed her admiration for the author of *L'Épithalame* whose sentiments "have, in addition to their profundity and truth, a poetic resonance which is very moving and astonishes and pleases me like a secret I would like to capture."[36] One can easily understand what would have pleased Irène in Chardonne's work: valorization of conjugal love (which Irène would treat in *Deux*, the most Chardonne-like of her novels) and attachment to the earth (which Irène would highlight in *Les Feux de l'automne* and in stories published at the end of the 1930s). In reading *L'Amour du prochain*, however, Irène could not possibly have been ignorant of the political ideas of its author. Although Chardonne claims to be apolitical ("I belong to no party"[37]), *L'Amour du prochain* clearly belies this neutrality. If his view of Soviet communism is fuzzy, his opinion of Nazi Germany is quite clear. He sees in Hitler's victory "new structures for a society one cannot yet name," a society that would be characterized by "the taste for grandeur [and] qualities of discipline" of a "patient, docile, and fervent" people.[38] After the Germans occupied France, Chardonne would unabashedly proclaim himself pro-Hitler. In 1940, he encouraged French collaboration "with this Europe which is formed over an earthquake";[39] later, in 1941, he accepted an invitation to participate in a trip for certain French authors organized by Goebbels. Finally, he explicitly lent his approval to German concentration camps, claiming that his own son, who had been interned (as a Resistance sympathizer) and then liberated through connections of the author, "[came] back full of admiration for what he [had] seen."[40]

Paul Morand, Irène's other principal literary acquaintance, is a more complex and perhaps more disturbing case than Chardonne. From all accounts it is Morand who first made contact with Irène, asking her for short stories he had read in *Les Œuvres libres*.[41] One can see clearly why this cosmopolitan author, who had traveled everywhere in Europe and written of his travels in several of his books (including *L'Europe galante, Ouvert la nuit*, and *Flèche d'orient*) would take an interest in a writer who had lived through the revolution in Russia, the flight to Finland,[42] and emigration to France. One can understand also how Morand, who took an active interest in the cinema, could have been impressed by the "screenplays" (stories incorporating the point of view of a cinematographic camera) Irène had proposed for the collection. Although Irène never spoke of Morand in her notebooks, she evidently knew him and his wife well. There are numerous references to Hélène Morand in both Irène's and Michel's correspondence.

Paul Morand's attitude toward Jews is quite clear. Irène must have been aware of the crudely anti-Semitic book Morand had had serialized in *Marianne* in December, 1933, *France la doulce* (France the Gentle). In it Morand accused French cinema of having been invaded by "pirates, naturalized or not, who have made a path from the obscurity of Central Europe and the Levant to the Champs-Élysées."[43] In fact, Michel Epstein's brother was himself a film producer and had contributed to the making of René Clair's *The Italian Straw Hat* in 1927. The protagonist of Morand's short novel, Max Kron, is a Jewish film director of Polish origin who makes the rounds of Europe (nose hidden in hand to disguise his Jewishness),[44] searching for material to exploit. "Roaming the world, ready and willing to do anything, this was his ancestral condition," wrote Morand,[45] rehabilitating the myth of the wandering Jew and applying it to the French cinema industry. Morand feigns astonishment that a crass businessman could succeed in making a French film titled "France the Gentle" while at the same time declaring to all concerned that he "[doesn't] give a damn for beauty where money rules."[46] The fault, Morand suggests, lies with the excessive generosity of the French who are unable or unwilling to bring an end to the immigration of the "riff-raff who swarm about here."[47] Using words that would have a terrifying connotation seven years later, Morand's protagonist congratulates himself for having found in France "the good Lord's concentration camp!"[48]

As anti-Semitic as he was, however, Morand was distrustful of politics, even as French ambassador in Bucharest, and kept a distance between himself and the occupying authorities after 1940. His wife, the Romanian princess Soutzo (whose real name was Hélène Chrissoveloni), was not so discreet. Hélène Morand was proud of her hatred for Jews, and during the occupation, her admiration for Nazi ideology led her to weave close relations with the German ambassador, Otto Abetz, and his wife. "Viscerally anti-Semitic, she would remain furious and deeply grieved when her grandson and sole heir, Jean-Albert de Broglie, married

Colette Nedela, a Romanian Jew," wrote one of Morand's biographers.[49] Surprisingly, given her attitude toward Jews, Hélène Morand is alluded to in a great deal of Irène's correspondence. When Irène was arrested in 1942, it is to Hélène Morand that Michel would appeal, perhaps because of her friendship with Abetz.

It is very likely that the severity of Irène's portrayal of Jews in her early works would have brought her to the attention of anti-Semitic authors. But she could not have been unaware that she was merely tolerated by the likes of Carbuccia, Morand, and Chardonne. In the course of the 1930's, Irène became an "acceptable" Jew, one who could be frequented by people who normally refused to tolerate Jews in politics and who shunned them in society. These anti-Semites could flatter their consciences with the notion that they had a Jewish friend who even shared some of their suspicions. It is thus no surprise that the right-wing press paid so much attention to her. The poet Henri de Régnier, writing in *Le Figaro*, lauded her novels in articles written just before his death in 1936. *Gringoire*, as we have seen, featured her works prominently. The left wing press, such as *L'Œuvre* and *Le Populaire*, which had reviewed her early novels, soon came to forget her.

Irène seems to have been oblivious to the tumultuous political events surrounding the final two decades of the Third Republic. The rise and fall of governments, the state of the franc, the debate about Germany's payment of war reparations, the harsh economic policies of Pierre Laval— none of these problems figure in her novels or short stories. There is no reaction to the riot in front of the Palais Bourbon on February 6, 1934, and no mention of Léon Blum's popular front or the industrial unrest that accompanied its coming to power in June 1936. But behind this apparent indifference lurks a very palpable sympathy for right-wing causes. Her espousal of traditional French values, evident in her later novels, is a case in point. There is also a troubling, if understandable, tendency to see Jews at the origin of the revolutionary activity in Russia that forced her family out. We find, for example, this note in her writer's notebook: "The aim of my life. If I live to an old age, if I have enough money to work slowly, I would like to document myself about Trotsky's life, as the sort of eternal Jew, always in revolt . . . a traitor, a bit of a bum, always finding a way out of tight situations . . ."[50]

Because of her close associations with the right, Irène probably believed herself to be immune from any difficulties she might encounter
at the beginning of the 1940s; she would, however, have the bitter experience of being abandoned by some of the very people who earlier
sang her praises. In the Paris of the 1930s, where the numbers of immigrants increased regularly, Irène could see herself as quite separate
from them: she was well integrated into the literary world, appreciated
as a French author and surrounded by people who seemed to be French
hospitality incarnate.

Nevertheless, as much as a large segment of the French press accepted Irène as one of their own, they never let her forget her foreign
origins. An anonymous interviewer asked her, in 1935, if she really felt
that she knew Paris; "perhaps I know the foreign contingent better,"[51]
was Irène's surprising confession. As she temporarily abandoned Russian
subjects to devote herself to novels and stories portraying the French
bourgeoisie, the press persisted in evoking her foreign origins. "A temperament, and a grasp of the world that are distinctly Slavic," noted
a critic after the appearance of the traditional and conservative novel
Deux.[52] Regarding the same novel, another critic suggested that, as a
foreigner (like Julien Green and Henri Troyat), Irène could not grasp
the totality of the French soul but rather "has worked exclusively on a
small agitated surface of French reality."[53]

Far more serious, however, than these reminders in the press of Irène's
foreignness was the refusal of the French government to naturalize her
or her husband. According to French law, they were eligible for French
citizenship as early as 1921, that is, three years after the beginning of
their stay in the country. Yet they did not request naturalization until
1938, when the climate had turned very much against immigration.[54]
Why did they wait so long? The only plausible explanation lies in the
worsening of the situation for aliens in France from 1938 on. Irène could
not have been ignorant of the anti-Jewish demonstrations of September, 1938; she had probably read, in April, 1938, of Robert Brasillach's
appeal "to consider Jews from foreign countries as aliens and to place
in opposition to their naturalization the most imposing of obstacles."[55]
She was certainly aware of the opinion of Emmanuel Berl, himself a Jew,
for whom "a statute for foreigners [was] necessary—and as quickly as

possible—if one wished to avoid more and more serious conflicts between Frenchmen and immigrants."[56]

It was therefore necessary to act quickly, and on November 23, 1938, Michel addressed a request for naturalization to the Service des Naturalisations de la Préfecture de Police. This request was supported by letters from Michel's employers (the Banque du Pays du Nord) and from Irène's admirers—Jean Vignaud (president of the Société des Gens de Lettres de France) and André Chaumeix (who had just been named director of the *Revue des Deux Mondes*). On December 1, Michel submitted the birth certificates of his two daughters (both born in France, hence French citizens) as well as his marriage certificate, but explained that both his and Irène's birth certificates had been "lost in Russia." Vignaud and Chaumeix wrote flowery letters. For Chaumeix, Irène was "one of the most original and strong talents among contemporary authors."[57] Five months went by without a response. On April 27, 1939, Irène and Michel were asked to re-produce documents they had already submitted. By September 1939, they had still not received an answer to their application. Vignaud wrote a letter to the Garde des Sceaux (France's minister of justice) reiterating his and Chaumeix's support of the couple, adding that "it must be present circumstances that have caused a delay in the favorable outcome of this request."[58] What circumstances? It is true that since September 1939, when Germany invaded Poland, the "phony war" had begun, but would this have been enough to impede progress of the application? The matter was never resolved. The application was simply ignored. It was a state of affairs that was to have deep repercussions on Irène and her family's position during the occupation, and it would forever cast a shadow on Irène's desire to assimilate.

5   *The Writer's Craft*

Irène Némirovsky's writer's notebook abounds with reflections and notations. During the course of the 1930s most of these notes gave rise to novels or short stories. Although she began as a painter of a distinctly Russian milieu, she quickly revealed herself to be an impressive observer of the French way of life, "a novelist with her eyes wide open," wrote Jean-Pierre Maxence, adding "posed before the exterior world, her observations penetrate and project beyond it."[1] And while none of her subsequent works achieved the success of *David Golder*, Irène succeeded in forging for herself a clear identity as a writer of distinction—mature, perspicacious, and pitiless for her characters.

"The true mystery of the world is the visible and not the invisible," Irène wrote in her notebook, borrowing a phrase from Oscar Wilde.[2] She attempted to describe with great precision the observable behaviors of her characters, analyzing them in their social contexts. As she did in *David Golder*, she began with what was closest to her. Paris, the Basque city of Hendaye, and the watering places she knew—this is where she chose to situate her novels and short stories. And as in *David Golder*, money would be the common thread that linked both the locales of her works and their characters. Disputed inheritances, petty jealousy, family disputes linked to money, and destitution form the themes of the largest portion of her work. "I tried to depict modern life with its harshness and subservience to money," she explained. "This is what is cruelest about our times, this struggle which many cannot endure."[3]

Important as it is, money is not the only subject that preoccupied Irène in the 1930s. Even while creating a reputation as a "French" writer, she began to re-create parts of the Russian world she knew. Two themes fascinated her: that of the impulse for violent revolution in czarist Russia and that of the pain felt by Russians who, for various reasons, were forced to leave their homeland. She also saw herself as a literary biographer of Russian authors and undertook works on Chekhov and Pushkin.

Irène's reputation in the 1930s was thus that of a writer caught between two worlds—Russia and France. But there is another world always waiting in the background—a Jewish world. It is both familiar and distant, and it perpetually haunts Irène. We find comments such as this in her notebook: "[A] French Jew . . . [a] stranger to the French, a foreigner [such as] Zyromski or Silbermann, which brings him many problems." That she would refer to a militant socialist (Jean Zyromski) in the same breath as the hero of Jacques de Lacretelle's novel (Silbermann) is significant. Jacques de Lacretelle describes the sad fate of a young Jewish boy who, despite a knowledge of French culture superior to that of his Christian classmates, is painfully conscious of his difference and becomes alienated to the point of leaving France. As for Zyromski, this Jewish socialist—who was to the left of Léon Blum and led the unsuccessful fight for French support of Spanish republicans during that country's civil war—was the object of the same kind of anti-Semitic attacks as those that hounded Blum. He was wrongly accused by the right-wing press of misuse of public property; like Stavisky, he became emblematic of a popular prejudice against Jews that linked them with the scandals that hounded the Third Republic.[4] Irène's continued preoccupation with the compatibility of her Jewishness and her French identity will lie smoldering during most of the 1930s, and not be turned into literary creation until later.

Writing Short Stories

Irène's reputation as a novelist was solidly established by *David Golder.* During the 1930s, she created an equally impressive reputation as a short story writer. Her first stories, those edited by Paul Morand under the title *Films parlés* (Talking Films), drew their inspiration indirectly from the film adaptations of *David Golder* and *Le Bal* and directly from the filmscript she wrote in 1931. "Madame Irène Némirovsky has just published a collection of short stories which are unquestionably linked to cinematographic technique," announced *Gringoire*.[5]

This collection, which appeared in early 1935, contains both stories that had been previously published in *Les Œuvres Libres* and two original pieces. *Films parlés* was an immediate success. Jean-Pierre Maxence in *Gringoire* pronounced Irène "a born writer of stories" and compared her to Maupassant ("the same vision of the totality of the subject"), to Mauriac ("these rash, dense, and bold dialogues"), and to Chekhov ("these lucid and melancholy notations").[6] If Edmond Jaloux, in *Les Nouvelles littéraires*, was somewhat less enthusiastic than Maxence ("Mme Némirovsky's stories have neither the originality nor the literary quality of those of Marguerite Yourcenar"),[7] Henri de Régnier was lavish with his praise of the "strange and unique beauty" of her work.[8]

One of the stories ("Film parlé") involves experimentation with a cinematic technique: the narrator is replaced by the eye of a camera, which records what it sees in a coldly objective fashion. But the importance of *Films parlés* is less its narrative technique (which Henri de Régnier found not to have much merit) than the subjects Irène brings to her work. Of the four stories in *Films parlés*, one, "Les Fumées du vin" (The Fumes of the Wine), is about the civil war in Finland, a subject that will reappear in another story, "Aïno," published in 1940, and that reconnects with the Russian theme of exile. Another, "La Comédie bourgeoise," takes place in a northern village in France and concerns the romantic life of an industrialist's daughter named Madeleine (likely inspired by Madeleine Avot) in a traditional society thrown into turmoil by post-war immorality. This story heralds other texts to come (both novels and short stories) that deal with the lost souls of the 1920s—those French men and women who could not adapt to modern values. In two other stories, "Film parlé" and "Ada," we have marginal individuals, wrenched from their homelands, trying to survive in the Paris of the 1930s. One of these characters is an old dancer of Eastern European origin, barely holding on to life; the other is a young girl from the provinces who comes to Paris in search of her long-lost mother, a prostitute in a bar close to the Opéra. In both cases, a world peopled with aliens (Jews, South Americans, and Russians) clashes with the implacable reality of a city that rejects them and where they are confronted, inevitably, with their own isolation.

Films parlés thus put Irène on the literary map for a variety of subjects, appealing to a variety of readers, but always within the confines of traditional French values. It is not surprising that conservative weeklies and reviews (*Gringoire, Candide, La Revue des Deux Mondes,* and *La Revue de Paris*) would consistently publish Irène's short stories. Given the good prices these publications were willing to pay, Irène made a point of writing as many stories as she could and keeping them in a drawer for future use. She would often submit stories she had written years earlier, and during the occupation, it was through the publishing of her short stories that Irène was able to survive. Some of these were re-issued in 2000,[9] but most of them remain in their original form, deep in the stacks of France's National Library.

Writing about Russia

The two Russian novels Irène wrote in the early 1930s take their inspiration both from her own experience and from her desire to understand the forces that led her country to civil war. The first of these works, *Les Mouches d'automne* (The Flies of Autumn), was published in an illustrated deluxe volume by Kra before being published by Grasset in 1932.[10] This is a nostalgic portrayal of an elderly Russian servant woman during the October Revolution and subsequent exile in France. It is a paean to old Russia, an apology for the caste system in which the old "baba" feels quite comfortable and happy to serve her masters with no thought for herself and her own needs. *Les Mouches d'automne* is as gentle towards its characters as *Le Bal* was cruel. Tatiana Ivanovna, the servant, raises the children and runs the household of her wealthy master in pre-revolutionary Russia. When the revolution arrives, Tatiana, at great risk to her own life, escapes with the family jewels, which she uses to enable her, her master, and his family to emigrate to France. But Paris of the 1920s does not sit well with Tatiana; she can accept neither the frivolity of the adolescent girls in her charge nor the long, snowless winters. On a foggy night that she somehow imagines as snowy, she ever so gently descends to the Seine, and there she drowns herself. "She had just enough time to make the sign of the cross, and when her raised arm fell backwards, she had expired."[11]

Irène's personal experience and her familiarity with the Russian community in Paris certainly contributed to the pictures she paints of the various different ways in which Russians coped with their exile. On the one hand there are the young people who, like the adolescents in this novel, give themselves up to a life of dissipation through alcohol and sex; on the other, adults, such as Tatiana's master, attempt to create a new life by working mechanically, with minimal thought to events gone by. But the oldest generation, those who had spent most of their adult lives under the Tsarist regime, can do little else but dwell on the past and images of a world disappeared. These are the victims of the revolution in Irène's eyes, for they cannot adapt to a new world, whether it be communist Russia or the capitalist west. The only exit for them is suicide.

Irène's novel touched the critics. "These few recollections of the Russian Revolution and the early years in Paris of a family of émigrés . . . are in fact much less rudimentary, much less facile . . . than *David Golder*," wrote a reviewer in *Les Nouvelles littéraires*,[12] a judgment seconded by Marcel Prévost, who wrote in *Gringoire* "this story [is], in my opinion, of superior quality to *David Golder*."[13] Certainly the portrait of the Russian "baba" is well executed; Irène recreates the ambiance of the Moscow countryside as well as that of the Passy quarter in Paris where the better-off émigrés took refuge. But there is a pathetic quality to Tatiana that was not evident in David Golder and which made the latter into a tragic figure. The tragedy in *Les Mouches d'automne* is rather that of Mother Russia, brought to rack and ruin by forces that, in the novel, are indefinable and inexpressible. It is not a politically based anticommunism that defines Irène's attitude but rather a nostalgic sadness, powerlessness in the face of events that are seemingly beyond human control. Michel tried to use *Les Mouches d'Automne* as proof of Irène's anticommunism when she was arrested in 1942, but in fact (as Irène's editor pointed out to Michel) the novel is anything but political.[14] Despite her sympathy for the right, Irène seems to have deeply distrusted politics as well as any sort of ideology. These misgivings would become very evident in the next novel she submitted to Bernard Grasset, *L'Affaire Courilof* (The Courilof Affair).

The writing of this novel coincides with the death of Irène's father Léon in Nice in September 1932. Irène chose to use her father's name for the protagonist of the novel, a Marxist revolutionary named Léon M . . . , and has him die in Nice. She chose her mother's first name, Fanny, for Léon's partner, who is also Jewish and a revolutionary. The historical premise of the novel is the series of assassinations of the tsar's ministers that took place in 1904–1911 (the assassinations of two ministers of the Interior, one minister of Public Education, and two governors).

The fact that Irène decided to write a novel about the years preceding the 1917 Revolution, rather than about the Revolution itself, is significant. She avoids any reference to mass confrontations or the economic reasons that led to workers' uprisings. Revolutionary conflict in the novel is distilled into the meeting of two individuals, one revolutionary and the other representative of the old regime. The novel begins in 1903. Léon, born to a family of terrorists, and member of a revolutionary group based in Switzerland, is assigned, as his first mission, to assassinate the Tsar's Minister of Education, a formidable figure named Courilof, responsible for the bloody repression of a student movement in St. Petersburg. Passing himself off as a doctor, Léon succeeds in penetrating the Courilof household and quickly becomes an intimate of the minister, who is battling the ravages of cancer as well as his political enemies. Léon inevitably is privy to the political and private dramas of Courilof's life. When the moment of action arrives, he is incapable of tossing the bomb. His partner Fanny, who only knows Courilof from the exterior, is called in and makes the fatal gesture. She is arrested and puts an end to her life in prison; as for Léon, condemned for a murder he believed in but could not commit, he escapes death and goes into hiding.

To be sure, Léon is perfectly aware of the political situation, but his motives are not political. His hatred for Courilof, called "the whale" because he is "ferocious and voracious,"[15] is based on the man's cruelty in ordering the killing of protesting students. Yet as Léon comes to know Courilof, he sees the situation in shades of gray rather than in black and white. Courilof is, in fact, a moderate, playing the political game of survival. He opposes the extreme right, those who espouse the cause of "Russia for the Russians," and who refuse railway concessions to Jews and foreigners. When Courilof sends troops to quell the student revolt he does not in fact order the soldiers to shoot. That command is given by the Minister of the Interior, who, we learn, has sent provocateurs to shoot at the police. Hence Courilof is innocent of having ordered the death of civilians, even though he opposes the student uprisings as the work of "professional revolutionaries, an infernal swarm, who would end up destroying all that was good and noble in Russia."[16]

As a revolutionary, Léon paradoxically understands Courilof's point of view; he agrees with him that "blood must be shed . . . for a just cause,"[17] even if he disagrees about the cause. There develops between the two men a reciprocal intelligence, even a complicity, which goes beyond any political consideration. "Perhaps [Courilof] had the same feelings toward me as I to him . . . comprehension, curiosity, an obscure fraternity . . ." thinks Léon.[18] Just as Léon begins to grasp the thought processes of the man he has been sent to assassinate, he begins also to admire him and becomes an apt pupil. Having failed to kill his new mentor, Léon will, after the October Revolution, find himself in exactly the same position as Courilof; his masters will be the Soviet rather than the Tsarist government. "It is in some measure to Courilof that I am beholden," he reflects ironically. "He taught me more than he knew."[19]

Irène thus made her one "political" novel a reflection on the moral corruption of all politics and ideology. Her attitude met with the disapproval of the press, which saw in her work an unwillingness to address the forces that motivate political movements. "There is here a certain confusion between the writer's detachment and that of the protagonist who is engaged in action . . . The assassination attempt in the end holds little interest, and the only tragedy is human stupidity," wrote the reviewer of *Les Nouvelles littéraires*.[20] But it is clear that for Irène, the motivation for political action is not substantially different from the motivation of the businessman; in both cases, self-preservation and the willingness to sacrifice others for one's own profit take precedence over human kindness and generosity. This attitude would show little change during the course of Irène's literary career.

Writing about France

"I continue to depict the society I know best, that is composed of misfits, those who have been expelled from their milieu, the place where they would normally have lived, and who do not adapt to their new lives without clashes or suffering,"[21] said Irène shortly after the publication of *Le Pion sur l'échiquier* (The Pawn on the Chessboard) in 1934. The lack of success of *L'Affaire Courilof* led her to abandon Russian topics and to turn once again to the world she could observe close by. She had been working on the semi-autobiographical novel, *Le Vin de solitude*, throughout the early 1930s, and this novel would be published in 1935. But the rest of her literary production during this decade would deal with characters drawn from everyday life, and privilege those who did not easily fit into French society. In addition to *Le Pion sur l'échiquier*, these novels include Jézabel (translated as *A Modern Jezebel*), published in 1936 (after being serialized in *Marianne*), and *La Proie* (The Prey), published in 1938.

In his report to Albin Michel, the reader responsible for *Le Pion sur l'échiquier* wrote: "The hero of this story, incapable of adapting to the sort of life imposed by this epoch, is brought to suicide."[22] This statement could serve as the paradigm for all three novels. Whether the protagonists be foreigners (or "cosmopolitans," as Irène would say),[23] like Christophe Bohun in *Pion sur l'Échiquier* or Gladys Eisenach in *Jézebel*, or whether they be Frenchmen like Jean-Luc Daguerne in *La Proie*, they inevitably find themselves at odds with the reality of their social milieu. For Bohun and Daguerne, the conflict is between their desire to overcome the mediocrity of their existence and the reality of the world of business and intrigue to which they are destined. For Gladys Eisenach, the clash is between the natural process of growing old and an irrational (though understandable) wish to be desirable to younger men. Each of these three novels ends in violence. In *Le Pion sur l'Échiquier* and *La Proie*, the protagonists, incapable of reconciling their lives with the financial and emotional demands of the world in which they live, have recourse to suicide. In *Jézabel*, Gladys kills her own grandson when he threatens to reveal her actual age to her young lover; this is in itself a sort of suicide, for Gladys knows that she will be condemned to death for her crime.

Many of Irène's short stories published in the 1930s reflect similar themes. A prostitute or a dancer (often foreign) looks for a way to shirk the obligation to earn a living;[24] a woman is imprisoned in a futile marriage to a man who cheats on her;[25] a retired school teacher cannot adapt to life in Paris after having once been a governess in Russia.[26] These diverse characters, while they do not always meet the tragic ends of the protagonists in the novels, display the same incapacity for assimilation into society. They can only adapt by means of subterfuge.

What characterizes these people is what Irène calls "a disturbing split between the outward appearance of these creatures and their interior lives."[27] Deeply troubled, on the surface they nevertheless resemble normal beings, even superior ones. Thus Gladys, who has killed her grandson, wins from the court a reduced sentence of five years (the judges are moved by "the charm, the beauty, the culture of this woman").[28] Similarly, Christophe Bohun seemingly leads the life of a bourgeois Parisien, even though his acute sensitivity to the futility of his own profession as a businessman drives him to suicide. Most of these characters are encumbered by a dark past that they must try to conceal. Gladys, daughter of a ship owner in Montivedeo, has lived in America, Poland, Italy, and elsewhere before landing in France. Christophe Bohun's father was born in poverty somewhere in Eastern Europe, and although not Jewish, he exhibits the same rapaciousness as David Golder. The protagonist of *La Proie* has no foreign parentage, but he is "poor, from an obscure family"[29] and has a difficult time moving in well-heeled circles. This is a theme dear to Irène, and one that will become more pointed as she deals further with her own Jewish heritage. For the critics, Irène "makes us feel that the real fatality of every man is that which he carries inscribed in his mind and in his body."[30]

Critics greatly admired Irène's pitiless stance with regard to her characters. They noted, for example, "the unspeakable pessimism which emanates from Madame Némirovsky's latest novel [*Le Pion sur l'échiquier*], a frightfully truthful book bearing witness to a vision that is so cruel in its sad lucidity that one is astounded to think that it stems from the pen of a woman, and one so young."[31] In an article written just before his death, Henri de Régnier commented: "With pitiless compassion and intensity, Mme Irène Némirovsky has erected, opposite a mirror that reflects life and all that is pleasing and displeasing in it, another mirror which reflects the soul."[32]

One wonders, though, if the critics understood the real intentions of the author. If Irène had acquired the reputation of an astute observer of misfits, it is in some sense in spite of herself. Her goal in painting the portrait of the monstrous Gladys Eisenach, for example, was "to paint a passion, a passion quite common to all modern women. When I began to write I was full of severity towards my 'criminal' . . . And then, as I wrote . . . I began to find all sorts of excuses for her."[33] This compassion is important in more than one sense. Far from turning a pitiless gaze on the unfortunate characters she creates, the author (through the narrator) searches for an explanation. Far from exhibiting unspeakable pessimism, her novels point to a way out of the misfits' dilemma. What the critics seem to have overlooked are the serene, stable, understanding secondary characters that Irène also puts into these novels.

These positive characters, as it were, take several shapes. In the short story "Film parlé," a prostitute has her daughter raised in the country by her sister; the young girl, who comes to Paris to find her mother, is seduced by a dishonest man, but ends up paying the latter's debts and introducing a measure of stability into their relationship. At the end of the story the girl has taken on "an air of repose and happiness" while the mother, in a drunken stupor, sits with "sunken staring eyes."[34] The same sort of character, in *Le Pion sur l'échiquier*, will take the form of a young woman in love with Christophe Bohun; she sacrifices her life to be close to the man who has rejected her to marry another woman. In *La Proie* this type of character is more thoroughly dissected. Marie, the mistress of a man who has been incarcerated through the fault of the protagonist, Jean-Luc Daguerne, incarnates a generosity of spirit that contrasts sharply with the egotism of Jean-Luc and his wife. Her quiet poverty, which she accepts, is understood by Jean-Luc as a "silent submission"[35] to her fate, and this man, who has always sought only wealth and recognition, begins to experience in Marie's presence a "feeling of peace"[36] and a "deep tenderness which neither his wife nor his child, nor any other person in the world has succeeded in arousing in him."[37]

Irène's intent thus appears less to be social criticism than moral enlightenment. Her secondary personages, even when these are victims of her protagonists, inevitably point the way toward an existence free of the pursuit of wealth, eternal youth, or physical pleasure. Where this other way—this moral way—was only hinted at in *David Golder* or *Le Bal*, the novels written later in the 1930s become ever more explicit. The tendency will be further developed as Irène moves further away from her family and more closely identifies with a world view that was essentially Christian.

Writing about a Jewish Childhood

Le Vin de solitude (Wine of Solitude) stands apart from the other works of Irène Némirovsky, for, although it was published in 1935 at the same time that *Jézabel* was serialized, it belongs to an earlier period of the author's literary production. Its portrait of the protagonists' parents (Boris and Bella Karol) echoes David and Gloria Golder. The novel's protagonist (Hélène Karol), a young girl with a penetrating discernment well beyond the norm for a girl of that age, and with an implacable hatred for her mother, recalls Antoinette in *Le Bal*. Finally, certain scenes in the novel concerning the love life and the adultery of Gloria have their roots in the early short story "L'Ennemie." Most important, the novel itself is a long reflection on the youth of a girl whose resemblance to Irène is not a coincidence.

In essence, *Le Vin de solitude* ties all the early novels together into an examination of Jewishness. Irène's discomfort with regard to her origins is palpable, as is her desire to paint Jewish characters in a light that borders on anti-Semitism. *Le Vin de solitude* both echoes its predecessors and goes beyond them, for it leads to the liberation of the protagonist from all the forces of her past and her origins and toward the possibility of choosing her own destiny.

For critics and journalists in 1935, however, it was the conflict between Hélène and her mother that held their attention. Their fascination centered on the hatred between mother and child as they both compete for the love of the same young man. "How a child who is loving, sweet and good, but who also carries within her a terrible perspicacity known to few young people, comes to the point of truly hating her mother: such is the subject of this beautiful novel by Mme Irène Némirovsky," wrote Henri de Régnier.[38] It is quite probable that Irène herself had a stormy relationship with her own mother,[39] even though she reveals little about her family in her personal letters. In a far more general sense, *Le Vin de solitude* is as close to autobiography as we can find in Irène's work.

Hélène's French governess plays a key role in the development of the novel, as we have seen. She alone is responsible for the young girl's education and sees to it that this education is not only in the French language but also inculcates French (not Russian and certainly not Jewish) values. The result is an increasing alienation of Hélène from her native city and its people. Kiev, "this sleepy provincial city, lost in the heart of Russia," becomes for the protagonist a place "of crushing sadness,"[40] whereas the annual trips she takes to France with her family are described as "a haven of light."[41] Hélène prefers to sing French songs, is steeped in readings about the life of Napoleon, replays the battle of Austerlitz with other children, and attends mass in a French church. She comes to bemoan her own identity: "Oh to be called Jeanne Fournier, Loulou Massard or Henriette Durand, a name that is easy to understand, easy to remember!"[42]

Hélène's alienation almost seems to be due to an error of birth: she should have been born in France of French parents. The particularly odious nature of the Karol family makes her situation only worse. If Hélène cannot bear the egotism and falseness of her mother, she finds the behavior of her father no more appealing, despite her affection for him. He abandons her at a casino in Monte Carlo, forgetting that they were to meet at the exit. He speaks the language of business, not of affection; "words [are] replaced by numbers."[43] As he lies dying, all he can find to say to his daughter is to ask her to look for his wallet, and to take out some money.

It is not only for his materialism that Hélène reproaches her father; it is also his Jewishness. This is the characteristic that turns him and his friends into men without scruples, indifferent to the suffering their machinations might provoke, and with no attachment to the country in which they live. Boris, the "little Jew who has come from nothing,"[44] has a friend and associate named Slivker, "a Jew with jet black eyes, whose arm shakes when he speaks, in a jerky motion, as though he still carried the stack of carpets he must once have sold in outside cafés."[45] For Slivker, as for Boris, "happiness . . . is war."[46] He has already sold spoiled food to the Russian army (causing the death of several soldiers) and is now preparing to sell them old Spanish cannons of dubious quality. "I have not the death of a single man on my conscience," says Slivker, and Boris Karol "laughs like a child" on hearing these words.[47] For Boris, Russia is not a native land any more than France is a sanctuary of freedom; he is the wandering Jew, observing with satisfaction as he crosses the Place Vendôme, "We make money at every step . . . we're rolling in it."[48]

Hélène's great disillusionment comes when the family is installed in Paris and she realizes her life is the same as it had been in Kiev. Rather than socialize with French people in the image of Mademoiselle Rose (now gone), the Karol family sees foreigners, among whom is an Armenian "with dull blue hair, a hooked nose and thick raspberry colored lips;" the latter, growing close to Bella, "transported by her eastern imagination," ruins Boris, who is already ailing.[49] With her father dead, Hélène at last sees herself "delivered from [her] house, from [her] childhood, from [her] mother, from all that [she] hated," and, in her "bitter and heady solitude," she breaks with the ties that linked her to her Russian and Jewish past, fleeing from her home into unknown quarters of Paris.[50]

In the context of this novel, France—the France of Mlle Rose, symbolized by the Arc of Triumph which Hélène sees when she leaves home—is the antithesis of the stateless world of the Jew, which Irène describes in terms that echo the anti-Semitism of the period following the Dreyfus Affair. "The Jewish race [is] forever devoured by a sort of fever, the fever of profit," wrote a Paris newspaper in 1898,[51] and Irène's description of Boris's character seems to confirm this judgment, as it confirms the views of the notorious anti-Semite and author of *La France juive*, Édouard Drumont, "the Semite is mercenary, greedy, scheming."[52] By lumping together Jews and Armenian, each one as greedy as the other, Irène echoes the racist notion, popular in the France of the 1930s, that immigrants from the east (what was called "the Levant") as well as Armenians, Greeks, and Jews all had common cultural characteristics that threatened a well-ordered society and were opposed "to reason, to subtlety, to prudence and to the sense of moderation which characterize the French."[53]

The criticism of Jews in this novel does not seem to have attracted much attention in 1935, although at least one journalist, Jean-Pierre Maxence in *Gringoire*, does remark on the "foreigners . . . ejected from their countries by the Revolution, who do business in one town and another."[54] Irène herself downplayed the Jewish aspect of the novel. In an interview shortly after the book's publication, she stated: "my ambition is to touch . . . those who have known despair at an age one normally characterizes as happy, but who have had the courage (or the good fortune) to continue living and loving life."[55] But Irène was being somewhat disingenuous in her public pronouncements. In the privacy of her notebooks, her Jewishness is consistently present. *Le Vin de solitude* is not only about a young woman's rebellion against her family; it is also about the author's rebellion against her ethnic and religious background.

Writing about Marriage

"It is curious to note that Madame I. Némirovsky, already author of a good ten novels, can legitimately affirm that, for the first time, she has devoted one of her works to the problems of love."[56] Such was the reaction to the publication in 1939 of the novel *Deux* (Two), which had been serialized in *Gringoire* between April and June of 1938. The critic's mild astonishment is understandable. After *Le Vin de solitude* and works based on the tragedies of misfits, a novel dealing with everyday problems associated with a rather banal marriage, in a world composed uniquely of French people "with old and opulent bourgeois roots,"[57] is remarkable. In *Deux*, there are no misfits and no foreigners. There is no money, and certainly no financial dealings. *Deux* is a novel about love, unfaithfulness, and the institution of marriage. It sold almost twice as many copies as any of the other novels Irène had published by Albin Michel (21,631, as opposed to 12,000 for *Jézabel*, 11,300 for *La Proie*, 7,000 for *Le Pion sur l'Échiquier*, and 10,000 for *Le Vin de solitude*).[58]

At the time of publication of *Deux*, Irène had already written several short stories on husband-and-wife relationships. She had drawn the portrait of a forty-year-old woman who, upon meeting the man she had always loved but had never dared approach before her marriage, finds that, despite the flame that is still not extinguished, this love will forever remain a secret within her.[59] In another story she described a couple in which the husband, "tired of success" and "tired of marriage," wants to take his vacation alone, while the wife, believing herself to be useless, worries about what the neighbors will say; in the end nothing is resolved and the day ends as it had begun.[60] In these stories, women are obliged to accept their lot and to repress any feelings of individuality or independence. Elsewhere Irène had a more egalitarian, if cynical view of the couple, and defined conjugal love as "the blood of two strangers, enemies, battling until one prevails."[61] In *Deux*, Irène takes up this same notion and delves more deeply into it.

The success of *Deux* doubtless stems from Irène's dissection of the evolution of a marriage. She turns upside down "bourgeois wisdom" which held that "marriage comes first, and love follows."[62] A man and a woman—Antoine and Marianne (drawn from life, according to the author)[63]—display an unbridled sensuality in the period just after the First World War. It is only after their desire for one another has waned that they decide to marry. Their marriage is clearly based on sentiments other than love, and it is these sentiments, so difficult to define, that are at the heart of the novel.

The novel begins with the passionate embrace of a young woman and a young man, and ends with the passion-less embrace of the same couple many years later. Between these two moments, Irène lets us see the movement of the relationship from youth to maturity, from the search for pleasure to the search for peace. What keeps the relationship alive, despite unfaithfulness on the part of both parties, is the ultimate sacrifice of the individual to the interest of the couple, seen here as a distinct identity. Marianne, the co-protagonist with her husband Antoine, is far from the traditional French housewife. She does not marry Antoine until long after they have become lovers; she has a romantic affair with one of her husband's best friends; she demands complete autonomy. Antoine also embarks on a love affair with Marianne's sister—with tragic consequences, for the sister commits suicide; it is an affair that will bring him face to face with death. Yet Marianne feels a need for Antoine at the very moment she is preparing to secretly meet her lover, and Antoine has a similar need for Marianne's company even while he is involved with her sister. Irène constructs a universe in which marriage only begins to exist after it has bled all the passion out of the relationship, and gains in strength as it is put to the test through extramarital affairs and deceit. "The conjugal bond" says Antoine to himself, "is so much the stronger for having been forged in hypocrisy and constraints."[64] Marianne's view of marriage is similar: "each couple tends to shape for itself and for others a legend of fidelity, mutual comprehension, union . . . this legend is a lie!"[65] Antoine and Marianne know, however, that at the moment of death they will each mourn the other much more than any of their lovers. Thus, writes Irène, "the years of life together had accomplished, almost without the couple being aware of it, their secret objective: two beings were transformed into one. They could fight, even sometimes hate one another, but they were one, just as two rivers who have merged into one."[66]

The idea that marriage can only survive after passion has burned out was nothing new. Léon Blum, the philosopher politician, had broached the topic in 1907 in his essay *Du Mariage*, in which he advised young people to first love one another and then marry.[67] Certainly in *Deux* there is an effort to find a way to save the institution of marriage, or "the human equilibrium of the family,"[68] as one critic observed. But unlike Blum, Irène is not putting forth a theory of marriage; rather she has created a work of fiction founded upon observation of a certain Parisian society between the two world wars. It is the accuracy of her observation, if we are to believe the critics, that gives merit to the novel, and which solicits comparisons with Jacques Chardonne,[69] whose imposing novel on the evolution of love, *L'Épithalame*, Irène so admired.

While *Deux* was not a literary event to the same degree as *David Golder*, the novel did bring a certain notoriety to its author. People wanted to know if *Deux* would be followed by more of the same. "In a few years I would like to write a sequel to this novel," declared Irène in a radio interview.[70] In 1939, however, she was preoccupied by other concerns. A war loomed on the horizon, and her attention turned away from the workings of a marriage to the survival of individuals in wartime situations. She began two novels on this subject, but they would not be published until after her death. *Deux* is, then, somewhat of an interlude in Irène's literary career. Its theme would not be taken up again. The perceptiveness of her observation of French society, however—and the pitiless nature of her gaze—are qualities that Irène would resurrect in the major work that she had planned for after the war, *Suite française*.

Boris and Eudoxia Némirovsky, Irene's great-grandparents

Michel Epstein and his
daughter Élisabeth

Fanny and Léon Némirovsky
(Irène Némirovsky's parents)

Efime and Élisabeth Epstein
(Michel's parents)

Irène Némirovsky and her daughter Denise

Irène Némirovsky and her brother-in-law Paul Epstein

Irène Némirovsky, Michel Epstein, and their daughter Denise

Mavlik, Michel Epstein's sister

Irène Némirovsky in Nice, 1920

Michel Epstein and Denise

Samuel Epstein, Michel's older brother

Élisabeth Epstein,
Michel Epstein's mother

Léon Némirovsky, Irène's father

Léon and Fanny Némirovsky, Irène's parents

Sr Germain 13-VII-30

Efime Epstein and Denise

Michel Epstein and his
mother, Élisabeth

Last family photo, 1939

6   *The Temptation of Christianity and the Persistence of Judaism*

The Temptation of Christianity

Irène Némirovsky, along with her husband and two children, converted to Christianity by becoming baptized on February 2, 1939, in the chapel of the Abbey Sainte-Marie de Paris.[1] Two clerics officiated at this ceremony: Monsignor Vladimir Ghika, a bishop of Romanian origin with friends among philosophers (Gilson, Maritain) and writers (Claudel, Cocteau),[2] and a French priest, Father Bréchard.[3] Irène never made clear what might have motivated this conversion; there is no reference to Christianity in her notebooks, and her letters to Albin Michel, written in 1938 and 1939, reveal nothing of a spiritual quest. According to Cécile Michaud, the governess who lived with the family, Irène converted because of fear of anti-Semitism;[4] she apparently thought that her family would be protected from persecution if they were not Jewish. The events of the end of 1938—the Munich Accords (September 29, 1938), Kristallnacht (the unleashing of German anti-Semitism on November 10, 1938)—would understandably have preoccupied Irène. Her status—and that of her husband—was still that of a stateless person, since the application she had made for naturalization in November 1938 had come to naught. But there is no indication that Irène believed that by converting to Christianity she would be better able to gain French nationality, nor is there any evidence that she naively thought that conversion to Christianity would protect her if the Nuremberg laws of Germany were ever applied in France.[5] On the contrary, the evidence available—primarily her literary works—would lead us to believe that Irène considered her conversion as something strictly personal, and that she spoke of it little or not at all even to her friends. Six months after her conversion, on August 28, 1939, her editor Albin Michel said in a letter to Irène, "you are Russian and Jewish." In her response, Irène said nothing to correct this impression.

Rather than a public act, intended to protect the family by giving it a Catholic identity (which would have convinced neither the Germans nor the Vichy French), Irène's conversion appears to have risen from a strictly personal spirituality, one that is foreshadowed in her writings of the period, which show a marked sensibility towards a Christian ideal of abnegation and suffering. We know from Cécile Michaud that "there was a priest who always came to the house." Could this priest have been Father Bréchard? Irène entertained a close relationship with Bréchard, whose death in combat would inspire a chapter of *Tempête en juin*. After Bréchard's death, Irène received a letter from his family that made mention of "the baptism of a young Jewish girl for whom Father Bréchard had said many prayers."[6] Bréchard was evidently accustomed to convincing Jews to convert to Christianity, and the frequency of his visits to Irène would help explain both her conversion and her friendship with the man.

That Irène would be attracted to Christianity is quite understandable. Raised far from Jewish practices, which she saw only from a distance, she felt an early affinity for the rites of Christianity. In France, her Judaism weighed on her, and her friendship with Madeleine Avot brought her close to a traditional Catholic family. Indeed, it would be no exaggeration to see in the pull of Christianity a counterweight to what Irène perceived as Jewish immorality, and about which she wrote in *David Golder* and *Le Vin de solitude*. If she does not seem to have had a spiritual revelation in the Pascalian sense, her Christian faith is the fruit of a profound questioning of the mores of the society in which she was raised and of the moral void she found there.

The literary text that most clearly reveals the path taken by Irène is contemporaneous with her conversion. It is a novel that was serialized in *Gringoire* in May 1939 under the title *Les Échelles du Levant* (The Ports of Call of the Levant).[7] Like Paul Morand in *France la doulce*, whose imposters come from "the obscurity of central Europe or the Levant to the light of the Champs-Elysées,"[8] Irène's main character is an impostor, a medical charlatan "of the Levantine type, with the troubled and hungry air of a wolf."[9] His name is Dario Asfar, and his origins are "a mixture of Greek and Italian blood;" he was born in the Crimea of a rug merchant father and an alcoholic mother,[10] and inherited the same kind of thirst for wealth that motivates the Jewish characters in Irène's earlier novels. "There is in me," admits Dario, "a whole line of starved elements; they are not yet, and never will be satiated! I will never be warm enough! I will never feel secure enough, respected or loved enough."[11] Fifteen years in France and a medical diploma from a French university have not effaced his "alien accent"[12] or his feverish search for wealth and stability. Haunted by the poverty of his youth ("images that rose in him . . . were bred by his flesh"[13]), Dario Asfar succeeds in fabricating a so-called psychotherapy that pleases his clients, rich women from Nice who confer upon him the ominous title of "Master of souls."[14] In cahoots with the wife of a wealthy businessman (Philippe Wardes), Dario has the man unjustly committed to an asylum and is named executor of his affairs.

But Dario Asfar's machinations come up against a force stronger than he, represented by the businessman's first wife, Sylvie. Incapable of reigning in a wandering husband, Sylvie at first resigns herself to leaving him in the hands of his mistress, whom he eventually marries. In this role, she opposes (unsuccessfully) Dario's evil plans, but she does so by offering Dario her friendship rather than by confronting him. Sylvie Wardes resembles in certain respects other serene and virtuous female characters in Irène's novels (such as Marie in *La Proie*), but she displays a spiritual dimension that is new to Irène's work. From the moment Dario meets her, he feels a "strange peace" descend upon him, "as though she had touched his feverish brow with her cool gentle hands." In the presence of this woman, Dario can hide nothing: "she forced truth from him."[15] Lest there be any doubt as to the character of the peace emanating from Sylvie Wardes, the narrator makes it clear that this is "a great and brilliant light"[16] that arises from her soul and allows her to accept all in the name of unconditional love. "I have with me a light that never deceives,"[17] Sylvie tells Dario, and adds that it is "an interior light, a God."[18] Sylvie's self-styled vocation is to illuminate the straight and narrow path, that of "her moral superiority" over those who attach "a large value to riches and vanity."[19] In short, Sylvie is the perfect incarnation of grace in the Christian sense. She acts not through strength but through humility and identification with the weak and downtrodden. "She is not looking for what we are seeking in life," explains Dario, "in extreme distress she would not defend her life."[20] Although Dario resists Sylvie's influence, his son Daniel will be saved by her. At the deathbed of his mother, at the very moment Dario, having had Wardes committed, is preparing to marry his former mistress, Daniel "knelt gauchely and quietly, and without being aware of it, prayed out loud . . . repeating in his painful stupor:—My Lord, forgive me . . ."[21] Under the influence of Sylvie, he has been redeemed.

In *Les Échelles du Levant*, the need to create a well-defined opposition between good and evil seems to have erased any notion of nuance in the presentation of the characters. Gone is the ambiguity that characterizes David Golder, supremely selfish but also so generous towards his daughter for whom he is consumed with a love that knows no bounds. Dario has only one dimension, that of the feverish pursuit of material wealth, and Sylvie can only be understood as the incarnation of selfless love. Hence the confrontation of these two figures takes on the character of a theological debate rather than a human interchange: "I know that you are a believer," Dario tells Sylvie. "Ah! You, you are children of the light. You have only noble passions, you are infinitely beautiful . . . But I, I am shaped by the shadows, by the clay of the earth. I do not trouble myself about heaven."[22]

In addition to this novel, two short stories written after Irène's conversion can be considered as Christian morality tales. In "Le Spectateur" (The Spectator), a story published approximately three months after the signing of the German-Soviet nonaggression pact in 1939, a man entirely disinterested in the events of Europe, an American "spectator," finds himself on the ship of a neutral country, torpedoed by a German submarine on the open seas. Forced to share a raft with Spanish refugees and Eastern European Jews, he quickly loses his arrogance and rediscovers love and charity among the poor and persecuted. He also learns, in the moments that precede the capsizing of the raft and his own death, the importance of sacrifice: "it was necessary to be opposed to evil . . . others would in turn feel exquisite scruples, would dress themselves in benevolent neutrality, would taste a delightful quietude."[23] The spectator, through his death, is redeemed.

The second morality tale takes place after the June 1940 defeat of the French. In "Monsieur Rose," Irène offers the story of a man who leads a "gentle life." He buys a house in Normandy when war is declared (in order to be far removed from the fighting) and is "one of the first Frenchmen to acquire a gas mask." He tries to protect himself from war, as he has always tried to protect himself from any commitment, but one day finds himself in a situation that will test his indifference. Running away from the advancing German army and searching for food, Monsieur Rose is forced to depart from his habits. He loses his chauffeur and car and, fleeing on foot, meets a young man who by his actions will teach him a lesson about sacrifice, for Monsieur Rose, despite all his faults, can be saved. When German airplanes begin shelling the lines of fleeing civilians, this stranger instinctively shelters Monsieur Rose's body with his own. For the first time in his life, Monsieur Rose is confronted with an act of pure selflessness, and he cannot remain indifferent to it. When a car approaches and offers him the chance to escape the danger of the shelling, Monsieur Rose refuses the ride because there is no room for his anonymous new friend. Both Monsieur Rose and the unnamed man remain with those who have no transportation and who are in immediate danger of being shelled to death. "Livid and trembling, he fell back with Marc, understanding dimly that life had just been accorded to him."[24] Through this act of solidarity with the poor, Monsieur Rose, like the spectator in the previous story, attains a state of grace that gives meaning to a life that he is now prepared to sacrifice.

Finally there is the model of Father Bréchard, transformed by Irène into a chapter of *Tempête en juin*. The priest, who was a lieutenant in the French army, was killed on June 20, 1940 by a German bullet as he tried to defend a village in the Vosges Mountains with a few soldiers from his regiment. Irène learned of the death of the curate from the man's mother, but it was only in July of 1941 that she discovered the circumstances. "On June 20, near 11 o'clock, at the approach of the Germans, Father B. was stationed with his men in a wooded area bordering the road at the entrance to the village . . . All the soldiers with the exception of one, fled at the approach of the tanks; Father B. remained alone with this soldier continuing fire. At one point the soldier tried to flee but was wounded and dragged himself toward Father B. to be cared for. It was while attending to the man's wounds that Father B. was struck in full face by a bullet; he clearly agonized for some time since he was found with his crucifix between his teeth."[25] The descriptions contained in this letter to Irène can be found almost verbatim in a chapter of the revised (unpublished) manuscript of *Suite française,* called "Un Pêcheur d'âmes" (A Fisherman of Souls). The chapter's title alone indicates the relationship that Irène saw between the priest's sacrifice and religion. Philippe Péricand, the fictional priest of the novel, is tormented by his role as a curate: does he have the right to promise dying people the possibility of salvation? Does he have the right to kill his fellow man? Can he judge between those who are worthy of Christ and those who are not? In the novel he lives out almost exactly Bréchard's fate. While he commands his men, he prays to be able to sacrifice his life for theirs: "Oh, Jesus, take me, take my life for theirs, for the least worthy among them." His fate, like that of his model Bréchard, signals his redemption. "He was not killed immediately. He had time to pick up his crucifix and place it on his lips."[26] Through total sacrifice of his physical body, and in complete resignation to death, this priest will show, by his example, his faith in God and the meaning of sacrifice.

In these examples of sacrifice and redemption there is a certain coherence, as Irène's prose resolutely leads us away from the world of businessmen, misfits, and monsters of egotism, into a universe peopled with characters whose are either pure, like Sylvie Wardes, or to whom moral purity is revealed, like Monsieur Rose.

The moral dimension of Irène's conversion to Christianity is obvious; less clear is any spiritual dimension. Irène's works show none of the theological aspects of Simone Weil, for example, whose conversion to Catholicism was accompanied not only by a commitment to help the poor and downtrodden but by also by great mystical impulses. Yet Irène's works of this period show, if nothing else, a yearning for a system of values that transcends the present and can lead to a higher level of existence than that of the world she sees around her.

The Persistence of Judaism

It is one of the great ironies of Irène Némirovsky's life that she had a renewed interest in her origins as a Jew just as she was converting to Christianity.

In February 1937, the weekly newspaper *Gringoire* published a short story titled "Fraternité." It is the first time this anti-Semitic weekly published one of Irène's stories about Jews, but there is nothing paradoxical about this phenomenon. One of the characteristics of anti-Semitism in the period 1930–1944 is an unhealthy obsession with all things Jewish. This brand of anti-Semitism sees in Judaism not a religion or a people guilty of killing Christ, but a separate race, subject to all sorts of sickness and psychological complexes, capable of exercising its nefarious influence on a sound society. Thus some newspapers of the time dwelled on the sexual behavior of Jews, accusing them of being homosexuals while at the same time being seducers of women, or "synagogue Don Juans" as one publication referred to them.[27] In September 1941, an entire exhibition was devoted to "The Jew and France" at the Palais Berlitz in which the physical and "racial" characteristics of Jews, their separate "language," their history, their rituals, and obviously their "plot" to take over the world were all detailed with sickening precision. Even as they sought to rid themselves of Jews, anti-Semites were clearly fascinated by them.

The readers of *Gringoire* were thus not surprised to find in their newspaper a short story dealing with Jewish identity. In the story, Christian Rabinovitch, a Frenchman, who is Jewish only in name and appearance ("my nose, my mouth, the only Jewish traits I have kept"), believes himself to be so perfectly integrated into French society, that he does not hesitate to accept a hunting invitation at the home of the Count of Sestres, whose daughter is to marry Rabinovitch's son. But while awaiting his train, Christian Rabinovitch sees on the station platform a man "dressed poorly, thin, badly shaved, with dirty hands," who "spoke with a foreign accent . . . who mangled his words." This man, accompanied by a child wearing "an ugly little very worn coat" reveals himself to be Jewish, an immigrant from Eastern Europe, now a hat maker living in Paris. This other Jew, by coincidence, is also called Rabinovitch. For Christian, the situation is one of anguish: "he felt quite distressed. What was there between this poor Jew and himself?" Christian decides they have nothing whatsoever in common: he was born in France and understands not a word of Yiddish. But the immigrant maintains that "all the Rabinovitches come from 'there,'" that is, somewhere in Central Europe, "Odessa or Berdichef, like me." Christian remains cold to this suggestion: "could it be possible that he be of the same blood as this man? There was no more resemblance between this man and himself than between Sestres and the lackeys that served him!" So he gives the immigrant a coin and steps quietly onto his train, "sure that culturally [he was] closer to a man such as Sestres." But once he is in his train compartment, his true identity as a Jew manifests itself. "He did not know it, but with a slow and strange movement, ensconced in his reverie, he swayed gently in his seat, forward and backward . . . his body finding thus . . . the swaying that had before him rocked generations of rabbis bent over their holy books, money changers over piles of gold, and tailors over their workbenches." Although "the painful impression brought about by his meeting with the Jew" begins to fade once he arrives at the count's, there remains in Christian a little doubt, a physical feeling of cold as though his body could never rid itself of this "old heritage" of Jewishness.[28]

A quite plausible reading of this story places it in the anti-Semitic tradition: The Jew can never entirely form an integral part of society, his difference being physical and indelible. Without a doubt many *Gringoire* readers understood the story in this light. But such a reading does not take into account the complexity of the descriptions of the two Rabino-vitches. In fact, for the first time in Irène's prose we see the Jew as victim of forces beyond his control. His otherness with regard to the French Catholic populace arises henceforth not from a deficiency of character, but from centuries of persecution.

If the Jew is preoccupied by money, it is because he never has the liberty to feel safe. "Where doesn't God cast the Jew?" asks the im-migrant Rabinovitch: "Barely has he earned, by the sweat of his brow, some hard bread, four walls and a roof over his head, than comes a war, a revolution or a pogrom or something else . . . and farewell . . . Pick up your bags and make tracks." The immigrant lost one of his sons in Palestine, where he went "to live in dignity" plowing the earth "like a peasant." The other son left to live in England; having begun his career in Germany, he had to flee when Hitler came to power. For the first time in her writings Irène uses the word "pogrom," makes reference to the oppression of Jews in Germany, and evokes the hope of Zionism for the Jews of Central Europe.

The context of the immigrant Rabinovitch's monologue, where the extreme precariousness of the Jew in Europe is detailed, helps us to understand Christian Rabinovitch's reaction. For the first time, a co-religionist, with the same name as his own, gives him a small lesson in Jewish history. Even if Christian can feign indifference and believe himself to be too French to have the same fears as his namesake, his body reacts viscerally to this lesson. "That is what I pay for in my body and my mind," he admits in stepping on the train, "centuries of misery, of sickness, of oppression."

But Irène hasn't finished giving her readers her own lesson in Jewishness. She credits the immigrant Rabinovitch with characteristics of courage and strength of character that Christian Rabinovitch, this cold and fearful man, does not possess. Thus the immigrant, with "his narrow chest . . . hollowed by a heavy and invisible weight" seems to be "endowed with an inextinguishable vitality" akin to "a candle lit in the wind . . . ready to go out [but that] burns again, humble and tenacious." It is thus the stateless Jew, not the assimilated one, who has the moral character traits necessary for survival.

Despite its appearance in *Gringoire*, "Fraternité" is not an anti-Semitic story. The physical characteristics of the Jewish characters may well be stereotypical, but their behavior is not. In each of them there is a complex individual, attempting to come to terms with an identity that is culturally, not physically, determined. This story marks a new stage in Irène's Jewish consciousness. While prior to 1937, she tried to separate herself as much as possible from her origins, seeing materialism in Jewish culture that seemed incompatible with the values of French society, she now recognized the complexity of the Jewish predicament, and saw the danger that threatened Jews in Europe. Is this new consciousness a result of the guilt of a converted Jew, trying to avoid the accusation of being a turncoat? Her writer's notebook suggests another explanation. Near an entry dated 1937 we see the following: "find for the Bal Hashem of Ernest Bloch that deep, wide and troubling sound and the first stroke of the bow linking this Hebraic melody to all the past." Clearly, Irène's own sense of her Judaism ran deep and was related to her view of the collective past of the Jewish people. Even as she found herself spiritually a Christian, she seemed to become particularly sensitive to her Jewish roots. Her notebook suggests that, as does her most Jewish novel, *Les Chiens et les loups* (The Dogs and the Wolves).

In the summer of 1938, Irène had begun to write a novel about two Jewish families; "I am working on another novel whose provisional title is *Enfants de la nuit* (Children of the Night), she said in an interview in September 1938.[29] In November 1939, she serialized this novel, which she called *Les Chiens et les loups*, in the weekly *Candide*. Albin Michel published it in 1940, only a few months after the appearance of the final episode in *Candide* on January 17. These dates are important for understanding the problems encountered by the novel as it appeared. On September 3, 1938, France declared war on Germany and entered into the *drôle de guerre* (or phony war) that would see the defeat of Poland and the fall of the Daladier government. Irène participated in the propaganda effort (under the direction of Jean Giraudoux) by writing articles for the Dutch press "which make known France's magnificent morale, which illustrate the quiet decisiveness of the combatants, the calm courage of the women."[30] The French public was thus already preoccupied by an uncertain war when the first installment of the novel appeared. The situation was no better in January 1940, when the novel was published as a book. On January 10, Hitler's plans for the invasion of Belgium were discovered; in February, food ration cards were distributed in France; in March, the Daladier government fell; in April, Germany invated Denmark and Norway. Two months later, France fell, Marshall Pétain became head of state, and the country was divided in two. During the summer of 1940, the press had more to deal with than a novel about Jews, no matter how well written. No reviews of the novel appeared in the press, except for a small article in *Gringoire*. In September 1940, Robert Esménard, Albin Michel's son-in-law, was forced to admit that *"Les Chiens et les loups* did not enjoy the success it should have after its appearance, very soon after the launching of the German offensive."[31]

"A Jewish-Russian family and perpetual Jewishness passing into . . . the French intellectual and the artist;"[32] this is how Irène defines the subject of *Les Chiens et les loups*. It is an astonishing book; not only does Irène revisit the Russian past she had described in *Le Vin de solitude*, she reworks the image of France she had presented in earlier novels. Here she turns her attention to an artist—a young Jewish woman who finds her inspiration not in the Christian world but deep within her Jewish consciousness, after she has arrived in Paris seeking refuge from the pogroms of Central Europe.

To the French reader of 1940, *Les Chiens et les loups*, appearing in an anti-Semitic weekly, would undoubtedly have given rise to another interpretation. This reading would see the novel's Jewish characters as a separate, wandering people, never to be assimilated into French society. This is indeed what the critic in *Gringoire* saw:

> This story of an impoverished young Jewish girl from Ukraine, coming to find refuge in France, finding a rich Jew who, even though married to a Catholic, suffers the influence of his race, is detailed with a striking lucidity, and in the firm, straightforward style that allowed the author of *David Golder* to enter the ranks of the great novelists. The torments of the Jewish soul, its perpetual sterile dissatisfaction, this morbid taste for money, are treated masterfully by Madame Irène Némirovsky . . . The character of Ben, with his aggressive intelligence, presents in four pages the plight of these recently arrived Jews among us, who despair, as states the author, "of finding a French type of happiness" and who are never at rest "because they want to be stronger than God himself."[33]

It is certainly true that the novel tells the story of Jews who, try as they might, cannot escape their Jewish destiny. Ada Sinner is the protagonist; she survives the bloody pogroms of Ukraine and comes to Paris accompanied by her cousin Ben, a young businessman always in search of money. At the same time, a distant cousin of Ada's, Harry Sinner, emigrates from Ukraine to France. Harry is the son of a rich banker; he moves to the 16th arrondissement and marries a Catholic Frenchwoman, herself the daughter of a banker. But although he wants to be integrated into French society, Harry is drawn to Ada, whose paintings remind him of his Ukrainian Jewish past. Even though he lives "in a rich bourgeois world" and frequents a "coterie" of young French people,[34] he has the same physique as his cousin Ben—the same "hooked nose," the same "frizzy hair," the same "weak and sickly" air.[35] In a chapter which must have greatly pleased the anti-Semites of the period, Harry, who has just left Ada, goes to the home of his long-standing French friends; this time, however, "he resembled an isolated bird, alone on a perch among others who are not of his race."[36] Ill at ease for the first time amongst French people, Harry, like Christian Rabinovitch in "Fraternité," unwittingly repeats the physical movements of his ancestors:

He held himself very calm and straight; but little by little, his arms dropped, his brow furrowed, his shoulders bent. Thin, weak, feeling the cold, pressing his elegant hands together, he rocked gently in the shadows, just as before him had rocked so many money changers at their counters, so many rabbis bent over their books, so many immigrants on the decks of ships.[37]

Harry comes back to his Christian wife, but nothing will be as before, since he now recognizes the "ascendancy" of his Jewishness. As for Ben, he is expelled from France for having been involved in a "scandal of a band of international financiers,"[38] and he opens stores in South America. Ada, pregnant by Harry, is also expelled, and sent to live in an unnamed city in Central Europe, on the eve of a new world war.

Indeed, this novel can be seen as the portrayal of what the *Gringoire* critic called "the torments of the Jewish soul." Ben appears to be "always moving,"[39] looking everywhere for "some sort of scheme." He is motivated by an unabated thirst for riches and possessions: "one begins by imagining all one can possess, and one ends by possessing, if one desires it strongly enough, more than one has imagined."[40] Ada also recognizes that "we are a greedy race, hungry for so long, that reality no longer nourishes us. We need the impossible."[41] But Ada is not a businessman like Ben, and what motivates her is not the pursuit of wealth. On the contrary, Ada is striving toward an esthetic that would permit her to bring to light the reality she lived in Ukraine. There is an important reason for which Irène chose an artist for a protagonist in this novel. She had already featured a young writer in the person of Hélène Karol (*Le Vin de solitude*), but this character affirmed her independence by distancing herself as much as possible from the Russian Jewish milieu from which she had sprung. In contrast, Ada asserts herself by painting the milieu of her childhood and accepting the fact that she belongs to the Jewish people. In other words, Ada draws from this "torment of the Jewish soul" an advantage that no other character in Irène's work knows.

The anti-Semitic interpretation by *Gringoire* clearly does not do justice to Irène's novel. We must put aside our distaste for some of the Jewish stereotypes which Irène uses, and which would not have shocked her reading public in 1940, and let the novel speak for itself. *Les Chiens et les loups* is an appeal to tolerance and an invitation to understanding.

For the first time in Irène's work, the anti-Semitic discourse is undermined from within. The French banker Delarcher, whose daughter Laurence is to marry Harry Sinner, becomes the spokesperson for this discourse in which one finds all the commonplaces of the anti-Semitism of the 1930s: Jews inspire in him "an insurmountable distrust," for their origins are obscure ("nothing clear there, nothing sure"); Jews, through their "international ties," constitute a "secret power" ready to control all of French finance; Jews are "men of small stature, greasy complexion, sharp features and beady eyes"; Jews are sickly and don't drink wine (they serve themselves only "a drop of Rhine wine" at the end of a meal).[42] But this speech is presented to us in the *style indirect libre* so prized by Flaubert; this style allows the reader to be distanced from the anti-Semitic discourse and thus to perceive its absurdity. Furthermore, the anti-Semitic banker mixes everything up: "Slavic, German, Jewish, it's all the same." He imagines that Harry Sinner's aunts are reading Nietzsche, an author he doesn't know but whose name signifies nothing good, and whom he confounds with "this tribe" of Jews. The anti-Semite is clearly presented as a hypocrite: "He was not xenophobic, but . . ." Moreover, this man, in spite of his "colossal" physique and his "booming" voice, is quite incapable of keeping his daughter from marrying the Jewish man whom he scorns so intensely.[43]

In another social milieu, but on the same level, the French tenants of the rooming house in which Ben and Ada live treat them "with a deep distrust," reproaching them for their abnormal culinary habits ("they never seemed aware of what constituted a hot meal, a stew, a well-simmered soup"), but above all for their doubtful origins ("floating beings, without roots, émigrés, suspicious types"). But here the narrator intervenes to state that there was, between the Jewish couple and the other renters, "an abyss of incomprehension" between the condescending disdain of the neighbors and the feverish life led by Ada in pursuit of her ideal.[44]

Each time the anti-Semitic discourse rears its head in this novel, there is a corresponding commentary that shows its incoherence. When Harry Sinner's Catholic wife criticizes Harry's mother for spoiling her son like a "Jewish mother," the elderly Jewish lady reflects that "I had to think first about protecting my child just as, before me, thousands of women of my blood had to protect their children from cruelty, famine, unjust hatred, disease, poverty . . . We are branded by this experience forever."[45] Nothing in this book is more moving than the description of the pogrom in Ukraine where the patriotic hymns and religious chants of the crowd become "a savage, an inhuman roar"[46] that terrorizes the two children, Ada and Ben. Irène clearly points the finger at the anti-Semites, themselves responsible for Jews' being expelled from countries, themselves guilty of refusing to look beyond the surface at the lives of the Jews among them.

What hope is there, given the situation Irène describes in this novel, for the integration of foreign-born Jews in France? The answer to this question can be found by comparing the final chapter of *Les Chiens et les loups* with that of *Le Vin de solitude*, written five years earlier. In the latter, a ray of sunshine illuminates Hélène's path near the Arc de Triomphe; in the former, an order for expulsion marks the end of a French life for Ada Sinner. Two Jewish immigrants; two different fates. The situation has changed, and Irène's optimism has waned.[47]

Along with an increased pessimism comes an increase in Irène's identification with the Jewish people. Irène takes the concept of a Jewish "race," so popular among the anti-Semites, and stands it on its head. In this novel, Irène sees the "race" as the result, not the cause of the difference between Jews and the peoples with whom they live. Jews are bound together by a common past, a shared history, and above all, centuries of oppression. According to Ben, "these Sinners with their riding stables and their illustrious collections, their fathers were, in their childhood, kids like me, hungry, beaten, humiliated, and *that creates a solidarity which cannot be forgotten, not that of race, not that of blood, but spilled tears.*"[48] For Irène it all comes down to images that evoke this past in a way that is unavoidable. This is why the protagonist of the novel is an artist; through her pictures Ada can call up a feeling of belonging and solidarity. Harry, seeing Ada's paintings in the window of a Paris bookstore, is "struck by a confused but strong impression" as though he "had seen somewhere in a dream or in his childhood" the scenes painted by his cousin. "It was his country, his past which he found," adds the narrator.[49] It is the beginning of an emotional voyage that Harry makes into his Jewish background, through his burgeoning love for Ada. At first, Harry shares with her memories of their youth in Ukraine, "the climate, the air from there . . . evenings on the banks of the river . . . little children with red hair.[50] But soon this imaginary voyage takes him to regions more hidden in his subconscious: "over there . . . what happened there, it's perhaps more important than you know, more important than the rest, than your life here, than your marriage. We were born there, our roots are there . . .

—You mean: in Russia?

—No. Further . . . Deeper . . ."[51]

This persistence of Jewishness takes on all of its importance in the last chapter of the novel, which is nothing short of a paean to Jewish solidarity, and especially solidarity among Jewish women. Ada, who is expecting Harry's child, is expelled from France and sent to "a small town in Eastern Europe" where, rather than "the Paris night illuminated by sign-posts and street lamps," she finds only "icy shadows, a cruel black night."[52] But far from living in solitude, Ada is surrounded by other Jewish women who are experiencing the same fate as herself. Her neighbor, for example, "had been successively cast out by America and Germany," and this woman's husband is in a "concentration camp."[53] This woman and other refugees "form a special class of people, outside of cast or race . . . where mutual help ruled."[54] These women help Ada to give birth: "Ada knew no one, she thought, but all knew of her condition, and she was more spoiled and pampered that day than ever in her life."[55] In this new life, in the midst of the hostility of a country where war and persecutions are a daily threat, Ada is full of hope:

Yes, her fate was hard and incomprehensible, but it seemed to her, she knew not why, that she was on the threshold of enlightenment, of a truth that would abruptly cast light on the injustice and resolve the problem. In this truth the child, without any doubt, played a part . . . ; she played another . . . She counted on her fingers, as a child enumerates riches: "painting, the baby, strength: with that one can live very well. One can live very well."[56]

Thus, the essence of Jewish identity can be found in solidarity, in artistic creation, and in a future represented by the birth of a child. Never before had Irène painted such a sympathetic portrait of the Jewish people. We are far from the salons of the Golder and Kamp families where men without conscience hatched shady business deals while their wives discussed the dresses and jewels they would buy. In this Eastern European exile, Jewish greed is transformed by Jewish women into courageous determination to surmount all the misfortunes of the present and the future.

The evolving situation of European Jews kept this novel from being recognized as an important part of Jewish literature. For there is a bitter irony in the fate imagined by Irène for the Jews expelled by France; like everyone else, Irène could not foresee the horror of the death camps. In telling Ada's story, was Irène thinking of herself? Did she also fear deportation to a Central European country? We should remember that in the spring of 1939, it became clear that Irène and Michel's request for naturalization would come to naught. In August 1939, Irène asked her publisher to furnish her with a letter of recommendation in the event that her status as a Russian Jew would create "problems" (to use Albin Michel's term)[57] for her. All this leads us to believe that the end of *Les Chiens et les loups* translates Irène's own anguish over deportation from France. It is in the context of this anguish that Irène feels solidarity, as a writer, with the destiny of the Jewish people.

While this solidarity does not go so far as a public declaration supporting Jews or against the discriminatory measures, from 1939 on, Irène clears from her work any anti-Semitic or racist connotation. In her description of the corruption of the financial world between the two wars, in a novel she wrote in 1941, *Les Feux de l'automne* (The Fires of Autumn), she no longer has recourse to Jewish or Levantine stereotypes; she emphasizes the powers of *French* finance, whose business dealings are at least as suspect as those she described in *David Golder* or *Les Échelles du Levant*. She no longer creates any Jewish characters. Was the Jewish situation, which she felt personally, too painful for her to make of it a subject for a novel or short story? It seems at any rate that she intended to take up the Jewish theme again after the war, but this time emphasizing the fate that awaited them; in November 1940 she wrote in her notebook: "A novel for a better time . . . under a pseudonym . . . Jewish . . . the debacle."

7   *Issy-L'Évêque*

Issy-L'Évêque is a small village in the department of Saône-et-
Loire, in southern Burgundy, nestled in the low hills of the Morvan region. It boasts a Romanesque church, built in the twelfth and thirteenth
centuries; it counts among its illustrious sons and daughters Madame
de Genlis, the first recognized author of children's fiction. But the real
claim to fame of Issy-L'Évêque is the Abbé Carion. In 1793, as mayor, he
declared the village to be the first revolutionary commune in France, and
he renamed it Issy-la-Montagne (the "mountain" replacing the "bishop"
of the original name).

In 1940, this village, having taken back its original name, counted
about 1500 people. As in many villages of the Morvan region, agricul-
ture was varied and intensive; with the exception of coffee and a few
other "imported" products, there was little the village could not provide
its habitants, even during periods of rationing. The population included
mainly farmers (peasants and tenant farmers) and artisans (for example,
there were seven blacksmiths). Electricity came to the village in 1929,
but people still went to their wells for water, since running water was
not brought in until 1963. Heat was mainly provided by wood, which
was abundant in the region. Bedrooms were unheated, and people used
hot water bottles or warm bricks to heat their beds. Winters can be severe in the Morvan, and in January 1942 the temperature went as low
as 30 degrees below zero.[1]

The train station in Issy-L'Évêque was closed in 1937. To get to the
village one had to take a car from Luzy, the nearest station. There was
only one hotel, the Hôtel des Voyageurs, located on the main street.

On the square across from the hotel was the shoemaker, Monsieur Lacombre. The tobacconist was Auguste Barre, and the village priest was Father Gauffre. There was a boys' school and a girls' school, whose director was Madame Molard. There was then (as now) a gendarmerie in the village.

When France was cut in half, in June 1940, Issy-L'Évêque found itself only a few kilometers from the "free" zone. The line of demarcation passed from Dole to the north to Chalon sur Saône to the south, and from there west to Moulins, through Digoin.

It is in Issy-L'Évêque that Irène Némirovsky lived with her family from May 1940 until she was deported.

Why Issy-L'Évêque? The Epsteins were familiar with the Riviera (and particularly with Nice) and the watering places of the Vosges mountains and the Basque country, where they spent their vacations. Why did they not take refuge in Italian controlled Nice or in Hendaye, for example, only a few kilometers from the Spanish border, which they could have traversed if they needed to? Irène had spent her summer vacation of 1939 in Hendaye.

The choice of Issy-L'Évêque was the result of a series of circumstances rather than a deliberate decision. Issy-L'Évêque happened to be the hometown of Cécile Michaud, the nurse that Irène had engaged just before her daughter Denise's birth in 1929, and whom she had kept on when Élisabeth was born in 1937. Irène sent her children to the Michaud family as soon as war was declared, in September 1939, and she herself often came to see her daughters during the winter of 1939–1940. In June 1940, during the German offensive, Irène decided not to go back to Paris, and Michel came to join her a few days later.[2]

At first Issy-L'Évêque seemed to have certain advantages over Paris, where German attacks were a threat, but the situation evolved rapidly after June 1940. German soldiers were billeted in the village and the movement of the population was restricted. After 1941, the situation got progressively worse for Jews in the entire occupied zone, and any trip to Paris required the permission of the German authorities.

Irène's family's stay in Issy-L'Évêque, thus, far from being a temporary respite from war and privation, became an exile for Irène. She found herself cut off from her family (in particular from her husband's brothers and sisters), from her Parisian friends, and from her publishers. Although she was able to continue writing, she had a hard time finding books; money was a constant preoccupation. With no experience of country living, Irène and her family had to adapt themselves to the hard life of Issy-L'Évêque.

Irène's stay in Issy-L'Évêque is the best-documented part of her life. She frequently sent letters to her publisher, Albin Michel, and to his son-in-law Robert Esménard as well as to their literary editor, André Sabatier. She resumed her correspondence with her childhood friend Madeleine Avot, who had become Madeleine Cabour. For his part, Michel wrote frequently to his family in Paris. All these letters, as well as a few other documents, have survived the war and allow us to understand not only Irène's day-to-day life, but also the evolution of her situation as the vise of the occupation tightened around her, just as it tightened around all the Jews in France.

In addition to her correspondence, Irène left numerous literary texts written while she lived in Issy-L'Évêque. There are ten short stories, three novels (including *Suite française*, published posthumously), and a biography of Chekhov. It is through these texts also that we can see Irène's reaction as France was defeated and occupied by Germany. We can also get some idea of how she would have evolved as a novelist, had she survived this period.

Living in Issy-L'Évêque

In August 1939, Irène, Michel, and their children spent their summer vacation in Hendaye. Around August 28, Michel suddenly returned to Paris and sent an express letter to Albin Michel:

> My wife is presently in Hendaye with the children. I am concerned about her in these difficult times, because she has nobody to help her in case of need. May I count on your friendship for a letter of recommendation which she could eventually show to the press authorities of this region?[3]

Two concerns seem to motivate this message: an uneasiness with recent events (the signing of the German-Soviet Pact on August 23), which could drive France into the war, and the possible difficulty of publishing Irène's short stories in provincial newspapers or weeklies. Michel was aware that Paris would be dangerous for some time, and that his wife would need to earn a living for their entire family in Issy-L'Évêque.

Like most people living in France, Irène and Michel were quite justified in fearing, in August 1939, that war was near. The reservists had been called up; civil defense precautions had been taken; the railway lines linking France to Germany had been cut.[4] Irène and Michel's situation was particularly difficult because their Russian origins and their stateless status might lead them to be counted—now that Russia and Germany had signed a pact—as enemies of France. Moreover, the general mood in France was hostile to immigrants. Even a moderate newspaper like *Le Temps* wrote, in March 1939, that "our liberal attitudes, which sometimes have gone too far, should be revised if [immigrants] threaten our security."[5]

Albin Michel knew very well that Irène was Jewish,[6] although it is unclear if he was aware that she was not a naturalized French citizen. In any case, he sent Irène a letter in which he showed his awareness of the "problems" that a foreign Jew could have in France:

> We are currently living through troubled times, which could become tragic from one day to the next. You are Russian and Jewish, and it is possible that those people who do not know you (but there are few of these, given your reputation as a writer) could cause you problems. Therefore, as it is always best to be prepared, I thought that a statement from me, as your publisher, could be useful. I am thus ready to attest that you are a woman of letters of great talent, as the success of your work in France and abroad shows. I am also ready to declare that, since October 1933, when you came to me after having published with my colleague Grasset some works—among which *David Golder* was a stunning revelation and led to a remarkable film—I have always had with you and your husband the most cordial relationship of an editor with his author.[7]

This letter certainly shows the friendship and admiration Albin Michel had for Irène, but it would be of no use to her. For one thing, Irène never had the occasion to present it to the French authorities who, in any case, did not disturb her before 1942; for another, as we shall see, the problems Irène encountered in attempting to publish her short stories in newspapers after 1940 were not of the type that a publisher, even one as well respected as Albin Michel, could solve.

The world situation got worse: on September 1 the Reich invaded

Poland. France and Great Britain declared war on Germany on September 3. This declaration of war found Irène and her children in Hendaye, where she was writing a short story—about life in Hendaye as war approaches—for the women's magazine *Marie Claire*. She quickly returned to Paris and sent the children to Issy-L'Évêque.

By the end of May 1940, Irène, who had made numerous trips between Paris and Issy-L'Évêque, went to the village to spend the Whitsunday vacation with her daughters. This time she stayed there. On June 14, the Germans entered Paris. Michel had taken a leave from his work for health reasons (septicemia), but he would not have been able to keep his position as an administrator in the Banque des Pays du Nord after the second Jewish laws were published in October 1941. Not wishing to remain alone and without work in Paris, Michel decided to join his wife and children in Issy-L'Évêque. This time, the trip was dangerous. What normally took one day now took three, because German airplanes were bombing the roads and the railway tracks. He left their Paris apartment in the hands of his brother Paul.

The decision to leave Paris seems to have been motivated first by the need to protect the children in case of air attacks (the first Paris air alert came on September 4, 1939, at 3:45 A.M.[8]); second, by a vague fear which was shared by almost everyone in Paris but especially by the Jewish population, three-quarters of whom, even before the arrival of German troops in June 1940, had fled the city.[9] This Jewish population did not necessarily flee to the "free" (southern) zone. Their objective seems to have been simply to exit Paris, for fear that the treatment that the Germans had given the Jews of the other conquered countries be meted out to them. Certain Jewish families—those who had friends in the government—were given stern warnings by those who had more information than they on the real intent of the Germans. Thus the police prefect Jean Chiappe warned the Jewish professor of medicine Robert Debré, in the summer of 1940, that the Germans would "put into effect an anti-Jewish policy" in Paris and that it was wise to flee and not to return "under any circumstances."[10] Is it possible that Irène and Michel would have received such a warning? No existing document shows this, but their right-wing journalist friends may have given them information that made their departure even more urgent.

In the village of Issy-L'Évêque, the defeat caused a rush of refugees from in and around Dijon, and, although the village was occupied by the Wehrmacht after June 18, it stayed out of the areas of active combat. "As far as I am concerned," Irène wrote Albin Michel, "the military operations, although they took place very near, have spared us."[11] The Epsteins, finding no available apartments to rent, took rooms at the Hôtel des Voyageurs, a modest inn just across from the small street where Cécile Michaud lived. It was an uncomfortable situation; Irène described it in a letter to Madeleine Cabour who herself had taken refuge in a village in the department of Loir-et-Cher:

We are living in a tiny village like you, with the same inconveniences (mortal boredom, loneliness) and the same inappreciable advantages, such as heat and excellent food. But you have one up on us because you have comfortable lodgings whereas we are living in a little village inn—very clean, but that's it. My daughter Élisabeth, who is 3½, doesn't know what running water is, not to mention an elevator. But she is none the worse for it. My eldest daughter goes to the school village. She is only 11, and it is working out well, but I hope that this situation does not last too long, because if it does, the only thing she'll be good for is to take care of cows, and I unfortunately do not own any cows.[12]

Irène and Michel had to stay at the hotel until November 1940. The children were close by, however, and little by little a certain routine took shape. Michel got dressed up every day, put on his hat, and went out to chat with other inhabitants of the village (especially with Auguste Barre, the tobacconist).[13] Irène spent a great deal of time writing in her room, with the shutters and draperies closed. When she went out, it was usually to take a walk with her daughters. Sometimes she went to speak with Father Gauffre, the village priest. From time to time, when the weather was good, she left the village and walked to the little wooded area nearby, where a statue of the Virgin was erected to commemorate the fact that the village was protected from the Prussian armies in 1870. Here, Irène wrote in her large notebook with her favorite pen; she wrote in very small letters because paper was increasingly difficult to come by. She would bring her manuscripts home and Michel would type them up.[14]

In this autumn of 1940, Irène and Michel seemed as preoccupied by their status as stateless Jews as they were the previous August when they asked Albin Michel for his letter of support. Is it a coincidence that, three weeks before the first law regulating the status of Jews in France was passed, and two weeks before the order was given for a census of all Jews—on September 13, 1940—Irène wrote directly to Marshall Pétain, the new head of the French State? Did Irène, through her friends, have an inkling about what was being prepared for the Jews by the Vichy government?

Marshall Pétain, in September 1940, had been head of state since July 10 and, despite General De Gaulle's call to resistance on June 18, the hero of Verdun enjoyed great popularity in a country whose population did not yet understand the real nature of his regime—which, though located in Vichy, made many laws applicable to all of France, north and south. Irène and Michel were not the only Jews in France to write to Pétain "with respect and sometimes even with veneration."[15] But whereas many French Jews used their status as military veterans or pleaded the infirmity of a relative in asking that a brother or sister be given permission to work despite Vichy's restrictions, Irène asked to be given a special status because of her reputation as a writer, and invoked the names of various important persons that she knew. And although she made reference in her letter to her status as a stateless person, she never mentioned her Jewish origins.

Monsieur le Maréchal, I had intended to ask Monsieur André Chaumeix, director of *La Revue des Deux Mondes*, in which I write, to draw your kind attention to my case. Unfortunately it is impossible for me to write to him, because he is in the free zone . . . Here is the problem: I have learned that your government had decided to take measures against stateless persons. I am greatly distressed by the fate that awaits us. My husband and I were born in Russia, and our parents emigrated during the Revolution. Our two children are French. We have been living in France for twenty years, and we have never left the country. My husband was an administrator at the Banque des Pays du Nord for fifteen years . . . If you would take the time to ask Monsieur Chaumeix, he would confirm that I have been writing for *La Revue des Deux Mondes* for many years. He could attest to my character, since he was recently willing to support my application for naturalization, a procedure that was probably interrupted due to the war. I am personally known to the family of Monsieur René Doumic.[16] Madame René Doumic and Madame Henri de Régnier will be happy, I am sure, to confirm this. I hardly need to say that I have never concerned myself with politics, and that I have written only literary works. Finally, whether it be in foreign newspapers or on the radio, I have tried my best to make France well-known and well-liked. I cannot believe, Sir, that no distinction is made between the undesirable and the honorable foreigners, those who have done everything possible to deserve the royal welcome France has given them. I ask therefore for your kindness in including me and my family in the latter category of people, so that we can reside freely in France and so that I may continue to exercise my profession as a novelist.[17]

The distinction Irène makes between "undesirable" and "honorable" foreigners reveals a certain sense of cultural superiority—the same superiority she felt in Kiev with regard to the poor Jews of the *podol*—but it must also be understood in the context of her fear of being deported. In fact, on October 4, the Vichy government took measures that allowed it to deport or to quarantine foreign Jews. This law was explicit: "foreign nationals of the Jewish race can . . . be interned in special camps by the decision of the prefect of the department in which they reside . . . [They] can also, at any time, be assigned to house arrest by the prefect of the department in which they reside."[18] Hence Michel and Irène would try to be treated, as Michel said in a letter to the director of his bank, "in the same way as French Jews."[19] Obviously, neither Michel nor Irène could have known in 1940 that the Vichy regime would, in the end, treat French Jews exactly as it had treated foreign Jews.

Irène's and Michel's strategy, thus, was to accept a situation that was imposed on them and hope for the best. They seem to have accepted their fate as if it was completely outside their control. Michel would go so far as to spend time with the German soldiers billeted in Issy-L'Évêque. The soldiers played billiards at the hotel, and Michel, who spoke and wrote German fluently, had a closer relationship with them than did most people in the village. Was Michel just naïve? Did he hope to get from these soldiers some sort of favor that might protect him and his family? He seems to have had motivation. He became friendly with two German noncommissioned officers, Ewald Hammberger and Paul

Spiegel; when they left for the eastern front, he wrote to Spiegel's wife and Hammberger wrote to him, reminiscing about the good times he had in Issy-L'Évêque.[20] Moreover, Michel managed to get a letter of recommendation from these soldiers just before they left the village, in June 1941. The letter, addressed to German soldiers or SS officers who might occupy the village later, reads as follows:

> Comrades! We have lived near the Epstein family for a long time and we have known them to be an honest and friendly family. We ask that you treat them accordingly. Heil Hitler![21]

This rather laconic letter would be of no use when Irène was later arrested. As for the letter previously written to Marshall Pétain, like so many others, it went unanswered.

On September 27, a German order was published forbidding Jews who had taken refuge in the southern, "free" zone to return to the occupied zone, and forcing all those in the occupied zone to be registered with the sub-prefecture within three weeks. Since the census was to take place in alphabetical order, the Epsteins (Irène used her maiden name only for her publications) went to register at the sub-prefecture in Autun on October 7. They never seem to have considered the possibility of not registering, as did many Jews at the time. The "Law on the Status of Jews," valid for all of France, was promulgated by the Vichy government on October 3. As we shall shortly see, this law would be used as a pretext for one of Irène's publishers to break his engagements with her. At the same time, the occupying forces ordered that the word "Jew" be affixed on all the identity cards of Jews in the occupied zone; this measure was to complement the census. For the first time, in a letter that Michel wrote to his former supervisor, the words "concentration camp" appear. This is a threat which, in 1940, did not yet have the same meaning it would have in 1942. At the beginning, a concentration camp was a place of detention for civil populations of enemy countries. We have seen how the writer Paul Morand used the term as far back as 1934; in 1939 the minister of the interior, Maurice Sarraut, did not hesitate to use the same term to characterize the internment camps built for Spanish, German, and Austrian refugees.[22] But even though Michel and Irène could not suspect that these French detention camps would become the anterooms of German death camps, internment, given the recent orders and laws affecting Jews, was a very real threat in October 1940.

Until the summer of 1941—when Germany invaded Russia—Irène and Michel lived a "phony exile," between routine and bad news, where periods of calm were followed by periods of anguish. To pass the time, Michel undertook a translation into French of a biography of Pushkin by the Russian writer V. V. Veresaev;[23] he sent it to Albin Michel in December 1940 but it was never published. In the winter of 1941, Irène obtained permission to take two successive trips to Paris to see her publisher; she returned convinced, as she explained in a letter to her friend Madeleine, that "returning to Paris with the children is currently impossible." In April 1940, Denise fell ill with acute appendicitis. "She had to be operated on in the middle of the night," wrote Irène to her friend, "and you can imagine the confusion. In the end, everything was for the best."[24] The lack of comfort in the small hotel inspired Irène to contemplate other places of refuge. She put aside any idea of living in Hendaye because, in her words, "finding food there is, apparently, very difficult." She asked her friend Madeleine to find her a "three or four room house, furnished, with a garden and heat in the winter" near Beaugency, in the department of Loir-et-Cher.[25] Madeleine managed to find her a house, but it would not be available until September and Irène was already in the process of negotiating a rental in Issy-L'Évêque.

While Irène and Michel were preoccupied with their children's health and their housing problems, more difficulties were being prepared for Jews in Paris and Vichy. On May 8, the German authorities blocked all Jewish bank accounts. More serious even, on May 14, 3700 foreign Jews were arrested in Paris and sent to the camps of Pithiviers and Beaune-la-Rolande.[26]

Writing in Issy-L'Évêque

Up until the time she was arrested, Irène never stopped writing. But the restrictive measures applied by the German occupation authorities as well as by the Vichy government imposed tighter and tighter limits on her existence as a "woman of letters."

Censorship was the most important measure that affected all French authors. Less than a month after the signature of the armistice, on July 1,

1940, a "notice relating to publications for sale in bookstores" required publishers to "submit to the Press Bureau of the German Military Authority all publications intended to be distributed or put on sale."[27] This measure was followed in August by the confiscation in libraries and bookstores of all books prohibited by the "Bernhard List," a document whose intent was to censor principally anti-Hitler German authors (such as Thomas and Heinrich Mann), but which also prohibited some French authors judged anti-German (for example Aragon or André Malraux).[28] Finally, on October 4, another list appeared, the infamous "Otto List." Officially titled "Works removed from sale by publishers," this list aimed at prohibiting the circulation of "books that, by their lying and tendentious character, have systematically poisoned French public opinion," and, in particular, "publications of political refugees or Jewish authors who, betraying the hospitality that France accorded them, have unscrupulously pushed the country into war in order to selfishly profit from the situation."[29] Those works prohibited include two novels by Joseph Kessel and a play by Henri Bernstein, *The History of England* by André Maurois, and some works by Léon Blum—all Jewish writers. All told, some 1060 titles were withdrawn from sale. Among the authors published by Albin Michel, one finds the names of Francis Carco, Roland Dorgelès, and Léon Daudet (none of them Jewish). Irène Némirovsky's name does not appear on the list.

A second Otto List appeared in July 1942, and was intended to replace the first. Titled "Non-desirable French Works," this list takes into account "certain works that may have escaped scrutiny when the first list was drawn up."[30] It includes some 1170 works, classified by publishers. As in the first Otto List, there is no mention of Irène Némirovsky. At the end of the second Otto List, however, the following sentence appears: "All books written by Jewish authors, as well as works in which Jewish authors have collaborated, are to be removed from sale, with the exception of works having a scientific content or for which exceptional measures have been applied."[31] It would be logical to assume that, as of the summer of 1942, Irène's books would not have been for sale. In fact, her books seem to have been taken off the market earlier, since in October 1941 (that is, eight months before the second Otto List was published), Robert Esménard told Irène that Albin Michel was no longer able to publish her works and insure their sale.[32]

When the third Otto List appeared in May 1943, the name of Irène Némirovsky figured in an "appendix giving the names of Jewish authors writing in French." But why were Irène's works not prohibited in the first Otto List? According to the Propaganda Frankreich, the German office charged with applying censorship, French publishers showed an "indifference . . . in making known publicly the names of writers of Jewish origin;" this problem led to "mistakes" in the first and second Otto Lists.[33] Is it thus possible that the German authorities simply forgot to include Irène's name on the first and second lists? It is more probable that Albin Michel himself neglected to make known to the Propaganda office Irène's name when the first list was being drawn up, in a kind of solidarity with one of his best authors, and in the hopes of continuing to sell Irène's books.

Even if Irène's books were not withdrawn as soon as those of other Jewish authors, the sales of her work went progressively down after the beginning of the occupation. Even in January 1939, Albin Michel, while agreeing to send Irène monthly checks of 4000F ($1385), had written to her that "we need to make a film. That appears possible to me, and it is on this hope that I base my agreement to advance you this money."[34] Not only was no film ever made, but the sale of Irène's books did not increase. In particular, *Les Chiens et les loups*, as we have seen, sold very poorly. Hence, in September 1940, Irène received a letter from her publisher stating that she would no longer receive any advances.[35]

In this early autumn of the German occupation, in her room at the hotel in a little Burgundian village, without any means of existence save her pen, Irène saw herself as "completely isolated from the rest of the world."[36] She seemed to have no other choice than to convince her publisher to continue to advance her money. Since Albin Michel was temporarily absent from Paris, she wrote to Robert Esménard, characterizing the letter she had received from his father-in-law as "incomprehensible," and she threatened to break off all her agreements with him, since, in her view, he had promised to extend his advances irrespective of the sales of her books.[37] Esménard answered her coolly that he had seen no written agreement in this sense, but he assured her that "in the absence of Monsieur Albin Michel, all his agreements will be scrupulously respected as if he were here."[38] Irène, in her response, agreed that "we had not confirmed our agreement in writing," but "[Albin Michel's] promise was firm, without any conditions whatever."[39] Esménard accepted her argument and confirmed Albin Michel's commitment, since, as he admitted, his father in law often made non-written agreements.[40] Moreover, he revised his pessimistic prognosis and declared that "the sale of your books is not positively bad, if we take into account the reduction in the number of bookstores that carry them."[41]

The question of monthly advances returned a few months later. Albin Michel had agreed to extend them until the end of the year 1940 at the level of 3000F per month; this was, he said, "the most that, at this time, a publisher can do in these most difficult conditions."[42] Despite the good will of Albin Michel, the money never arrived in Issy-L'Évêque. In March 1941, Irène complained to Esménard that "since January 1 I haven't received a penny."[43] Months went by; in May, the money still had not arrived. The German edicts of April 26, excluding Jews from any profession related to publication, worried Irène. "I admit," she wrote to Esménard, "that the recent edicts concerning Jews make me fear that there may be difficulties in my receiving this payment . . . and that would be a disaster for me."[44] Finally, Esménard advanced all the money that had been due at the end of June, some 24,000F ($6000).

But generosity was far from being the rule among publishers. Irène also needed to find weeklies for her short stories and for the serial publication of her novels—a system, as we have seen, that earned much more money than the simple publication of a novel in book form. Before the war, she had signed a contract with the publisher Arthème Fayard who was to serialize the novel *Jeunes et vieux* in his weekly *Candide*. Fayard had earlier, as we have seen, published Irène's first two novels and many other texts in his monthly *Les Œuvres Libres;* as late as May 1940, Irène's essay titled "La Jeunesse de Tchekhov" (Chekhov's Youth) had appeared in this publication. The director of the weekly *Candide* was Fayard's son-in-law, Fernand Brouty. In June, Brouty left Paris and brought his two newspapers (*Candide* and *Ric et Rac*) to the "free" zone—first to Clermont-Ferrand, then to Marseilles.

There is little doubt that Brouty knew that Irène was Jewish, or that he supported her in her efforts to be published. On July 25, he wrote from Clermont-Ferrand, asking her to send him "a short story as soon as you can;" but he also added "as far as the novel is concerned, there is no hurry because the paper shortage and the limit in the number of pages do not allow us to publish serial novels."[45]

Irène then sent him a short story ("Monsieur Rose"), which he published in *Candide* on August 28. A few months later she received a check for 3000F. Irène had more stories for Brouty, and in October she asked him to accept them: "as winter approaches, the boredom of the countryside begins to be frightening and only work can help me pass the long hours."[46] She even asked Brouty to consider her using a pseudonym, if that would help her stories get into print.

While waiting for an answer from Brouty, Irène wanted to know more about the agreement she had signed for the serial publication of the novel. The contract provided an advance of 60,000F, half of which was to be paid when the contract was signed and the other half when the manuscript was submitted. As the rent of her apartment in Paris came to 10,000F a month, and as she had to pay for the hotel in Issy-L'Évêque, this contract was extremely important to her.

This time she ran up against a wall. She wrote directly to Jean Fayard in Paris. He repeated what Brouty has told her; it was impossible to publish the novel in serial form because of the "very special conditions" which were "the reduction in the number of pages of newspapers." "If you are in a hurry to have your freedom [to publish elsewhere]," he added, "I would prefer to abandon this publication and to allow you to keep the half of the advance you have already received."[47]

Irène saw what Fayard was getting at. She began a letter thus: "I worked for you at an agreed price. When my work is submitted, this price must be paid to me whatever the circumstances." But she judged this language to be too harsh and rewrote the letter, which she sent on October 11.

As far as the novel is concerned, I understand perfectly well that it is impossible for you to publish it at this point. We will, as you propose, wait for the present conditions to change. I only ask that you please pay me the thirty thousand francs upon submission of my manuscript, as it had been agreed between us.[48]

As she had done with Brouty, she proposed to Fayard the use of a pseudonym (Pierre Nerey, which she had used before in *Les Œuvres libres*). By now, the pseudonym had become a necessity. In early October, the Vichy government had passed a law that had immediate consequences on a large part of the Jewish population in France—whether of French nationality or foreign—and deprived many of them of their professions. This measure was particularly severe for those who lived by their pen. "Jews are unconditionally and unreservedly prohibited from exercising any of the following professions: director, manager, editor of journals, reviews, agencies, or periodicals, with the exception of strictly scientific publications," said the directive.[49]

In Fayard's eyes, the existence of this new law precluded his publishing anything more written by Irène. On October 14, he sent her a letter in which, for the first time, he mentioned "a case of *force majeure*, which prevents me from publishing your work for the time being (a pseudonym is useless, since we are obliged to know our authors). I would thus ask you to wait until the question has been resolved. You will understand that it is difficult for us to pay for a novel that we cannot publish. Please note that I . . . freely admit that the 30,000F already paid to you represent no obligation on your part and that I give you complete freedom to publish this volume elsewhere, if you can."[50]

For the first time, Irène felt threatened as a Jew and foresaw future problems she might have. She wrote a response to Fayard's letter, mentioning a "unilateral rupture of a contract between us," but then found that this language was not strong enough. She wrote a second letter, and sent this one to Fayard on October 17.

I am stupefied by your letter, which I have just received. I cannot believe that, whatever the circumstances, your publishing house would renege on a freely-signed agreement.

I ask you to recall that, on July 25, 1940, Monsieur Brouty sent me a letter from Clermont-Ferrand in which he not only asked me to send him some short stories, but brought up the subject of my novel, mentioning only that there was no need for me to finish it right away because of the paper shortage. Never did he make the slightest mention of the possibility that my contract would be broken.

. . . Do you realize that, by your decision, you are leaving me absolutely bereft of money—since my husband is ill and cannot work—with two children to support? Those 30,000F to which I have a legitimate right were meant to allow me to get through the winter. Is there thus a law that forbids the publication, in the free zone, of the works of Jewish writers? And is there a law that allows publishers to consider null and void their contracts with these writers?[51]

But Fayard was unmoved by the human drama that Irène was living. On October 22, he told her that he was "surprised by the tone of your letter" and reminded her that the law was "valid for all Frenchmen, hence without any distinction of the zone they live in." He added, "you will admit that, in these conditions, it would be unthinkable to pay for a novel that we do not have the right to publish."[52] He was right about the law's validity in all of France, but Irène claimed that it only prohibited Jewish journalists, and that, despite the fact that her novels appeared in newspapers, she was an author, not a journalist. She decided to ask the Société des Gens de Lettres for their opinion, and wrote to the director of the society in Paris, Monsieur Georges Robert. She had obviously obtained a copy of the law as it was promulgated in the *Journal officel*, the official publication that contains all laws and decrees of the government, from which she quoted at length. She made a point of citing article 4, which allowed Jews "access and the exercise of liberal professions,"[53] and she continued,

The fact of publishing a novel in a weekly does not, in my view, put the author in the category of "directors, managers, or editors of journals." The very spirit of this law appears to invalidate such an interpretation, because Jews are authorized to exercise liberal profession and, thus, nothing would prohibit me from publishing a book to appear in a bookstore.[54]

Georges Robert received Irène's request and submitted it to the judicial council of the society, presided by a certain Monsieur Peytel. This council rendered its opinion on October 29, and its judgment was favorable to Irène. It claimed that "Madame Némirovsky . . . has been involved with periodicals only from the time that these became accustomed to publishing entire novels in their newspapers" and that, as a consequence, "it is impossible to assimilate the great author Madame Némirovsky, independent and free in her own right, to writers employed by newspapers. The contract in which she cedes the rights of publication of a novel to a journal cannot be assimilated to a contract of employment."[55]

Irène was relieved. She sent her brother-in-law Paul to the offices of the Société des Gens de Lettres de France in Paris, where he was warmly received. As far as Irène was concern, justice had been done.

But she had not counted on Fayard's reaction. He was taken aback; he never expected that Irène would go so far as to approach the Société des Gens de Lettres, and he had no intention of retreating from his position. He intercepted a letter that Irène had sent to Fernard Brouty (she had to send it via Paris since mail between the two zones was forbidden). This letter contained the text of the judgment given by the member of the judicial council. In it, Irène wrote, "as you can see, according to the text of this consultation which is reproduced in detail below, I was justified that no existing law prevents my novels from appearing in the press. Monsieur Fayard has thus made an error in his interpretation, and this has caused me grave prejudice."[56]

For Jean Fayard, whose friends and colleagues at the Société des Gens de Lettres de France had put him in the wrong, this was an affair for him personally, not for his son-in-law Fernard Brouty. Fayard decided to express his disappointment directly to Jean Vignaud, president of the Société des Gens de Lettres. In his letter to Vignaud, Fayard conveyed his astonishment that "this unofficial opinion was given without the advice of the government on the question," and added that he did "not interpret the law in the same way as those of your colleagues who answered Madame Némirovsky's request." He proposed that the Société des Gens de Lettres seek from the government a "formal text" that would authorize him to publish the work of Jewish authors—a request he knew very well to be useless and ridiculous. "If the government, consulted on this point, produces a formal text authorizing *Candide* to publish the work of Jewish authors, I will follow through with the terms of the contract," he added.[57]

Vignaud, unlike Robert, remained faithful to his friend Jean Fayard. Peytel's opinion in this matter was most bothersome, and Vignaud decided to overrule him. He backed up Fayard unconditionally; for him, the publisher's contract was invalid simply because the author was Jewish.

Irène protested: "according to your own judicial council, the act of publishing my novel in *Candide* would not make me a journalist." As for the idea of submitting the question to the government, Irène found it laughable: "I admit that I never had the idea of asking the government, as Monsieur Fayard suggests, to decide if, yea or nay, my novel can appear in *Candide*, since it appears to me that the government has more important matters to deal with."[58]

This was too much for Vignaud. He refused to allow Irène to take issue with his judgment and that of Fayard. He decided to put the author in her place by reminding her, if indirectly, that she was stateless and Jewish:

> Monsieur Georges Robert sent you the opinion of a member of our judicial council, relating to your collaboration with the newspaper *Candide*. I would like to emphasize that the conclusions presented in this brief do not conform to the reality of the situation, at least not in the occupied zone. I can assure you from my own experience that we have had to furnish proof that those who collaborate with our newspaper—that is, novelists and short-story writers (some of whom are famous)—are neither foreigners nor Jews. In the present circumstances, Monsieur Fayard is perfectly justified in his action—he is even generous, since he agrees to let you keep your advance, which is equal to half the price of your novel. At the same time, he leaves you completely free to publish elsewhere. Finally, Monsieur Georges Robert has asked me to tell you that, when he sent you the judgment of our judicial council, he had asked you not to take your case further or to be litigious, and that you had promised him you would not. This is to say that I cannot approve your complaint against the editors of *Candide*. You forget too easily, I believe, the situation in which we are living.[59]

Candide never published the novel *Jeunes et vieux* or any more short stories written by Irène.

If Irène could no longer count on Jean Fayard to help her publish her work, another publisher was willing to brave the law of October 3, 1940, and print her novels and stories. In one of those contradictions that mark the period and indicate the complexity of the human spirit, this person was Horace de Carbuccia—a collaborator and a notorious anti-Semite, who, as we have seen, had great respect for Irène beginning in the mid 1930s. Carbuccia, alone among French editors, was able to bring out Irène's fiction until February 1942.

Carbuccia took his weekly newspaper *Gringoire* to the "free zone" after the defeat of the French army. He left his publishing house, the Éditions de France, in Paris, and entrusted its management to Camille Ferri-Pisani. Pisani was an active collaborator and published, among other works, *L'Amérique juive* (Jewish America) by Antoine Cousteau. As for Carbuccia, his collaboration with the Nazis seems to have been motivated by self-interest rather than ideology, as was the case with Ferri-Pisani.[60] Carbuccia had evidently had enough of collaboration when he decided to put an end to his newspaper in 1942.[61]

Irène seems to have suspected that Carbuccia would prove to be helpful. In January 1941, she wrote to him:

You were so friendly to me when I was writing for *Gringoire* that I turn confidently to you now. I firmly believe that if you could do something for me, you would do it. I have to earn my livelihood. Reviews and weeklies refuse me the right to publish my novels and stories. Yet there are, in other liberal professions—medicine or law, for example—certain Jews who have the right to earn their living. These exceptions are motivated, as you well know, either by their former military service or by their own merit. Could one not argue for an exception in the case of writers like myself, who have never been involved in politics? . . . You alone, Monsieur de Carbuccia, could, through the influential position you enjoy, intervene on my behalf with the government. Frankly, I don't know what will become of me; all the doors seem closed. It is so cruel, so unjust, that I cannot help thinking that people like yourself will understand and come to my aid.[62]

Although no answer to this letter can be found, we know that Carbuccia was sympathetic to Irène's situation, because she sent him manuscripts (using the intermediary of the Éditions de France in Paris), and Carbuccia managed to send her money.[63] In April 1941, *Gringoire* began publishing installments of a novel titled *Les Biens de ce monde* (The Wealth of This World), and called it a "new work by a young woman," omitting Irène's name. The installments lasted until June. Carbuccia went even further in flouting the law; between March 1941 and February 1942, he published more stories by Irène than he had even done before, a total of six. Five of them appeared under pseudonyms that Irène had used before: Pierre Nérey (or Neyret) and Charles Blancat; the sixth appeared as "a novella written by a young woman."

The words of the historian André Kaspi ring true here: "During these somber times, Jews had few friends, but not everyone was their enemy. The truth is neither white nor black. It is gray."[64] Irène found more help in Carbuccia than in any other publisher, even Albin Michel who, despite all the sympathy he poured out in his letters, published nothing of hers until after the war. It is not clear what were Carbuccia's motivations; his memoirs only cover the period 1919–1924. To be sure, nothing that Irène sent him would have ruffled the feathers either of the Germans or of the Vichy regime. As we have seen, *Les Biens de ce monde* sings the praise of the rural world of eternal France. Irène mentions Germans only once, in a short story titled "L'Inconnu" (The Unknown). Here, a French soldier kills a German soldier only to learn that the German was his half-brother; the soldiers' father had deserted the French army during World War I and had made his life in Germany with a new wife. Although the French soldier in this story refers to Germans in a derogatory way (calling them "a bunch of rickety anemics"),[65] the tale takes to task war in general, not German militarism.

Irène's motivations are more transparent than Carbuccia's. In addition to her need to earn money, she was also trying to keep up her contacts with people who could be useful to her; her relations in the political right before 1940 allowed her to call upon these same people, many of whom had now become collaborators. She seems not to have been aware of clandestine publishers (like the *Éditions de Minuit*) or of the journals of the Resistance. She was living closed up in a world of people who, like Albin Michel, caved in to censorship rather than go into hiding and publish clandestinely.

In fact, Albin Michel found himself in a position which led him to call upon his collaborationist friends to help him avoid problems with the German authorities. The Germans threatened to remove him from his publishing house if he could not give them proof of his status as an "Aryan." Publishers like Calmann-Lévy, Ferenczi, and Fernand Nathan—all of them Jewish—had been removed and replaced by Aryan administrators. The same thing happened to Albin Michel; an administrator was named in January 1941, until the proper proof of his birth could be presented to authorities. His son-in-law Robert Esménard put together all the necessary documents that proved that neither he nor his father-in-law were Jewish; "Monsieur Michel has no Jewish ancestry," wrote Esménard to René Philippon, president of the Publishers Union, who was in charge of the case. Documents showing that Albin Michel was not Jewish were presented to the Office of Provisional Administrators, but to no avail; not until Pierre Benoît, a collaborationist author who belonged to the "Comité France-Allemagne" (whose job it was to promote German and French authors favorable to the Nazis) intervened in favor of Albin Michel was he allowed to continue to be in charge of his publishing house.[66]

Despite Albin Michel's reticence to publish Irène's works during the occupation, he and his staff were of continued moral support. Their relationship became closer after December 1940, when André Sabatier, Albin Michel's chief editor, returned from military duty in Lebanon.[67] Sabatier, a small, thin man with a mustache and glasses, had left Bernard Grasset in 1936 for Albin Michel, at about the same time as Irène.[68] He was a close friend of Jacques Benoist-Méchin, a historian and great admirer of the German military (author of a history of the German army as well as an explanation of Hitler's *Mein Kampf*). Benoist-Méchin fled Paris to Vichy after being freed from a prisoner-of-war camp; in the Vichy government, he became secretary of state for Franco-German affairs and, later, ambassador of the French State in Turkey. He was sentenced to death after the war, in 1945, but his sentence was later commuted to house arrest.

The relationship between Sabatier and Irène went far beyond simple cordiality. More than Albin Michel or Robert Esménard, Sabatier became a personal friend, someone in whom Irène could confide and to whom she could speak freely. As soon as she had word that Sabatier had returned from military duty, she sent him a letter to describe her situation in Issy-L'Évêque:

As for me, I have no good news for you. Since last May I have taken refuge in this little village, in the most uncomfortable circumstances but where, at least, my whole family can be together and can easily find food. I have worked hard. I finished the Life of Chekhov. I wrote a novel (the odyssey of which I shall tell you later), and I have begun another; I have written many stories, but for the moment none of these bring me any money, for reasons you can easily understand. My situation is thus far from brilliant, and I must make changes at all costs.[69]

Sabatier's reaction to Irène's letter was one of sympathy and compassion: "It is with a great deal of emotion that I received your kind letter, for I had suspected all the difficulties and sadness your exile in the provinces causes you, especially in the present circumstances," he wrote.[70] By encouraging her to continue to write and to send him manuscripts, Sabatier perhaps hoped to do what Esménard had refused,[71] that is, publish Irène's biography of Chekhov and perhaps one of her novels. Sabatier played an important role in convincing Albin Michel to extend Irène's monthly allowance of 3000F for the year 1941. "I know that I can count on your faithful friendship," Irène wrote to him in December 1940.

It may seem paradoxical that a Jewish author like Irène would live in the period of the occupation by calling upon friends and acquaintances who had no scruples about cooperating with the Nazi requirement that they show evidence of being Aryan or who openly collaborated with the Germans. But Irène's situation is a complex one. She had made her reputation as a writer primarily among people on the political right; as a Russian fleeing the revolution, she saw in communism a threat every bit as real, for her and her family, as nazism. These two ideologies, she wrote in 1942, are "for me, equally inimical."[72] But by counting on the support of these people to protect her from the anti-Semitic measures taken by the Germans and the Vichy French and by refusing to leave Issy-L'Évêque, Irène was erecting a wall around herself, a wall that would end up imprisoning her.

Writing under the Occupation

When one looks at Irène's literary production during the early period of the German occupation, one notices her faith in the essential goodness and generosity of the French. Even when she was unable to get her texts published, even when she could not travel without special approval, France remained for her the country of courage and sacrifice in the face of the adversity and hardship imposed by war. Later, when she writes *Suite Française*, this faith will be sorely tested.

Among the short stories Irène had published in *Gringoire*, some—like "L'honnête homme" (The Honest Man), published in 1941, "Les Revenants" (The Ghosts), published in 1941, or "L'Incendie" (The Fire), published in Feburary 1942)—are inspired by the life of the countryside around Issy-L'Évêque. Stories about houses that hide family secrets alternate with problems of inheritances and daily life in rural France. There is no war in these stories and no foreign occupation, even if the end of "L'Incendie," where an artist and his work are consumed by fire, could be seen as evoking the pillage and destruction of works of art by the Germans.

More interesting than these country stories is a short work called "Destinées" (Destinies). Irène recounts a dinner party given by an author who lives (as did she) on the sixth floor of a Parisian apartment building, surrounded by (as she was) Spanish and Russian immigrants who live on the Basque coast. The story takes place on May 10, 1940, during an air raid alert. This group of immigrants to France cannot forget, on the eve of war, their own experiences in the Russian revolution or the Spanish civil war. Each of them tells a story, and each story serves as an allegory indicating a reaction to the coming conflict. For the Spanish refugee, a woman, the coming war recalls the story of an old lady and her masseuse: when the Spanish civil war came, the masseuse denounced her former wealthy client, not for political reasons but out of jealousy, and looked on "without the least bit of emotion" as the lady was gunned down. For a Russian refugee, the situation evokes the story of a "foreign statesman who became a Germanophile because he had been cuckolded by his French mistress." This diplomat convinces his head of state to make an alliance with Germany, thus imposing a foreign policy based on a personal grudge. These stories remove politics entirely from the coming conflict. In "people-to-people hatred," says the narrator of the story, "there is always at bottom a question of self-interest or wounded love." But can the origins of the Spanish Civil War or those of the coming world war really be reduced to personal disputes? No, says the narrator, but personal responsibility is engaged in any conflict or revolution. "In public calamities, nobody is innocent," says a Russian refugee, "Everybody pays for the faults committed in the past and forgotten. It is as if a race or a class, or a country, gave birth to monsters that would turn on it and crush it."[73]

In "Destinées," Irène describes "the smiling courage [of the French], their generous restraint, and their wish always to give more than is asked of them—not only in aid but in encouragement."[74] But we know from other works Irène was writing in Issy-L'Évêque and that were published after her death that she was preoccupied with what she saw as France's own responsibility for its defeat in 1940. This idea is implicit in two works that were published posthumously: *Les Feux de l'automne,* which evokes the period between 1914 and 1941 in the context of Paris; and *Les Biens de ce monde,* which deals with the same period, but in a provincial context.

Les Feux de l'Automne is basically a chronicle of the youth in a country that has lost its soul and thus cannot avoid being defeated in 1940. Irène creates a petit-bourgeois Parisian family whose eldest son, having become a physician, is killed on the front in 1916, the day following his marriage. His younger brother, Bernard, enrolls in the army despite his parents' objections; he too is shot, but, unlike his brother, he survives the war. But the period following World War I sees the decline of spiritual and patriotic values and the rise of hedonism—the pursuit of wealth and pleasure. When Bernard returns from the front, he is tempted by the easy money and casual sex his friend Raymond Détang, a politician involved in more than one dishonest deal, proposes. Yet Bernard, for all his love of the easy life, marries his brother's widow, out of a sense of fraternal duty. This is a solid, moral woman whose Catholic faith is unshakable, a character not unlike Sylvie Wardes in *Les Échelles du levant.* Bernard's friendship with the dishonest Détang proves, however, to have tragic results. His eldest son is killed while piloting a defective airplane, made in the United States, which Bernard himself had sold to the French air force in a shady deal perpetrated by his friend Détang. In a state of despair, Bernard re-enrolls in the army and, in June 1940, is captured by German forces. When he is finally freed, he comes back to his wife who, "entirely consumed by love and expectation," is waiting for him. Bernard has found redemption in this woman's unflinching love and self-sacrifice; under her influence, he is now "changed, matured, a better person."

In writing *Les Feux de l'automne,* Irène had researched the case of the minister of the air force in the Daladier government, Guy La Chambre. La Chambre took over from Pierre Cot in 1938 and, for two years, tried to rearm the French air force. In particular, he decided to purchase from the United States a quantity of Curtiss P-36 fighter planes, a decision that produced debate in the government since some politicians claimed that these planes were defective.[75] The Vichy government put La Chambre on trial in Riom, along with General Gamelin, Édouard Daladier, Léon Blum, and the controller general Jacomet. The trial took place in February 1942, at the very time that Irène was writing this novel. She was thus able to consult the interrogatory of La Chambre, published in the press.

But this "aircraft affair" is only one aspect of the errors which, in Irène's view, had led France to defeat. More important is the attitude of an entire generation that turned their backs on the patriotism and sacrifice that characterized the France of the pre-World War I period. Irène's original title for this novel, *Jeunes et vieux* (The Young and the Old), reflects a generational conflict. The Paris she depicts, that of the years following World War I, has become unrecognizable for the generation that fought the war; it has become a city "full of people speaking foreign tongues," where "Frenchmen no longer feel at home."[76] "New morals" have replaced traditional values of "frugality, marital faithfulness, and virginity."[77] The world of this older generation is falling apart and is being replaced by "a mass of corruption and venality" where power is "in the hands of business and industry."[78] The defeat of 1940 is thus a moral defeat. "The battle for France has been lost for twenty years," Bernard recognizes this at the end of the novel. "It was lost when we came back from battle in 1919 and wanted to have a good time to forget those four lost years in the trenches; when we became corrupted by easy money; when an entire class of men said 'I don't give a damn, so long as I get mine.'"[79]

This novel echoes some of the elements that Pétain and his government advanced during the "national revolution" that was supposed to rekindle the French spirit. The cult of the mother and the family, reflected in posters put up all over France, preached an attitude like that of Bernard's wife, whose values were "a husband, a home and many children."[80] Like the government, the Catholic Church also blamed immorality and a deficit of family values for the 1940 defeat, and particularly attacked the politicians of the Third Republic who had, in its view, conducted sleazy affairs with corrupt businessmen.[81]

In *Les Biens de ce monde,* Irène concentrated on what she considered the positive values inherent in the French character, and tried to show how these values could survive military defeat. What characterized the France of the countryside, for her, was its permanence. She told the story of the Hardelot family, which survives each crisis and finds, at the end, the same social structure, the same friends, the same values that they grew up with, even if their home and village have been destroyed. "In this world," wrote Irène, "everything stayed the same . . . Until the end of time, the Hardelots would continue to furnish the shops in the Pas-de-Calais and in the North with solid, unequaled white linen paper for their registers . . . they would buy land, marry their children, lead a frugal life and die in their beds."[82]

This novel is also a hymn to conjugal love, and recalls in this respect *Deux.* The relationship between Pierre Hardelot and Agnès is strong precisely because it has to resist the criticism of Pierre's family (since he and Agnès come from very different social backgrounds), the war, and the passage of time. This love is what holds the family together; mother and father project their values to their children who, in turn, become part of the web of love that unites the family with a stability that even the world wars cannot shake. Pierre's attachment to the family paper factory—for which he risks his life during a bombardment—is seen here within the context of his love for his father. Pierre's sense of responsibility is related to his wife's sense of sacrifice; Agnès is yet another self-abnegating, moral, religious wife. *Les Biens de ce monde* ends with an evocation of the harvest and of a future in which suffering will find its reward:

> [Agnès] felt neither pain nor fatigue. It was as if she had harvested all the richness in her life, all the love, the happiness, and the tears that God gave her; now that all was ended, she ate the bread that she herself had made, drank the wine from the grapes she had pressed. All the good of the earth had been put in store for her, and all the bitterness and sweetness of the earth had borne fruit.[83]

Les Feux de l'automne and *Les Biens de ce monde* are important not so much as major literary works but because they show a point of view that fits in well with the Vichy regime. In writing these novels, Irène was undoubtedly hoping that her publishers would take them; the reality, as we have seen, is that they would not even look at them. Yet these novels do not really reveal Irène's attitude at the time. She does not seem to have been brainwashed by the Vichy government's ideology any more than most of the French people. If we look closely at the other texts unpublished in her lifetime and at other literary projects, we see evidence of doubts about the Vichy government and its ideology, as well as a sometimes harshly critical attitude toward those who cooperated with the regime. It is no wonder then that Irène did not speak of this project in detail to Sabatier or Albin Michel. The manuscript was carefully hidden by her family after Irène's arrest.

The project that most preoccupied Irène from 1940 until her death was a major work, a *roman fleuve* that would be titled *Suite française* (French Suite), whose first two volumes—the only ones written before Irène's arrest—were not published until more than sixty years after her death. This project was born in the summer of 1940, during the defeat; there were to be, at first, five volumes and a total of 1600 pages. "What interests me is the history of a world confronting danger," wrote Irène in her notebook. In particular, she wanted to examine in detail the reaction of various levels of French society—the upper middle-class, the intellectuals, the working class—to the defeat and occupation. "My idea," she wrote, "is to make the story read as if one were looking at a film. But the temptation is great—and I have given in at times—to give my own point of view." Here, history would be the background against which she would examine the human heart. "The most important and interesting thing is the following: historic facts, revolutions, etc., must be touched upon, whereas what will be developed is daily lives, human feelings, etc.—especially the human comedy."

Irène worked on the first volume, called *Tempête en juin* (Storm in June), during the summer of 1941, and had her handwritten manuscript typed by Michel.[84] She created a bourgeois family (the Péricands), in which the grandfather (a rich industrialist) is the founder of a charitable organization for unruly Parisian children in the wealthy 16th arrondissement; an affected and hypocritical intellectual author (Gabriel Corte); an unscrupulous bank president (Joseph Corbin); a peasant family (the Labaries); and a family of modest means (the Michauds), whose son is wounded during the war. Each of these characters lives out his or her own adventure during the debacle of June 1940.

In contrast to the two other novels of this same period, *Tempête en juin* is a vehicle for Irène to put a distance between herself and the collaborationist writers she knew in Paris and to take an ironic view of the industrial middle class. Her presentation of the wealthy Péricand family contrasts sharply with that of the Hardelot family in *Les Feux de l'automne*; with the exception of Péricand's two sons, his family is perfectly hypocritical and the charitable organization of which they are so proud exists only to give themselves a good conscience. As she looks at the lines of Parisians fleeing the city on foot, Madame Péricand, who has an automobile at her disposal, says, "Do you see how good our Lord Jesus is? Just think, *we* could be those miserable wretches."[85] Irène goes at the literary world with equal ferocity. "Hit the writers hard," she had noted in her notebook, "example: AC . . . we have never attacked some authors, like A.B." We cannot be sure to whom she is referring; was AC Alphonse de Châteaubriant, minister of education and art in the Vichy government, and a great admirer of Hitler? Is AB Abel Bonnard, member of the Académie Française, supporter of Pétain, and participant in the infamous voyage of French authors to Germany, organized by the Reich in October 1941? Whatever the case, Gabriel Corte is "violently collaborationist." His egotism and love of comfort make him count on friends in the Vichy government. It is hard to avoid seeing in this cynical author, who gets from his highly-placed friends "thousands of the small favours that make life easier,"[86] Irène's bitterness at being shunned by some of her own friends with contacts in the government. Similarly, the injustice done to Jeanne Michaud, fired by her banker boss for not being able to flee Paris fast enough to join him in the southern zone, could easily have been inspired by Irène's own experience with the broken Jean Fayard contract.

But the real importance of *Tempête en juin* is not in the settling of old accounts. Far from portraying defeated France as a country united in its misfortune, as the Vichy regime would have wanted, Irène describes it as a splintered country, where the rich profit from the debacle on the backs of the poor. "But why are we always the ones who have to suffer?" asks the courageous Jeanne Michaud. "If war is declared or the franc dcvalues, if there's unemployment or a revolution, or any sort of crisis, the others manage to get through all right. We're always the ones who are trampled!"[87] Rumblings of revolt can be heard in defeated France. The young delinquents of the Péricand foundation, having understood that their benefactor is using them to protect himself from danger during the exodus, turn on him and kill him. "The End of a Philanthropist," is how Irène ironically titles this chapter.[88]

The France that Irène saw in 1940 is made up of a few heros (such as the soldier Jean-Marie Michaud), quite a few profiteers (the Péricands, Corte, Corbin), and many victims. The latter are the most admirable; poor peasants save the life of the wounded and abandoned Jean-Marie Michaud and nurse him back to health. "It is curious that the mass, so 'detestable,' is made up of these decent people," wrote Irène in her notebook. But she resisted, especially in the second part of *Suite française*, giving too flattering a picture of French peasantry and workers. Cowardice as well as courage could be found at every level of the population. During the debacle, most French people simply wanted to protect themselves. Politics became irrelevant; the characters in this novel are hardly aware that the French government has fled to Bordeaux and then to Vichy. Nobody seems to have heard Maréchal Pétain's message of June 17 or De Gaulle's call for resistance of June 18. Some characters, such as the author Corte, talk vaguely of a "new regime" and "reversals of loyalties," but their principal interest is their own survival in an increasingly confusing world. For other characters—the poor who suffer the most—the only solution is to find peace within themselves and to believe that this, too, will pass. Maurice Michaud, unemployed and believing his son has been killed in battle, finds his strength in "my certainty that deep down I'm a free man . . . It's a constant, precious possession, and whether I keep it or lose it is up to me and no one else . . . I desperately want what has begun to finish. In a word, I desperately want this tragedy to be over and for us to try to survive it, that's all."[89]

Tempête en juin begins in Paris, in the summer heat of June 1940, and ends with the cold of the following winter in a little village in southern Burgundy. *Dolce*, the next volume, takes up the stories a few months later, during the spring of 1941, when a German regiment arrives in this village named Bussy, but quite transparently, Issy-L'Évêque. The fictional hotel in Bussy has the same name as that in which Irène and her family resided (the Hôtel des Voyageurs); the town itself has the same layout as Issy-L'Évêque, and it is situated only a few kilometers from the "free" zone; some of the fictional characters even have names approximating those of the real inhabitants of Issy-L'Évêque.[90]

In contrast to *Tempête en juin*, *Dolce* is a less ambitious and, in some ways, more successful novel. Irène does not attempt to give as wide-ranging a portrait of France as she does in the first volume; here she focuses on one village, and shows how its citizens accommodated themselves to the German occupation. She concentrates on three families: the Count and Countess of Mortmort, who adapt very quickly to the occupation despite an anti-German prejudice left over from the Great War; the Labarie family, which had nursed Jean-Marie Michaud back to health in the first volume, and who are wary of the Germans as they would be of any foreigner; and Madame Angellier and her daughter-in-law, a middle-class family (Madame Angellier's son is a prisoner-of-war), whose reaction to the German soldiers is the most complex and the most interesting.

A reader encountering *Dolce* for the first time will be reminded of the famous clandestinely published novel by Vercors (the pseudonym of the Resistance fighter Jean Bruller), *Le Silence de la mer* (The Silence of the Sea). Vercors' novel also presents a French family—a man and his niece—who have to come to terms with an intelligent, cultivated German officer billeted in their home. Their refusal to engage in conversation with him and to respond to his professed love of their country and its literature was considered a model to follow by those in France who refused collaboration. Published in 1942, *Le Silence de la mer* has more of a polemical intent than *Dolce*. It also lacks the ambiguity and complexity of Irène's novel, which does not advise a certain type of behavior but rather describes and analyzes a range of behaviors. What interests Irène is not the occupation as such but rather the individuals—both French citizens and soldiers in the Reichswehr—who have to live in a situation in which they are both actors and victims.

At the heart of Irène's novel is an absolute respect for human life, be it French or German. Irène wrote in her notebook that she would give a parallel portrayal of the death of a French and German soldier, and added that they both should show "a painful nobility." In fact, the only death occurring in *Dolce* is that of a German soldier, the company's French interpreter, killed by the peasant Benoît Labarie for having made eyes at Labarie's wife. With the exception of this interpreter, whose behavior is roundly condemned by his superior, the conduct of the Germans is irreproachable. They respect the life and property of the inhabitants of Bussy (they even protect and return the personal effects of a family that had fled the village), and they are confused by the distrustful attitude of many of the villagers.

Apart from the Count and Countess, whose appreciation of orderliness leads them to collaborate closely with the occupying forces, the villagers of Bussy realize that this regiment of German soldiers represents more than the sum of its parts. It is an evil force, a danger to their very lives. Their distrust—and for some of them, their resistance—comes not from a response to Charles de Gaulle's appeal or moral outrage at what Germany has done to the populations it has conquered. It comes, rather, from the "obscure movements of the blood," as Irène described it, that urge Madame Angellier not to let the German soldier play her cherished piano, or Lucille (her daughter-in-law) not to give in to the advances of Captain Von Falk, despite his physical appeal and his civilized manner. When Benoît Labarie, having killed the German officer, turns to the Angelliers for help, he is immediately hidden and protected. This gesture, which, in the context of the occupation would be seen as one of resistance and would be punishable by death, comes naturally to the Angelliers, not for political reasons but because Benoît is one of them—he is of the village and thus deserves their protection.

Collaboration between the French and the Germans in Bussy is impossible because it is simply not in the order of things. As she had in *Les Mouches d'Automne*, which dealt with the Russian Revolution and its aftermath, Irène avoids any political interpretation of the great events in history. In *Dolce*, the occupation is like a hurricane that forms "a sort of circle whose edges are made of wind and rain but whose centre is . . . still."[91] Bussy is in the eye of this hurricane; the calm of 1941 is illusory and will soon end. At the end of the novel, the German soldiers are leaving for the Eastern front, and Benoît Labarie is fleeing to Paris, there to join some "politicized" friends. The storm that began in June 1940 is still blowing.

The volume of *Suite française* that Irène planned to follow *Dolce* was to be called *Captivité* (Captivity) and was to make even more explicit Irène's attitude toward the occupation and collaboration. The protagonist and hero of this novel would be Jean-Marie Michaud, and he would be increasingly hostile to the policies of the Vichy regime. Although Irène never had time to complete this part of *Suite française*, she gave a good indication in her notebook of what she would have written. Jean-Marie was to reject the corporatist idea of "community," one of the principal building stones of the National Revolution of the Vichy government. In her writer's notebook, among the words that she would put into his mouth, we find the following: "I intend to find out why I am asked to die, and why I, Jean-Marie Michaud, would die for P. Henriot [Philippe Henriot, propaganda minister in the Vichy government] and P. Laval and other lords, just like a chicken is eviscerated to be served at the table of these traitors." She proposes this metaphor for Henriot and Laval: "The first is a tiger, the second a hyena; one smells on the first the odor of fresh blood, and the stink of dead bodies is on the other." She goes even farther and, using Jean-Marie as her mouthpiece accuses the collaborationists of treachery and opportunism:

He [the collaborator] feels neither jealousy nor deceived ambition, nor any real desire for revenge. He is scared. Who would do the least harm to him (not in the future but right now and in the form of kicks in the ass and slaps)? The Germans? The English? The Russians? The Germans beat him but the beating is forgotten and now the Germans can defend him. That is why he is for the Germans.

By contrast with the first two volumes of *Suite française*, *Captivité* was to be openly political and would directly attack the Vichy regime. But for all her dislike of Laval and Henriot, Irène, like many others, spared Pétain himself. Nor did she approve the armed Resistance. Irène's opinions, which she never expressed in her correspondence, appear in her notebook; the Resistance proclaims its "patriotism, love of liberty, etc." in order to hide its "cowardice" and its true motivations, which are to "take everything" from those who own the riches of the country—in other words, to foment social revolution in France.

Unlike many Frenchmen and women, and the many foreigners who joined the Resistance and actively fought the occupation forces, Irène stayed away from any organized movement. Undoubtedly, her anticommunism made it difficult for her to join with forces close to the Communist party, which had just thrown itself into the fight against the Nazis after Germany invaded the USSR. Irène's analysis of the situation was very clear. Until the English win the war (an event that will happen, she wrote, "after my death") and establish a middle-class liberal democracy, Europe is governed by "two forms of socialism:" that of the USSR and that of Germany (National Socialism). "Neither of the two appeal to me. But there are facts! One of them rejects me, therefore . . . the other . . . but this is out of the question."

There are no Jews in *Suite française*. Indeed, the France Irène describes—the transposition of her own village—has no Jewish refugees, either hidden or, like the Epsteins, living out in the open. Irène wrote her novel throughout the years 1941 and 1942, yet there is no reference to the laws against Jews (although we know that Irène was preoccupied with this law) or to the census of Jews in September 1940 (another subject of much anguish for the Epstein family). It is doubtful that the projected volumes of *Suite française* would have taken Jews into account; the notes Irène left behind do not reveal any Jewish characters or any reference to deportation. After the publication of *Les Chiens et les loups* in 1940, Irène kept Jewishness out of her writing. As an author, she continued to create for herself a purely French identity, and left no trace of her origins in her later fiction.

Irène's Russian origins, however, did inspire a work of nonfiction during the occupation period. This is the *Life of Chekhov*, which Irène wrote in 1940 and 1941 and which Albin Michel published in 1946. Irène felt a great affinity with Chekhov, and not only because of his skill as an author. Like her, he had his texts published in a journal whose director (Souvarine) was "a reactionary and especially an opportunist"[92]—a description that fitted nicely Horace de Carbuccia. Then too, Chekhov, far from Moscow, seemed to find the same sense of exile as Irène, far from her former life in Paris. Irène admired Chekhov's dedication to the downtrodden of Russia on the Island of Sakhalin and his way of "meditat[ing] unceasingly on his art" and "search[ing] for simplicity above all."[93] Like Irène, Chekhov was a great Francophile and once said of France, "How it suffers, how it pays for everyone, this people who is more advanced than any other and sets the tone for European culture."[94] The occupation of France served only to magnify this feeling of despair for a culture that was being raped. In her comparison of Chekhov's time and her own, Irène could hide her hopelessness: "One cannot imagine a period as different from ours as [the period of Chekhov's life]. People then appeared happy. They had no idea of the evils from which we suffer. They wished for freedom. They did not know the tyranny that is weighing on us."[95]

More than anything else, Irène wished for *La Vie de Tchékhov* to be published during her lifetime. She had asked Sabatier to look over the manuscript to "avoid any misunderstanding with the censors."[96] There is nothing in the text that would have disturbed the German authorities except, of course, for the author's Jewish origins. Irène was able to publish an excerpt from this biography in *Les Œuvres Libres* in May 1940.[97] The desperation with which Irène pursued her efforts to have this book published reveals not only her will to continue to write under the occupation, but also to be recognized as an author whose talents went beyond fiction. It is significant to note that, if Irène accepted the use of a pseudonym for the stories she wrote during the occupation, she steadfastly refused that her book on Chekhov appear under any name but her own.

In the summer of 1941, Irène's life changed dramatically in Issy-L'Évêque.

"Unbelievable heat," she wrote in her notebook on June 25. "The garden is decked out in June colors—azure, pale green, rose. I have lost my pen. There are still other worries such as the threat of the concentration camp, the status of Jews, etc. An unforgettable Sunday. The thunder clap of Russia falling on our friends after their 'mad night' on the shores of the pond."

This "mad night" was the party held for the soldiers of the Wehrmacht before their departure for the "thunder" of the eastern front where they were headed; this party makes its way into the second volume of *Suite française*.[1] Four days before, on June 21, Germany had invaded Russia. The German-Soviet pact was broken and the war had entered a new phase. It is not surprising that these soldiers, happy to be in the safety of Issy-L'Évêque, would give a party for the town as they were about to leave; nor is it surprising that Irène and Michel would regret their departure. Michel had become close to some of the young German soldiers. His excellent command of German had facilitated this rapprochement; he would later receive letters from them and from their families.[2] Irène's principal preoccupation was the human drama of the young soldiers leaving for a brutal battle:

They are leaving. They have been feeling down for 24 hours. Now they are gay, especially when they are together . . . They are sending packages home. They are very excited, that's evident. Admirable discipline, I think, with no ideas of revolt at heart. I am resolving now never to hold rancor, however justified it might be, toward a group of people, whatever their race, religion, conviction, prejudices, errors. I am sorry for these poor boys.

But Russia was far away. There were "other worries" that would become more pressing to Irène. Deportation to a detention camp was a continuing threat, though at Issy-L'Évêque no one was as yet aware that these were death camps. The status of Jews had just undergone a modification for the worse in that more professions were forbidden (including, as we have seen, writing articles for magazines). In April, a German decree forbade Jewish economic activity; on May 28, another decree denied Jews access to their bank accounts.

Irène would have known, since her brother-in-law Paul was still in Paris, that on May 14, 1941, Jews were rounded up for the first time in Paris. More than 3500 people were arrested and sent to camps in Pithiviers and Beaune-la-Rolande. This round-up targeted mainly foreign Jews; it was widely sanctioned by collaborationist newspapers and met with general indifference on the part of the public.[3] Irène and her husband had good reason to fear deportation, even more now that the war between the USSR and Germany would place them, as natives of Russia, firmly in the camp of the enemies of the Reich. They feared less for their children, who were born in France and thus legally French in accordance with the *droit du sol* principle—the automatic granting of French nationality to anyone born in France.[4] They could not imagine that, despite this law, Jewish children born in France would eventually be deported to the death camps.[5]

On June 22, 1941, Irène sent a letter to Julie Dumot, her father's former companion, a woman of little education but of exemplary fidelity to the family. "On learning that Russia and Germany were at war," she wrote, "we immediately feared the concentration camp." She asked Julie to come to Issy-L'Évêque to take care of all the family's business, for she was sure she and her husband would soon be arrested. "When you come, if we are no longer here, move in with the children at the Hôtel des Voyageurs . . . where we have been living for a year. It is a modest little inn, but you will be well fed and the proprietors are people in whom you can have confidence."

This extremely detailed letter shows that Irène and her husband had saved enough money to be able to put some aside. Irène would leave Julie 25,000F (about $6000) in banknotes and another 60,000F (about $14,500) with a notary. She had rented a very large house, which the family was to occupy beginning in November. She kept in reserve for resale a certain amount of jewelry and furs that she had taken from her mother's apartment before moving to Issy-L'Évêque. Furthermore Albin Michel had agreed to make monthly payments of 4000F ($975) to her in 1941, a total of 48,000F ($11,600) even though he published none of her works during that year.[6]

Irène also planned to leave her rough manuscript of *Tempête en juin* (with her penciled corrections) and ask that it be sent to Carbuccia for publication; she hoped in this way to earn "approximately 50,000 francs [$12,150]." But the novel, she wrote, was not yet quite finished and only "in the direst of circumstances" should Julie have recourse to this source of income.[7]

Irène was so sure she would be deported that she sent a letter to the rental agent of her Paris apartment on June 23. "At the moment you receive this letter we will be separated from our children whom we have entrusted into the care of Mademoiselle Julie Dumot," she wrote. "I hope this state of affairs will not last and that influential friends will succeed in freeing us."[8] Fortunately, she did not immediately have to put these friends to the test, for neither she nor Michel were arrested in the summer of 1941. Julie Dumot did arrive, however, and remained with the family.

The month of June 1941 passed in relative calm in Issy-L'Évêque, but it was not so in Paris. During the summer of 1941, round-ups in Paris continued: on July 16, 4000 Jews were deported, both children and adults; between August 20 and 23, 4000 more were arrested and the detention camp at Drancy was opened. In occupied France, from August 13 on, Jews could no longer own radios. On September 5, an exhibit called "The Jew and France" opened in Paris. Its catalogue reads: "Jews are at the root of all the troubles, all the perturbations, all the conflicts, all the revolts of the modern world."[9] For the time being, however, Michel's brothers and sister were safe.

As for Irène's mother, she had fled Paris, armed with a false certificate of Latvian nationality[10] (Latvians being one of the "protected nationalities" of the Nazis). Irène had more or less lost touch with her; their strained relations did not allow for much communication. When Irène's mother learned that Irène had entered her apartment and taken her furs, she sent a letter, through an intermediary, asking for them back. Irène was coolly ironical in her answer to the intermediary's query: "it is in fact I who took the furs . . . and other objects. I immediately sold it all, allowing [my mother's] granddaughters and myself to survive a while longer. I think she will be thrilled to have been able to help me . . . She must have known I had neither money nor work when she fled Paris . . . PS: I unfortunately gained little from the sale of the furs, for they were in a pitiable state."[11]

Autumn

The autumn of 1941 was bleak in Issy-L'Évêque. Irène's exile from Paris weighed heavily and banking restrictions made life extremely difficult. Moreover, her friend Madeleine Cabour had already returned to Lille; "I would give anything to be home again, but Paris, for many reasons, frightens me," wrote Irène to Madeleine.[12] She nevertheless tried to get permission to go to Paris with Michel, who explained, in his letter to the authorities, that he needed to "take care of [his] wife's business with her editor" and to "visit the oculist who has always taken care of [his] wife."[13] But the authorities held to the letter of the law, and permission was not granted. "These are very hard times," wrote Irène to André Sabatier. "These are the facts. It's impossible to work, but I have to provide for four people. To that are added other stupid vexations: I can't go to Paris, and I can't have things sent to me, things you can't do without, such as blankets, beds for the children etc., not even my books. There is a total prohibition with regard to apartments inhabited by any such as myself. If I'm telling you all this, it's not to make you sorry for me, but to explain why my thoughts can only be black."[14] Irène did see the situation as somewhat harsher than it really was. The law of July 22, 1941, restricting the businesses, goods and assets of Jews, mainly concerned Jewish bonds, for which an "Aryan" administrator could be named. "Apartments or private dwellings" were specifically exempted. Besides, Irène's Paris apartment was inhabited by her brother-in-law Paul in her absence,[15] and he was allowed to send furniture from Paris to Issy-

L'Évêque as late as May 1942.[16] Nonetheless, the situation in Paris gave Irène much cause for concern. Her rental agent refused her request to have the rent lowered by 50% owing to the "extreme diminution of my resources due uniquely to the fact of the war."[17] This was another rebuff that only deepened her feelings of exile and frustration.

To these vexations was added another, which stemmed from the German order on April 26 freezing Jewish bank accounts. On October 27, 1941, Irène received a letter from Robert Esménard telling her that henceforth he would be "obligated to deposit into a frozen account any payments due to a Jewish author."[18] In such a situation Irène would not be able to withdraw the monthly advances her editor had promised her. She proposed a way around this hurdle: "I wonder if under these conditions it wouldn't be simpler to pay my friend Julie Dumot who lives with me and who is the author of a novel entitled *Les Biens de ce monde*, the manuscript of which is in Monsieur Sabatier's possession . . . Mademoiselle Dumot has also published various short stories in *Gringoire* under the pseudonym Charles Blancat. It is under this pseudonym also that she would like to publish *Les Biens de ce monde* and any subsequent works . . . Mademoiselle Dumot is unquestionably Aryan and can furnish proof of this."[19] Esménard was prudent; he consented to the scheme but never spoke of it in his letters, which ran the risk, as did all letters, of being opened by the censors. On December 17, 1941, he gave Julie Dumot a contract for the publication of a novel, *Les Biens de ce monde*, and agreed to pay her (actually Irène) a salary of 3000F ($730) per month. Henceforth it was "Julie Dumot" who was the author and who was paid money that went into Irène's pocket.

In spite of this subterfuge, however, Albin Michel did not think it wise to publish either the biography of Chekhov or the novel. Irène tried to convince Esménard, writing "A little while ago I saw that works by Daniel Halévy and Jean Fréville have appeared, I don't remember with which publisher. Since they are both Jewish (certainly the latter whom I have known since childhood), I wonder if it would be possible to arrange for publication of my own works as well."[20] Irène was mistaken about Halévy; although he had distant Jewish ancestry, he was nevertheless born of a Catholic father and a Protestant mother. Once a defender of Dreyfus, he became a supporter of Marshall Pétain and was able to

publish several works during the occupation. As for Fréville, this re-
puted journalist of the Communist *L'Humanité* was indeed a Russian
Jew (Eugene Schklaff), but for political reasons was not able to have anything published during the occupation. Esménard answered Irène that
he still had to find the "propitious moment" to publish her works, and
to "again apply with utmost discretion on your behalf" to the German
authorities for permission.[21] On December 9, still with no answer, Irène
once again asked Sabatier: "Will you soon start off your 1942 program
with my Chekhov? That would indeed be agreeable to me, I confess, for
people would then see that I am not taboo." But in fact she already was
"taboo." In February 1942, Sabatier told her that the Chekhov biography
would appear soon, but on February 23, Irène still had not received the
proofs. Finally, in May 1942, she acknowledged that all her efforts had
met with "closed doors."[22]

On November 11, Irène and her family were at last able to leave the
Hôtel des Voyageurs, where they had been living for sixteen months, and
move into the house they had rented. It was a very large house located
in the lower village, behind the monument commemorating the war
dead, on the Route de Grury. With its four bedrooms, there was more
than ample room for the family, Julie Dumot, and Francine the cook.
Behind the house was a vegetable garden with an apple tree; from the
veranda, protected by an awning the length of the ground floor on the
south side, one could see the hills of the southern Morvan. Water was
drawn from a well behind the house and the facilities were also in back.
There was a chicken coop from which Irène could count on gathering
at least six eggs every morning. The garden was Michel's domain; he
grew radishes and lettuce, and the following spring many sorts of other
vegetables. Behind the house there were also cherry trees and pear trees,
whose fruit they hoped to harvest next season. The situation was considerably more comfortable than living in the hotel. The family ate well
and was even able to send packages of butter, noodles, and vegetables
to Michel's brother and sister in Paris.[23]

Albin Michel continued paying 3000F a month through Julie Dumot
and in October there were new developments: Julie received an offer for
the purchase of the film rights to *Les Biens de ce monde*. A film production
company had contacted Carbuccia (since it was he who had published

the novel in installments), asking him for rights to the novel. All Julie had to do was show she was not Jewish, since the second statute regarding Jews strictly forbade them from engaging in any cinematographic activity. Irène, writing to Albin Michel as Julie, stated, "I would like you to know that I am 100% Aryan and French, and that I am at your disposal to furnish any proof of this you deem necessary."[24] The film project, however, was never to be realized.

Winter

It was a cold winter, but Irène had ordered fifteen "moules"[25] of wood, and the house, at least the ground floor, was cozy. But this was little consolation for Irène. She was becoming impatient with the publishing situation. Using the "Aryan" Julie Dumot as a stand-in identity was practical, but it deprived Irène of her own identity as a successful woman of letters, an identity she had worked so hard to achieve during the 1930s. It was also frustrating to earn so little. "It is discouraging to write knowing that so much effort does not even allow one to subsist; my children are being raised like peasants and the future remains black," Irène wrote to Sabatier in February 1942. The previous December, she had tried one last time to have her stories published by Carbuccia and had sent him the manuscript of a piece called "Un beau mariage" (A Beautiful Marriage). But this time, Carbuccia stalled. He had brought *Gringoire* to the "free" zone, where he was subject to the censorship of the Vichy regime rather than the Germans. Irène, believing (incorrectly) that Albin Michel had already obtained permission from the German authorities to publish the Chekhov biography, expected Carbuccia would have no problems with Vichy.[26] Carbuccia duly submitted Irène's project to the authorities in Vichy, and wrote her, "As soon as I have a response I will certainly contact you."[27] He never did, and he never published anything more written by Irène.

The winter of 1941-1942 saw a worsening in the situation for Jews in France. On December 12, 300 non-French Jews and 750 French Jewish personalities were arrested; among them was the writer Jean-Jacques Bernard, son of the Jewish playwright Tristan Bernard. "Never have I seen so many Jews together in one place," wrote Bernard, who was deported to the Royallieu camp near Compiègne.[28] Among the Jews arrested in this group, 977 would be deported to Auschwitz in March 1942.[29] On December 14 the Germans imposed on the Jews of the occupied territories a fine of one million francs. On February 7, they ordered a special curfew; henceforth Jews could leave their homes only between 8:00 P.M. and 6:00 A.M., a situation that made obtaining food almost impossible. On February 10, another order, this one from the Vichy government, made it illegal for Jews to change their names.

Irène had frequent contact with her brother-in-law in Paris and was surely aware of these measures, but she did not mention them in her letters or write about them in her notebook. Nor did she make any reference to the American entry into the war in December 1941. She still seemed to believe that, whatever the situation may bring, her "influential friends" would make sure that she and her family were not harmed. In February, she received a message from one of these friends, the "radical" politician, now senator Joseph Caillaux. Caillaux, one of the more colorful figures of the Third Republic, began his political career in 1898 and served the republic in various capacities (as minister of finance, prime minister, deputy prime minister, and senator) since the beginning of the century. His views, as a left-leaning radical, earned him a great many enemies, in particular that of the editor-in-chief of the influential *Figaro*. In 1914, Caillaux's wife, infuriated that *Le Figaro* had published some of her husband's personal letters, shot the newspaper's editor dead. Caillaux himself was convicted of "intelligence with the enemy" in 1920, but rebounded into politics again in the Briand government (1926), and later, as a senator, played an important role in defeating the first Blum administration in 1937. As a senator, he supported Pétain and presided over the senatorial commission of finance until retiring to Mamers, near his native Le Mans. Caillaux's hostility toward the Popular Front and Léon Blum had led him to make some rather anti-Semitic statements, and particularly to accuse Blum of not having "enough French earth beneath the heels of his shoes" to claim to represent France. This would later be taken up by anti-Semites such as Maurras and Darquier de Pellepoix.[30] Caillaux's attitude toward Irène was quite positive, however. In December 1941, he sent her a personal note in which he expressed "all the admiration" he had "for the great novelist you are," and mentioned his own and Madame Caillaux's fond memories of Irène.[31] One can easily understand, in the light of a letter such as this, how Irène could have believed herself to be sheltered from danger.

It is not surprising, then, that Irène and Michel believed they could get permission to travel to Paris, despite the restrictions placed on Jews (who were subject both to a ban on travel and the new curfew) and the danger that the journey represented for them personally. Irène wrote to the military commander (Kreikskommandantur) in Autun on February 11, 1942, and Michel translated the letter into German. She was requesting permission to spend a month in Paris to see her editor, conduct business with the rental agent of her apartment, and take her eldest daughter, Denise, to the oculist. "I was born in Russia but I have never been sympathetic to the Soviets," she argued, adding "I am Catholic but my parents were Jews."[32] She was under the illusion that the German command would make an exception for her. She seems also to have been under the illusion that Albin Michel was on the point of publishing her biography of Chekhov and well as reissuing other works. "My new book is about to appear,"[33] she wrote to the commander, adding, "the German authorities in Paris have given my editor permission to reissue my books."[34] In the end, this request for permission to travel would be refused.

Spring

Since Irène could not come to Paris, André Sabatier agreed to visit her in Issy-L'Évêque. Irène had been trying to get Sabatier or Esménard to come to Issy-L'Évêque since December 1941. "While I cannot promise you great comfort, I can at least assure you that you will eat more or less as you did before the war," she wrote to Sabatier.[35] On February 20, Sabatier announced his visit for the month of April.

At the end of March, Sabatier's travel plans took shape. Irène was overjoyed, and regreted only "that [he could] remain just a short time."[36] His itinerary was trying; Sabatier would have to take the train from the Gare de Lyon at 6:00 in the morning and wait several hours to change at Nevers for Luzy, a village located eleven kilometers from Issy-l'Évêque. Here, Irène and Michel would meet him in a rented vehicle. The return trip would be just as difficult, for Sabatier would have to go through Dijon, and there was only a night train between Luzy and Dijon.

In spite of these hurdles, Sabatier made the journey. He left Paris on Wednesday, April 8, and spent two nights with Irène and Michel. He brought reading material (newspapers, reviews, books) and above all his friendship and sympathy; he could not bring the guarantee that any of her works would be published. "I never doubted," wrote Irène after his visit, "that you were a true friend, but what a comfort to actually see it and be sure of it."[37]

As soon as he returned to Paris, Sabatier tried once again to open doors for Irène. He served as an intermediary to send short stories, under the pseudonyms Jacques Labarre and Pierre Monjeu, to a magazine called *Présent*, situated in the unoccupied zone. He also tried to make contact with the editors of *La Revue des deux mondes*, which had moved to Royat, also in the "free" zone. But he could do nothing about the Chekhov biography or the novel *Les Biens de ce monde*.

Only one of the stories Sabatier sent on behalf of Irène was published. Sabatier did, however, succeed in convincing Albin Michel to raise Irène's monthly allowance (officially paid, of course, to Julie Dumot) from 3000F to 5000F ($1000). By the end of 1942, Albin Michel had advanced her as much as 89,000F ($17,800). Why, under those circumstances, was Albin Michel unwilling to publish Irène's biography or her novel? Until the appearance of the second "Liste Otto" in July 1942, expressly prohibiting works by Jewish authors, the editor *could* publish Irène's books. Indications are that Albin Michel was unwilling to take the risk of publishing a Jewish author, particularly as the company was prospering financially during the occupation. In August 1941, Esménard commented that "business is going extraordinarily well" and quoted, as an example, books by Pierre Benoit,[38] which were "selling off the bookshelves at an astonishing speed."[39] But at the same time, Esménard told Irène that in 1941 and 1942 "[he] could publish nothing."[40] Perhaps there was also a financial consideration in the decision not to publish Irène's work; *Les Chiens et les loups*, as we have seen, did not sell well. It seems probable that the continued monthly payments were based to some extent on the editor's intent to publish Irène's work once the war was over, but most of all on a very admirable sense of compassion and friendship. At least, this is how Irène understood the situation; the monthly stipends were "advances . . . benevolently agreed to," in the words of her husband Michel.[41]

Despite the increase in monthly allowances, Irène's and Michel's economic situation was getting worse. "Neither my wife nor I at the present time have any income whatsoever," wrote Michel. "We are not in a position to pay our rent and we possess no fortune."[42] Are we to believe that the 85,000F put aside had been spent, and the furs sold? It seems that Michel and Irène, who had lived well in Paris and had rented a large house in Issy-l'Évêque, had debts everywhere. They owed their Paris rental agent 7000F[43] and the revenue service "a fat sum"[44] for back income tax. Their Parisian accounts (frozen by the Germans) were in the red.

No solution to this situation could be found except the selling of some of Irène's work. Once again, a trip to Paris, in a desperate attempt to convince Albin Michel to publish some work, was planned. Since neither Irène nor Michel could get permission to travel, it was decided to send Julie Dumot along with Irène's daughter Denise, in April 1942. As a minor (she was twelve), Denise could travel accompanied by an adult. It was a trip that would last one month, with several days spent in the Bordeaux region (where Julie was born). Denise described the trip in great detail in letters to her mother.

It is evident from these letters that, despite the privations suffered by everyone and in particular Jews, during this trip Denise and Julie were able to live more than adequately. They dined on "oysters, filet of beef, cauliflower, salad, camembert, oranges, coffee . . . good white wine, red Burgundy, liqueur and cognac."[45] Mavlik, Michel's sister, invited Denise to see "La Symphonie fantastique" at the cinema (which was not off limits to Jews until July 1942). For the child Denise, this was a trip full of fun and adventure: "While we were in Paris there were two alerts. The first time I heard nothing, but the second time I heard only the beginning and I was so happy I jumped for joy." Julie, however, had business to conduct. She went to the apartment in the Avenue Constant Coquelin to get books, linens, and clothing that she sent to Issy-L'Évêque. On Tuesday May 26, she had a meeting with Esménard, in the course of which he agreed to again raise Irène's allowance (from 5000 to 6000F, or $1200) and to extend the payments through to the end of 1943. He was still unwilling to promise any imminent publication of her work. Nonetheless, Irène was relieved. "Julie has just come back bringing good news," she wrote to Sabatier, "I can see just to what extent I am beholden to you."[46]

Summer

The summer of 1942 became, for the Jews of the occupied zone, the beginning of a new phase of life. From June 7 onward they were forced to wear the yellow star of David. The notion of requiring Jews to bear distinctive garb probably had its origin in the Council of Latran which, in 1215, imposed special attire on Jews; in France the obligatory wearing of yellow cloth or a hat of the same color was in effect in certain areas, such as Avignon, up until the French Revolution. The Germans imposed a special armband on the Jews of Poland in November 1939; they required the yellow star on the garments of the Jews of the Reich in September 1941. The German order applied to any Jew in the occupied zone over the age of six. Although Irène never spoke about this requirement in her letters or notebook, she would have had to sew the star onto the clothes of everyone in the family except her youngest daughter Élisabeth.

The imposition of the Jewish star was conceived as a way of identifying Jews in the street and insuring that they comply with existing interdictions. In Paris, at the beginning, the yellow star produced results the Germans did not expect: some non-Jews also sewed stars on their clothing along with their names or provincial origins, and some Jews kept their stars hidden or even refused to wear them.[47] At Issy-L'Évêque, where Irène and her family were the only known Jews,[48] the wearing of the star only confirmed what was already common knowledge.

For Irène, the imposition of the star was the final stroke. She now abandoned all hope of continuing to be a published author. She wrote to Sabatier, "I have abandoned all [my efforts] in order not to think about the future any more and to work on this project of several volumes I spoke to you about. Really I'm now no longer hoping for anything."[49]

Something had changed in her view of her own and her family's situation. It was as though she had a premonition that a tragedy was about to occur. A deep despair overcame her. Not only was she certain of not being able to publish, she began to doubt that she would ever finish the second volume of *Suite française (Dolce)* of which she had already written eighty-two pages. "To think that I have not yet finished the second part [of *Dolce*]"she wrote in her notebook on June 12, "the fourth and fifth are in limbo, and what a limbo! It is truly in the lap of the Gods, since all depends on what will happen." Three weeks later, on July 3, she wrote: "Decidedly, it just keeps going on and getting more complicated! Would that it just be over, for better or for worse!"

And then we have this journal entry, without a date: "My God! What is this country doing to me? Since it rejects me, let us think about it coldly, let us watch it lose its honor and its life. And others, what are they to me? Empires die. Nothing is important. Whether one looks from a mystical point of view or a personal one, it's all the same. Let us keep a cold head. Harden our hearts. And wait."

What happened? Irène had written a curious sentence in her notebook, without a date: "If, on July 13, those who have promised to come actually come, that will have, among other consequences, two, or at least one less part [of *Suite française*]." Had Irène been warned of her imminent arrest? It is certainly possible, but nothing indicates that she or her husband took any measures to hide from the authorities. Their daily life was certainly more difficult. On July 8 the Germans issued a ninth order, this one obliging Jews in the occupied zone to make all their purchases only between 3:00 and 4:00 in the afternoon and never to be seen in public places (libraries, theaters, restaurants); they were also forbidden to have telephones or even to telephone from a public booth. Furthermore, as expatriate Russians, Irène and Michel were required to obtain the signature of the German authorities every week. A letter with no heading, but clearly from the sub-prefecture at Autun, speaks of a request made by Michel on July 7 to take a trip; "your status as a Jew will cause your request to be rejected," it says.[50] Where was Michel looking to go and to what purpose? One can only hypothesize. If he and Irène wanted to escape and go into hiding, he certainly would not have asked permission from the German authorities. Irène was worried that she had not heard from Sabatier for a long time. On July 11, she sent him her last letter: "I have not had news from you for a long time. I hope all is well. Here life goes on as you saw, monotonous . . . fortunately! Think of me if you publish any interesting novels. Reading is the only distraction possible. I have written a lot lately. *I suppose they will be posthumous works, but at least they make the time pass.*"[51] The words are dramatic. The situation was becoming dramatic as well.

In Paris, German authorities were preparing "Opération Vent Printanier" (Operation Spring Wind), the biggest round-up yet of Jews. They were aided by French authorities and police. Both non-French and French Jews would be sent to camps in Drancy, Compiègne, Pithiviers and Beaune-la-Rolande and from there to concentration camps in Poland.

There was no celebration of July 14 (Bastille Day) in 1942. The French delegation to the occupation authorities made this decision "because the country is in mourning," they announced.[52] Newspapers spoke of Russian forces retreating before the German army in the battle of the Don. *Le Progrès de Côte d'Or,* a local paper read in Issy-L'Évêque, reported on a gathering of the Ligue Française in Dijon. The president of this league declared, "After our defeat, the Jew took refuge in London and in America, and by radio he continues his shameful work . . . Do you wish the guilty to be punished? Do you want to get rid of the Jews?" According to the reporter, the crowd responded with a resounding yes.[53]

The hunt for Jews was gearing up.

The Arrest

On Monday, July 13, Michel sent a telegram to Robert Esménard and André Sabatier in Paris: "Irène gone today suddenly. Destination Pithiviers (Loiret) Hope you can intervene. stop. Tried without success to telephone—Michel Epstein."[1]

Irène Némirovsky was arrested on July 13, 1942, by the French police. They confiscated her food-ration card and wrote on the back of it: "taken to Toulon s/Arroux on July 13, 1942 on order of the French authorities."[2] A schoolteacher from Issy-L'Évêque recalled the event some thirty years later:

On the day of [Irène's] arrest by the Gestapo, Madame Molard [the principal of the girl's school], came to warn me in a panic and I immediately took the girls [Denise and Elisabeth] to my house where my mother was. Nothing serious happened at the school, at least I don't remember that there was any investigation that day, but we were all frightened. Luckily Madame Michaud was there! I remember that the gendarme Besson tried to warn [Irène] and even asked her, "don't you want to say good-bye to your children?" She answered, "one adieu is enough."[3]

It is clear from the correspondence that, at the time Irène was arrested, Michel still firmly believed he could get her freed by their "influential friends." It is clear also from the correspondence that the French authorities announced to Irène that her arrest was part of a "widespread measure taken against expatriate Jews between the ages of 16 and 45," and that she would be taken to the camp at Pithiviers.[4]

Irène was first brought to Toulon-sur-Arroux, approximately 13 kilometers from Issy-L'Évêque, where she remained imprisoned for three nights. The evening of her arrival she scrawled a brief note in pencil to Michel: "For the moment I am at the police station where I ate black currants and red currants waiting for them to come and get me . . . I am convinced it won't be long. I thought we could also approach Caillaux and Abbé Dimnet, what do you think?" Caillaux was, of course, well known; Ernest Dimnet is a more obscure figure. A popular philosopher, and close friend of the collaborationist author and journalist Alphonse de Châteaubriant, he had probably met Irène while she was writing for Bernard Grasset, who was also Dimnet's publisher.[5]

Irène spent two days in prison; on Thursday, July 16, she was transferred to the internment camp at Pithiviers. This camp, which had been built by the Germans in 1940 for French prisoners of war, had already received more than 2000 Parisian Jews in May 1941. Along with Beaune-la-Rolande, Pithiviers was managed by Vichy in collaboration with the Germans. Before July 1942 it was mainly a camp for men, where the prisoners, in spite of insufficient food and abominable sanitary conditions, had succeeded in creating an active cultural life with speeches, concerts, meetings, and religious services. One could receive packages, in limited quantities, and some people managed to gain their freedom, mainly for health reasons.[6] But in July, everything changed. Visits, as well as leaves, were prohibited. The Gestapo was tightening its grip.

When Irène arrived in Pithiviers, the camp had already taken in Jews from the Paris round-ups—men, women and children—the result of the "spring wind" operation that had just begun. Obersturmführer Dannecker, head of the Jewish section of the S.D. (Sichherheitsdienst, the German security service), had proposed a deportation of 40,000 Jews in three weeks, with three convoys leaving every week, each one carrying approximately 1000 Jews from the Pithiviers and Beaune-la-Rolande camps. Already on June 26, a convoy (no. 4) with 999 Jewish men crowded into railway cars had left for Auschwitz. But the camp did not have enough prisoners for Dannecker's plan to be carried out. The huge arrest of Jews in Paris was intended to "remedy" this situation.

The regulations of the camp allowed inmates one letter a week ("written *only in French*")[7] and two packages a month, but all were inspected.

Irène was able to send Michel a postcard on Wednesday, July 15, in which she wrote: "There is disorder at the moment, but the food is *very* good. It even surprised me."[8] It is doubtful that this note revealed the truth. One must read between the lines and imagine the sense of the word "disorder," for conditions prevailing in the camps in the aftermath of massive arrivals from Paris were known to be atrocious.[9]

On Thursday, July 16, convoy number 6 prepared to leave for the Auschwitz concentration camp. Like previous convoys, it was required to be made up of 1000 prisoners. The camp commander, Lieutenant Le Vagueresse, had signed the deportation order the same day: on the list, as number 96, is inscribed the name Epstein, Irène, born 2-11-1903 in Kiev, profession "woman of letters." A total of 119 women and 809 men were on the list.[10] Irène sent a postcard to Michel: "I think we are leaving today."[11] But the convoy was actually scheduled to leave the following day.

On Friday, July 17, Irène was awakened very early, before sunrise. She waited on the platform with the others. Beside her were Chana Grinberg, salesclerk from Aunay-sur-Serein in the department of Yonne; Linda Rezelbach, worker, from Sens; Anita Oppinheimer, hairdresser, from Dijon; Thérèse Katz, student, from Dijon; Rachel Pronin, pianist, from Paris. At the last minute, Jacqueline Ribstein, a hairdresser from Paris, was scratched off the list by the occupation authorities.[12] Almost all the prisoners were foreign born, most from Poland, and the majority were aged between 33 and 42; children under 16 were supposedly not eligible for deportation. There was, however, a 15-year-old boy, Gérald Souweine, who wrote a note before leaving: "Everybody, women, men, sometimes old men, a few sick people and children (girls of 13) are loaded in . . . and me along with them. I don't know where. I'll go to the East in any case."[13]

The convoy left Pithiviers at precisely 6:15 A.M. It took two days to get to Auschwitz. On July 19, Irène, like all the others in the concentration camp, was indelibly marked with a number on her forearm. The women of convoy 6 all had a number between 9550 and 9668.[14] Irène was assigned to a bunk; because of her age she was not gassed immediately on arrival. One month later an epidemic of typhus (a frequent occurrence at Auschwitz) broke out. More than 200 prisoners fell ill, among them Irène Némirovsky. She died in the camp on August 19, 1942, at the age of 39.

Why was Irène arrested and deported? At first sight the answer is simple: she was on the list of foreign Jews included in the census of September 1940. On July 2, René Bousquet, secretary general of the ministry of the interior for the police since May 1942, had promised the Germans that the French police would arrest foreign Jews. This decision was confirmed by Pierre Laval himself in a communication he sent to Berlin on July 6. The wave of arrests was meant to target mainly nationals from Eastern Europe, including Soviet Russians and White Russians, men and women between the ages of 16 and 55.[15] Irène fulfilled all these conditions. Unlike other Jews, who had gone into hiding, Irène was not denounced to the authorities. Imprudently, neither she nor Michel hid themselves or their origins. Everyone in Issy-L'Évêque knew her; the German authorities knew her.

Irène's arrest fell within the framework of a much vaster operation unleashed by the French police on the orders of the German authorities in the Saône-et-Loire department. Those slated for deportation at that time were all registered Jews without French citizenship. Thus the commissioner of police of the Renseignements Généraux of Autun was able to write in March of 1943 that, "Jews of foreign nationality have all been arrested and sent to concentration camps."[16]

What is curious and unexplained about Irène's arrest is the fact that her husband was not taken into custody at the same time; he would not be arrested until October. No document exists to clarify this odd occurrence. Perhaps there were administrative reasons; it was necessary to fulfill quotas on certain convoys. Michel's convoy, number 42 on November 6, was made up of 998 men, women, and children.

The Reaction

As soon as Irène was arrested, Michel began trying to gain her release. He turned to Albin Michel for help; he had no other contacts in Paris except for his brother. What happened later—vain attempts to liberate Irène, fruitless contacts with celebrated individuals, moving letters addressed to the Germans—shows clearly the nightmare lived by those who were temporarily spared and the total incomprehension of all, Jews and non-Jews alike, before a situation whose real horror they could not imagine.

Irène's arrest brought Michel to a state of panic. "I tried in vain to reach you yesterday on the phone" he wrote on July 14 to Sabatier. "The gendarmes took my wife away yesterday. Destination, it seems, the concentration camp in Pithiviers (Loiret). Reason: general measures taken against stateless Jews between 16 and 45 years old. My wife is Catholic and our children are French. Can anything be done for her?"[17] Michel apparently believed that, despite the fact that the French statutes defined Irène as Jewish (since she had at least three Jewish grandparents), she would be recognized as Catholic. The same day Michel received a letter from an acquaintance of Julie Dumot, Jean Giomarc'h, living in Paris, whom he had informed the day before of Irène's arrest: "I am confused. What can I do? I immediately thought of Madame de C. [Chambrun], but Monsieur Paul Epstein has an appointment with the count [de Chambrun] this evening. I will see your brother tomorrow at noon and we will join efforts. I will take his advice and perhaps inform Madame de Régnier."[18] "Madame de C." was Josée Laval, daughter of Pierre Laval, in charge of the Vichy government under the authority of Pétain. That Michel's brother Paul was able to secure an appointment with René de Chambrun, her husband, shows to what extent the doors of "influential people" close to the Vichy régime were open to Irène, Michel, and their family. To be sure, some Jewish artists and writers did succeed in getting released from the camps. Maurice Goudeket (husband to Colette), for example, was released in 1941 after the intercession of Hélène Morand, who made his case to the wife of Otto Abetz, Germany's ambassador in Paris.[19] Jean-Jacques Bernard was freed from the camp in Compiègne. Michel was therefore not entirely mistaken in believing that, by appealing to certain highly-placed individuals, he could get for Irène the treatment that was given to some others. But between the sympathy expressed by these people for Irène's predicament and their willingness or ability to get her released, there would be an insurmountable gap.

During the days immediately following Irène's arrest, Sabatier, quite unaware that she was being deported to Auschwitz, tried all means at his disposal to free her, while seeing to the material needs of her family. Michel and the children needed to be provided for, and Sabatier continued to send payments to Julie Dumot. He was also astute enough to realize that his letters could be read, so he was highly circumspect in referring to Julie Dumot. He advised Michel to destroy "all correspondence on this subject, business or personal, which appears superfluous to you." "You understand me," he added.[20]

At the same time, Sabatier wrote to his friend Jacques Benoist-Méchin, secretary of state to Laval:

> Our author and friend I. Némirovsky has just been transported from Issy-L'Évêque, where she lived, to Pithiviers. Her husband has just informed me of this. She is a White Russian, Jewish as you know, who never engaged in political activities; she is a novelist of very great talent, who always served her adoptive country honorably, and she is the mother of two young daughters, aged five and ten years. I BEG you to do ALL that you can.[21]

In an undated telegram to Michel (probably sent July 16) Sabatier spoke of other contacts he had had with people who could prove useful: Paul Morand, Bernard Grasset, and Albin Michel, who, he said, were taking "collective steps" on Irène's behalf with the Vichy authorities.

After Michel received Irène's card informing him of her departure from Pithiviers for "an unknown destination,"[22] the situation became clearer, but also more desperate. Michel communicated the latest developments to Sabatier, who responded on July 24: "All that is necessary has been done. I saw my friend [Benoist-Méchin] who told me there was nothing more to do but wait. I stressed to him the French nationality of your children after your first letter, and [Irène's] possible departure for the Loiret camp after your second."[23]

But Michel could not, as he was advised by Sabatier, simply wait. He had to act and find a way to convince the authorities that they had made a mistake. He now realized that claiming Irène to be Catholic was useless; he wondered therefore if he should point out to the authorities that his wife implicitly supported the anti-Communist policies of the German régime. This was the question he put to Sabatier on July 26:

> Regarding the situation of my wife, perhaps it is necessary to point out that she is a White Russian who has always refused to accept Soviet nationality, and who, after much persecution, fled Russia with her parents, and whose entire fortune was confiscated. I myself am in the same situation and I believe I do not exaggerate when I name a figure of approximately one hundred million pre-war francs that were taken from us there, from both myself and my

wife. My father was president of the Association of Russian Banks and delegated administrator of one of the biggest banks in Russia, the Commercial
Bank of Azov-on-Don. The authorities concerned can therefore be assured
that we have not the slightest sympathy for the present [Soviet] régime. My
younger brother, Paul, was a personal friend of the Grand-Duke Dimitri of
Russia, and the imperial family living in France was often received at my
father-in-law's house, in particular the Grand-Dukes Alexander and Boris.[24]

Michel enclosed with this letter the recommendation written for him by
the German officer before his departure from Issy-L'Évêque. He may
have known that his brother Paul had also been arrested, although that
news would not be confirmed for a few days. In any case neither he nor
Sabatier could know, in the summer of 1942, what awaited Irène or Paul
in the "East" to which they had been deported. They imagined work
camps—a hard life certainly—but even those who had heard rumors of
the gas chambers could not actually believe they existed.[25] Accordingly,
it was imperative that Irène, who suffered from asthma, be kept from the
harsh conditions that would put her health in danger. Making a point
of Irène's health problems is thus a tactic that Michel would use.[26] Another tactic was to try to demonstrate to the Germans that, despite her
Jewish origins, Irène was anti-Semitic. He wrote to Sabatier: "Do you
want to see *Les Échelles du Levant* for which you have the manuscript
and which appeared in *Gringoire?* The book is quite hard on the hero
who has a Jewish background and is a charlatan of a doctor; but I don't
remember if my wife specified that he was Jewish. I think she did . . .
[27] In fact Michel is in error regarding *Les Échelles du levant*, for Dario
Asfar, although he comes from some obscure country in the east, is not
Jewish, but of mixed Greek and Italian ancestry.

Sabatier found that the example given by Michel "does not . . . in any
way appear to respond"[28] to proof of anticommunism or anti-Semitism.
Michel persisted in his efforts to show that Irène represented no threat
at all to the Germans or to the French state. On July 27, he drafted a
letter to Otto Abetz, the German ambassador in Paris. Michel clearly
believed in the logic of a régime that had no logic except that of terror.
He reasoned that, because the Germans were staunchly anticommunist,
they must have sympathy for the White Russians who fled the Soviet
régime. Furthermore, since the Germans detest the Jews, by the same

logic, they must respect those authors who harshly scrutinize the Jewish character. Michel also seemed to believe that Abetz, whose virulent anti-Semitism was well known, would be moved by the plight of his wife. His letter expresses his deepest despair:

I know that by addressing you directly, I am perhaps overstepping my bounds. I nevertheless am taking this step since I believe you alone can save my wife. I place in you my last hope. Please allow me to express the following . . . On Monday, July 13, my wife was arrested. She was taken to the concentration camp in Pithiviers (Loiret), and from there to an unknown destination. This arrest took place, I was told, because of general instructions regarding Jews, given by the occupying authorities. My wife, Madame M. Epstein, is a well-known novelist, I. Némirovsky. Her books have been translated in a great number of countries, and at least two of them, *David Golder* and *Le Bal*, in Germany. My wife was born in Kiev (Russia) on 2.11.1903. Her father was an important banker. My own father was president of the central committee of the Banks of Commerce of Russia, and delegated administrator to the Bank of Azov-on-Don. Our two families lost considerable fortunes in Russia. My father was arrested by the Bolsheviks and imprisoned in the Saint Peter and Paul Fortress in Petersburg. It is with great difficulty that we succeeded in fleeing Russia in 1919; we then took refuge in France and we have never left since. All this must reassure you that we have nothing but hatred for the Bolshevik régime. In France, no member of our family has ever been involved in politics. I have been a managing clerk of a bank; as for my wife, she has become a respected novelist. In none of her books, which incidentally have not been prohibited by the occupying authorities,[29] will you find a word against the Germans, and although my wife is Jewish she speaks of Jews without any tenderness . . . I also am taking the liberty to point out to you that my wife has always kept away from any political party, and that she has never profited from any favor either from the left or the right, and that the magazine to which she contributed as a writer, *Gringoire*, whose chief editor is H. de Carbuccia, has certainly never been kind to either Jews or Communists . . . I know, Mr. Ambassador, that you are one of the most eminent men in the government of your country. I am convinced also that you are a just man. It therefore seems unjust and illogical to me that the Germans would imprison a woman who, though originally Jewish, has no sympathy, and all her books show this, either for Judaism or Bolshevism.[30]

In order to be certain of the letter's delivery, Michel sent it to Sabatier, asking him to entrust it to the Comte de Chambrun as well as to Hélène Morand, a great friend of the Abetz family. Sabatier complied on July 28, adding, probably for form's sake, that the letter contained "interesting precisions" but that "certain sentences are unfortunate."[31]

On July 29, Michel received a letter from his sister, Mavlik. Paul, she informed him, had been arrested; she was the only member of the family still living in Paris. This letter attests to the confusion that reigned for all concerned. "I was mad with despair but I got the better of it and am running about all day trying to get news," wrote Mavlik. She was certain that her brother, Samuel, was imprisoned in Beaune-la-Rolande, that his mistress Germaine was going to see him, and that, at the same time, she would be able to see Irène in Pithiviers. She was wrong on all counts. Visits to the camps were not authorized in July 1942; neither Samuel, his wife, nor his brother, Paul, were at Beaune-la-Rolande. They were at Drancy.[32] They would all be deported to Auschwitz at the end of July 1942. Not one of them returned. Letters sent from the internment camps sometimes spoke of conditions there as not being so bad. Thus in her letter to Michel, Mavlik quoted other friends writing from Drancy: "they are well treated and fed."[33] Mail from these camps often reflected existing propaganda rather than reality.

Mavlik's letter helped keep Michel from imagining the worst. Irène, he now believed, was "in a camp somewhere in France under the guard of French soldiers." But on August 9, he learned "from a very dependable source" that three weeks previously, all those detained at Pithiviers "[had] been sent to the German border, and from there on toward the East, Poland or Russia most likely." Deportation "to a barbaric country under conditions that are probably atrocious, without money or food, among people whose language she doesn't even know, that is intolerable," he added.[34] The last sentence is curious, for Irène certainly spoke Russian, although not Polish. At any rate, twenty-three years in France, in Michel's eyes, had turned them both into French people. Russia had become a foreign country to them.

As far as Sabatier was concerned in early August, everything possible had been done for Irène, and it was up to Michel to be patient. "Madame P. Morand is tireless in her dedication," he wrote. "She is multiplying her efforts. Your letter [to Otto Abetz] is in her hands, and the gist of it is being communicated, along with a medical certificate, by one of the friends she has at the embassy, at this very time." According to Sabatier, Hélène Morand had suggested that Michel no longer take "steps in scattered fashion" and that he consult the "Union Israélite (Jewish Union), which alone, through its diverse functions"[35] could enlighten him as to Irène's fate. The Union Générale des Israélites de France (UGIF), to which Sabatier alluded, was an organization created by the law of December 2, 1941, with the encouragement and approval of the Germans. Like the German Judenrat, it was financed in part by funds confiscated from Jews. The UGIF played a rather controversial role during the occupation, for it was required to cooperate with the Gestapo; it occasionally helped save some Jews, but the Germans expected it would be complicitous in implementing the "final solution."[36]

More useful than the advice to consult the UGIF was the analysis Sabatier gave of the situation. He saw clearly that it was futile to take any further action on Irène's behalf. He tried to clarify things to Michel:

1. The measure which impacts your wife is a general order (here in Paris it seems to have affected several thousands of stateless people) and that explains in part the impossibility of obtaining any special consideration, but it also allows us to hope that nothing particularly unusual has happened to your wife.

2. The measure was taken by certain German authorities that are all powerful in this area, and upon whom other German authorities, military or civil, and French authorities, even those that are highly placed, seem to have little possibility of influence.

3. The departure for Germany is credible, not for camps, according to Madame P. Morand, but for Polish cities where they are grouping stateless people.[37]

Hélène Morand was only repeating here a fiction believed by both Jews and non-Jews in 1942. Even Pierre Laval maintained publicly in September 1942 that deported Jews were being taken to cities in the south of Poland.[38] It remains to be seen just what Hélène Morand actually did for Irène. In examining Sabatier's letters, which are the only indications we have,[39] we note two facts: first, that Hélène Morand did not feel it prudent to give Michel's letter directly to Otto Abetz, but rather communicated the "essence" of it, that is, her own interpretation of Irène's situation; second, that even before contacting the German ambassador, Hélène Morand knew—and told Sabatier—that it was impossible to obtain for Irène "a measure of special favor." She clearly was dubious as to the efficacy of anything she could do, and it was doubtless a half-hearted effort that she put forth on Irène's behalf. Furthermore, if other "influential friends" such as Benoist-Méchin ever attempted anything, Sabatier never spoke of it. We must conclude that Irène's situation did not warrant, in the view of Hélène Morand or others close to the German authorities, any kind of serious intervention.

On August 23 a bailiff arrived at Michel's house. He carried in a sealed envelope a summons addressed to Irène for the unpaid rent on the Paris apartment. Because Michel and Irène were married under the system of the separation of property, only Irène was legally responsible for the rent. Since Paul had been arrested and no one remained to look after the apartment, Michel decided to write to the lawyer who had been dealing with the dispute between his wife and the landlord, asking him specifically, "of what use is a summons addressed to a person interned in a camp?"[40] The lawyer did not react to the desperate irony in Michel's tone and responded dryly: "It will be up to the judge . . . to decide if he must still pass judgment on this affair in the absence of your wife. If you are unable to pay anything, I fear the landlord will try to obtain an annulment of the rental agreement and the sale of the furniture . . ."[41] Thus the apartment furniture would be sold and, like so many other Jewish lodgings in Paris, other belongings pillaged.[42] Michel's financial situation went from bad to worse. He had to liquidate his reserves; in September 1942, he possessed only three shares of stock in the Bon Marché department store, which were in his wife's name, and was living on a small annuity allowed him by his former employer, the Banque des Pays du Nord, along with the monthly payments sent by Albin Michel.[43]

From the end of August 1942, Michel no longer spoke of liberating Irène, but rather of trying to lessen the harshness of conditions for her in the camps or in the city where he believed she was. "I have undertaken no new steps," he wrote to Sabatier. "If the Red Cross could at least have clothing, money, and books sent to Irène before the coming of winter."[44] Another idea: "What if we changed places, if they took me instead of my wife?"[45] Sabatier answered that "an exchange is at the moment impossible. It would only make for an added internee."[46] Sabatier suggested coming to see Michel in Issy-L'Évêque; Michel thanked him but said he had "nothing new . . . to report."[47]

Toward the end of September, Michel noticed that his identity card would expire on November 18. To renew it he had to see the prefect of the Saône-et-Loire department in Mâcon. He was, however, loathe to take this step: "I would not wish this request to bring new worries upon us,"[48] he wrote to Sabatier. He asked Sabatier to intercede with the prefect in Mâcon. Sabatier answered: "Don't do a thing. Any steps taken seem to me extremely imprudent."[49] Michel then asked Sabatier if he should "give the children a change of scene,"[50] that is to say, send them away from Issy-L'Évêque. Sabatier's advice was twofold: on the one hand he noted that when Irène was arrested, she was "in complete compliance" with existing laws, but "that did not change anything"; on the other, since the children were French (and Sabatier could not conceive that French children, even Jewish, would be sent to camps), he was not of the opinion "that a change of scene is indispensable."[51] But Sabatier was deluded; while in the beginning, round-ups in the occupied zone only involved foreign Jews, from mid-July 1942 onward, many French Jews, including children, were being arrested. In total, in 1942, one-third of all Jews arrested were French, and more than 6000, out of 76,000, were children under the age of twelve.[52]

Epilogue

On Friday October 9, Michel Epstein was arrested by the French police. He was taken to the city of Le Creusot and from there to the camp at Drancy. On November 6, he was deported to Auschwitz. The German authorities did not record the date of his death; most likely he was gassed.

Irène and Michel's two daughters, Denise and Élisabeth, were not deported.[53] Julie Dumot took them to Cézac, near Bordeaux, where they were kept hidden until the end of the war.

For many years, Albin Michel continued to send monthly payments to Irène's daughters.[54] In December 1945, Robert Esménard organized a committee to come to the children's aid and to allow for a monthly stipend to be paid to them over and above the royalties due to their mother.

After the war, the children were placed with the Dames de Sion (The Ladies of Zion), near Paris; subsequently Denise was helped by Jean-Jacques Bernard and Élisabeth went to live with the family of Madeleine Cabour's brother. Élisabeth became an editor, translator, and novelist; she was especially known for *Le Mirador,* a fictional biography of her mother, and *Un Paysage de cendres,*[55] a novel based on her experiences during the occupation. She died in 1996. Denise lives in Toulouse where she works to preserve the memory of her mother and all Jews who perished in the Holocaust.

Conclusion

Irène Némirovsky's tragic end has obscured any real criticism of her work, as it has masked any real analysis of her attitude towards Jews.[1] Most of the articles written about her before the publication of *Suite française* focus on the injustice of her fate and the importance of rehabilitating a forgotten and martyred author.[2] The few good questions asked remain unanswered. "In revolt against her background . . . did Irène Némirovsky turn her back on her origins?" asked the journalist Myriam Anissimov in 1985, "Not in the least," she answered, "since she declared herself Jewish when the Nuremberg laws on race were promulgated in France."[3] It is true, as we have seen, that Irène never hid her Jewish origins during the occupation, but her relationship to Judaism is infinitely more complex than Ms. Anissimov implies here. More recently, Paul Renard asks: "How can we explain this sometimes racist vision in the work of Némirovsky, who is herself Jewish? The will to become integrated into French society? . . . The influence of certain friends such as Bernard Grasset, Morand, Brasillach, Horace de Carbuccia?"[4] The answer to this question is intricate and lies deep beneath the literary texts. It seems to us in fact that the problem of the "racist vision" in the work of Irène Némirovsky can only be explained in the context of the body of a literary work that serves as a vehicle for her own personal vision of a moral order.

Irène Némirovsky is nothing if not a moral writer. She rages against the injustice done to an artist by greedy parents in *Un Enfant génial.* Just as odious to her is the situation of the two children in *L'Ennemie* or the case of Antoinette in *Le Bal;* in both circumstances it is money that, as it enriches the parents, corrupts the values of the family. Injustice in Irène's work is always tainted with money. The suffering of Hélène Karol, like that of Cristophe Bohun (*Le Pion sur l'échiquier*) or the daughter of Gladys Eisenach (*Jézabel*) results from a perversion of paternal or maternal instincts by money. The nature of man (and above all woman), which is to love without reservation, is inevitably led astray by the pursuit of wealth, a pursuit which is nothing other than a manifestation of self-love and leads inevitably to solitude.

It is in this perspective that *David Golder* takes on its importance. For while Golder, at the beginning of the novel, pushes his associate Marcus to commit suicide and seems to be without scruples in business, he is the only character in the novel to be conscious of his actions and to be able to look at himself from the outside. He does not cause Joyce to suffer; he in fact causes no one other than his business rival to suffer. On the contrary, he is painfully devoted to the daughter who is not even his own, but for whom he is ready to sacrifice his life. This is what makes for Golder's originality and distinguishes him from Balzac's Père Goriot, to whom he is often compared. Where his offspring is concerned, Golder displays the best of his generous nature. It is this paternal love that extracts him from the solitude into which he had withdrawn and throws him out onto the world—not to pursue wealth for its own sake, but to make the ultimate sacrifice for his daughter's sake.

To be sure, some of the Jewish characteristics that Irène gives David Golder, along with the more stereotypical descriptions of Soifer and Fischl, are troubling. But Golder is significantly different from the other Jewish characters in the novel. He alone wants to separate himself from his milieu; he alone returns to his birthplace in Russia. These differences are crucial to our understanding of Jewish characters in the work of Irène Némirovsky. For, despite his formidable business acuity, and unlike his cronies, Golder is not entirely perverted by the pursuit of wealth; he has much in common with Ada (in *Les Chiens et les loups*), who, like he, is tortured by her link to her Jewish origins and who, finally, returns to the Eastern European region from which she came.

There are two types of Jewish characters in Irène Némirovsky's work: those who obey an instinct of generosity and who, like Golder and Ada, draw their strength from a long history of courage in the face of persecution, and those who have been corrupted by the need to grow rich and remain confined within a certain negative stereotype. Two caveats are important. First, the negative stereotype is not confined to Jewish characters; Dario Asfar, a Levantine Christian in *Les Échelles du Levant*, has characteristics similar to Jewish personages such as Soifer or Fischl. Second, Némirovsky takes pains to show that the precarious situation of Jews in their countries of adoption makes almost inevitable this perversion of their basic nature. Jewish characters in her novels inevitably find themselves faced by two choices: either they follow the roles that Christian Europe has for centuries given them and become modern "money changers," or they reject this imposed materialism in an effort to center their lives around human relationships.

This brings us to the theory of "Jewish self-hatred" suggested by Sander Gilman in his study of the German literary world.[5] Gilman suggests that Jewish anti-Semitism results from the internalization in the Jewish writer of the negative image of the Jew in society and its projection onto the literary work.[6] The result in Némirovsky's novels and stories is the appropriation of a certain stereotypical image of the Jew in French society. While internalizing the stereotypes that repel her, Irène also creates another image of the imaginary Jew, one who is "pure" and whose characteristics are consequently exactly opposite to the stereotype.

The anti-Semitism of Irène Némirovsky seems thus less an effort to deny her origins than a desire to reinvent them. Nothing is more significant in this respect than *Les Chiens et les loups*. Here we see a Jewish renaissance in the true sense of the word, when Ada gives birth to a child in whom "she saw . . . *no known trait.*"[7] It is a "new Jew" that Irène Némirovsky is creating in an ultimate attempt to free herself from the negative stereotype. If, after writing this novel, she turned toward Catholicism to find the antithesis to Jewish materialism, it is because, after a long effort, she was finally able to put aside her own ambiguity regarding her heritage. The break, on the spiritual side, is complete; the behavioral models found in Catholic iconography as well as in displays of sacrifice (such as that of the Abbé Bréchard) have become the central element in Irène's moral vision, a vision she will henceforth express in her work. As for her Jewishness, it remains as an identity, a mark of distinction, a difference, and, to a great extent, a solidarity with a people in whose culture she recognizes her own origins.

Through her work and her tragic fate, Irène Némirovsky can be compared to no other major author of the twentieth century. Although she is far from the only writer of Russian Jewish origin to adopt the French language (one thinks of Nathalie Sarraute, Joseph Kessel, or Romain Gary), she alone made the problem of Jewish identity a central feature of her work. Némirovsky alone among the many Russian Jewish writers who lived in France during the German occupation was deported and perished at Auschwitz.

Némirovsky's case is interesting also because it poses the question of the relationship of an author's cultural identity with his or her national or legal identity. When Irène wrote in her notebook that France had rejected her, it is because suddenly she realized that her true identity did not coincide with the cultural identity she had forged for herself as a writer. In this respect, Némirovsky's situation is quite different from that of French Jewish writers. The Jewish playwright Jean-Jacques Bernard, for example, never doubted his French identity even when he was imprisoned at Compiegne.[8] It would not be an exaggeration to see Irène Némirovsky as a Frenchwoman only in her imagination. By internalizing the image of "French writer" that she saw reflected in contemporary criticism in the 1930s, she grew further and further removed from her Jewish-Russian identity. Only when she was subjected to the census—the counting of Jews under the occupation—did she became acutely aware of her foreignness and her statelessness; only then, and even as a convert to Catholicism, did she find it increasingly difficult to believe herself integrated into French society. In this light, we can understand the wish, expressed in her letter to Marshall Pétain, to be treated as "an honorable foreigner," or better yet, as her husband requested, as a French Jew. For she is not just trying to avoid deportation, she is also trying to have her cultural identity recognized as a national identity. This is why it is inconceivable that she be deported—as she assumed foreign Jews were—to her "country of origin." For Irène, in 1942, the country of origin is already forgotten; it is France that has given her a language and a culture that have become, at least in her view, virtually native.

In March 1940, after twenty years in France, at the pinnacle of her career, Irène Némirovsky was asked who she was: a French author or a Russian author writing in French. This is how she responded:

> I hope and I believe I am more a French than a Russian author. I spoke French before speaking Russian. I have spent half of my childhood and all of my young adulthood and married years in this country. I have never written anything in Russian except for my schoolwork. I think and I even dream in French. All is so totally amalgamated into what remains within me of my race and my native land, that even with the best will in the world, I would be incapable of knowing where one ends and the other begins.[9]

This response reveals the dilemma of this author who died without ever having resolved the question of where she belonged. Irène Némirovsky's quarrel with her heritage and her creation of a very individualized literary identity are reflections of the twentieth century, which saw so many writers and artists flee their native lands, not to live in exile, but to establish themselves definitively in another country and to adopt its language and culture. Is their assimilation ever complete? Does there not remain in every transplanted author this amalgam of cultures of which speaks Irène? For beyond her literary work and her tragic end, Irène Némirovsky shows us, in the ambiguity of her relationship to France, the terrible difficulty of living in an adopted culture and choosing one's own destiny.

Notes

Notes to Preface

1. "'Some Trust in Chariots' and other works of recent fiction", *New York Times*, November 23, 1930.

2. See Mordaunt Hall, "A French Drama Film," *New York Times*, October 20, 1932.

3. Dorothea Kingsland, "Riviera Worldlings," *New York Times*, March 7, 1937.

4. Charles Cestre, "The Literary Scene in Paris," *New York Times*, October 6, 1940.

5. See Edgar Reichmann, "La Comète Némirovsky," *Le Monde*, 7 February 1992.

6. See *La Revie littéraire* (Literary Revival), Actes, no. 6, 2000, published by the Université de Bourgogne.

7. Paul Gray, "As France Burned," *New York Times*, April 7, 2006.

8. Ruth Kluger, "Bearing Witness," *Washington Post*, May 14, 2006.

9. "Like Anne Frank, Irène Némirovsky was unaware of neither her circumstance nor the growing probability that she might not survive." Sharon Dilworth, *Pittsburgh Post-Gazette*, April 30, 2006.

10. Alice Kaplan, "Love in the Ruins," *The Nation*, May 29, 2006.

11. Jane Stevenson, "A Personal History in the Making," *The Observer*, March 26, 2006.

12. See Jonathan Weiss, "An Old Tale of Shame for Today's France," *Los Angeles Times*, November 14, 2004.

13. See Peter Kemp, "The Secrets of the Notebook," *The Times*, March 5, 2006.

14. See Andrew Reimer in the *Sydney Morning Herald*, March 23, 2006.

Notes to Introduction

1. *Suite française* (French Suite) was published in France in October 2004 by Denoël. It was published in the United States as *Suite Française*, translated by Sandra Smith. New York, Alfred A. Knopf, 2006.

2. Léon Poliakov, *Histoire de l'antisémitisme*, Paris, Calmann-Lévy, 1981, vol. 3, p.464.

3. Paris, Presses de la Renaissance, 1992.

Notes to Chapter 1

1. February 11 according to the old calendar replaced in 1918.

2. *Adresnaya I spravochnaya kniga ves Kiev* (Address Registry of Metropolitan Kiev), published in 1909.

3. Today this is 9 Goroditsky Street. We are indebted to Iulia Komska for having researched in Kiev all the information concerning the origins of the Némirovsky family.

4. *Le Mirador,* p.135.

5. Interview with Frédéric Lefèvre, *Les Nouvelle littéraires,* January 11, 1930, p.1.

6. See Alice Stone Nakhimovsky, *Russian-Jewish Literature and Identity,* Baltimore, The Johns Hopkins University Press, 1992, p.8.

7. *Les Chiens et les loups,* Paris, Albin Michel, 1940, p.7.

8. *Les Chiens et les loups,* p.8.

9. According to Michel Epstein, Irène's husband, "My wife's grandparents as well as my own were of the Jewish religion. Our parents practiced no religion." Letter to Otto Abetz, July 27, 1942.

10. *Les Chiens et les loups,* p.38.

11. One can find period photos of the *Podol* in the book by Anatoly Konchalovsky and Dmytry Malakov, *Kiev Michaela Bulgakova,* Kiev, Mystechtvo, 1993, pp.46, 47, 50, 51.

12. *Les Chiens et les loups,* p.7.

13. *L'Énfant genial,* in *Les Œuvres Libres,* v.70, 1927, p.357.

14. See Nakhimovsky, p.10.

15. This book was re-edited in 1992 by Élisabeth Gille under the title *Un Enfant prodige* (Paris, Gallimard, 1992).

16. *L'Énfant génial,* in *Les Œuvres Libres,* v.70, 1927, pp.332, 334, 357.

17. *Un Enfant prodige,* pp.56–7.

18. *Un Enfant prodige,* pp.72–3.

19. *Un Enfant prodige,* p.69.

20. *Un Enfant prodige,* p.81.

21. Interview with Frédéric Lefèvre, *Les Nouvelles littéraires,* January 11, 1930, p.1.

22. *Le Vin de solitude,* Paris: Albin Michel, 1935, p.126.

23. "Le Sortilège," *Gringoire,* February 1, 1940, p.6.

24. *Les Chiens et les loups,* p.7.

25. "Le Sortilège," p.6.

26. The title has a double meaning in French. The expression *entre chien et loup* is used to refer to the moment that the sun sets, when it becomes so dark that it is impossible to distinguish between a dog and a wolf.

27. *Les Chiens et les loups,* p.39.

28. *Les Chiens et les loups,* p.44. The pogrom that Irène describes takes place when Ada is eight years old; Irène herself would have been eight in 1911, the year in which the young Jew Mendel Beilis was accused (and later acquitted) of the ritual murder of a Christian child. This event had the effect of lighting the fires of anti-Semitism always present in Russian society.

29. *Les Chiens et les loups,* p.54.

30. *Les Nouvelles littéraires*, January 11, 1930, pp.1–2.

31. "Le Sortilège," p.6.

32. Quoted by Roger Bourget-Pailleron, "Une Nouvelle Équipe: Madame Irène Némirovsky." *La Revue des Deux Mondes*, 1936. Apart from this reference to the portrait of the governess, Irène never spoke of any autobiographical content in *Le Vin de Solitude*. Nevertheless the novel, which tells the story of a young Russian woman who would become an author, follows Irène's itinerary of flight to France after the revolution almost exactly. The fictitious family, whose parents have the same first names as Irène's grandparents, ends up living at the same Paris address as the Némirovsky family. These similarities in detail are confirmed in interviews given by the author.

33. *Le Vin de solitude*, pp.34–5.

34. *Le Vin de solitude*, p.40.

35. "You have taken Alsace and Lorraine, but despite you we shall remain French," a defiant song following the defeat at the hands of the Prussian army in 1870.

36. "Love's pleasures only last an instant," the perennial French ballad.

37. *Le vin de solitude*, p.37.

38. *Les Nouvelles littéraires*, January 11, 1930, p.1.

39. *Le Vin de solitude*, p.37

40. *Le Vin de solitude*, p.82.

41. *Les Nouvelles littéraires*, January 11, 1930, pp.1–2.

42. Interview with Jeanine Bouisounouse, "Femmes écrivains, leurs débuts." *Les Nouvelles littéraires*, November 2, 1935.

43. *Les Nouvelles littéraires*, January 11, 1930, pp.1–2.

44. "Les Conrads français," *Les Nouvelles littéraires*, March 30, 1940.

45. Foreword of *La vie de Tchekhov*, Paris, Albin Michel, 1946, p.8.

46. *Les Nouvelles littéraires*, January 11, 1930, pp.1–2.

47. *Les Nouvelles littéraires*, January 11, 1930, pp.1–2.

48. *Les Nouvelles littéraires*, January 11, pp.1–2.

49. *Les Nouvelles littéraires*, January 11, 1930, pp.1–2.

50. "Aïno," *Revue des Deux Mondes*, Volume 55, January 1, 1940, p.149.

51. "Aïno," p.158.

52. "Aïno," p.149.

53. "Aïno," p.150.

54. "Aïno," p.155.

55. "Aïno," p.150.

56. "Aïno," p.150.

57. "Aïno," pp.151, 152.

58. "Aïno," p.159.

59. "Les Fumées du vin." *Films parlés*, Paris, Gallimard, 1934, p.214.

60. "Les Fumées du vin," p.266.

61. *Les Nouvelles littéraires*, January 11, 1930, pp.1–2.

62. "Aïno," p.149.

63. *Les Nouvelles littéraires*, January 11, 1930, p.1.

64. *Le Vin de solitude*, p.219

65. Interview with Jeanine Bouisounouse, *Les Nouvelles littéraires*, November 2, 1935.

66. *Les Nouvelles littéraires*, November 2, 1935.

67. *Le Vin de solitude*, pp.310–311.

Notes to Chapter 2

1. See Michaël Marrus and Robert Paxton, *Vichy France and the Jews*, New York, Basic Books, 1981, p.25.

2. See Nancy L. Green, "Les Juifs étrangers à Paris," in André Kaspi and Antoine Marès, *Le Paris des étrangers*, Paris, Imprimerie Nationale, 1989, p.111.

3. Green, pp.116, 352.

4. Green, p.115.

5. See Ewa Bérard-Zarzycka, "Les Écrivains russes—Blancs et Rouges—à Paris dans les années vingt," in Kaspi and Marès, *Le Paris des étrangers*, p.352.

6. In Robert Bourget-Pailleron, "La Nouvelle équipe," *La Revue des Deux Mondes*, no. 591 (1936).

7. *Annuaire du téléphone*, 1921.

8. *Les Nouvelles littéraires*, January 11, 1930, p.1.

9. Ralph Schor, *L'Opinion française et les étrangers en France 1919–1939*. Paris, Publications de la Sorbonne, 1985, p.154.

10. Schor, p.153.

11. The novel was published by Plon in 1922.

12. These names are written in the outside pages of Irène's notebook, begun in Russia and continued in France.

13. Letter of December, 1921.

14. See the interview with Frédéric Lefèvre, *Les Nouvelles littéraires*, January 11, 1930, p.1. In her application to become a naturalized citizen, made in 1938, Irène identifies herself as having a *licence es lettres* from the Université de Paris, but she omits to give the date.

15. Undated letter.

16. Undated letter.

17. Interview with the author, January 26, 1999.

18. Letter, July 29, 1922.

19. Undated letter.

20. Choura Lisiansky, a friend of Irène's (information provided by Denise Epstein).

21. Undated letter.

22. Undated letter.

23. Undated letter, "Paris this Thursday."

24. Undated letter, "Paris this Sunday."

25. Letter of May 15, 1922.

26. "In social gatherings the gigolo, as one said at the time, was decorative . . . For the party to appear dazzling and sumptuous, it was necessary to have stirring about the doors, the buffet table, the smoking room, a crowd of young men with lacquered hair and tireless legs. Women would have three or four of them in their wake. These gigolos were nice boys who did their jobs accordingly. In this society the gigolo was

not paid, but he was fed." *Les Feux de l'automne*, Paris, Albin Michel, 1957, p.113.

27. Undated letter.

28. Undated letter.

29. Undated letter.

30. Undated letter.

31. Mila Gordon (whose sister would marry the journalist Pierre Lazareff). The quote is from an undated letter.

32. Undated letter.

33. Letter, November 11, 1921.

34. Undated letter.

35. Letter, September 23, 1922.

36. Undated letter.

37. Undated letter.

38. The novel would be serialized in *Gringoire* from April 10 to June 20, 1941, but not published in book form until after Irène's death, in 1947.

39. The fictitious city of Saint-Elme would have actually been Elnes, which is close to Lumbres. See Paul Renard, "Irène Némirovsky, Une romancière face à la tragédie," *Roman 20/30*, no.16, December, 1993, p.167.

40. *Les Biens de ce monde*, Paris, Albin Michel, 1947, p.28.

41. Undated letter.

42. Letter, April 24, 1924.

43. Letter, January 22, 1930.

44. Letter, December 4, 1940.

45. Undated letter.

46. Author's interview with Natacha Duché, March, 1996.

47. *Les Nouvelles littéraires*, January 11, 1930, p.1.

48. *Les Nouvelles littéraires*, November 2, 1935, p.3.

49. *Les Œuvres Libres*, no. 56, February, 1926, pp.221–344. The novel was subsequently edited by Fayard in the "Collection de Bibliothèque" in 1930 and in the collection "Feuillets littéraires" in 1932.

50. *Le Malentendu*, Paris, Fayard, 1930, p.11.

51. Irène used her newly born daughter's name here: "I would love to show you my daughter whom you don't know. She is fourteen months old and is called Denise-France—Catherine or Minouche in private." Letter to Madeleine, January 7, 1931.

52. *Le Malentendu*, p.148.

53. *Le Malentendu*, p.108.

54. *Le Malentendu*, p.137.

55. *Gringoire*, April 11, 1930, p.4.

56. *Les Nouvelles littéraires*, January 11, 1930, p.1.

57. *Les Œuvres Libres*, No. 70, April, 1927, pp.331–375.

58. The novella was retitled *Un Enfant prodige*. Gallimard, 1992.

59. *L'Ennemie*, in *Les Œuvres Libres*, No. 85, July 1928, pp.279–379.

60. *L'Ennemie*, p.281

61. *L'Ennemie*, p.283.

62. In spite of her discretion, Irène's correspondence with Madeleine and later

with a friend of her mother's shows rather pronounced personality conflicts with her mother. Their strained relations were confirmed on several occasions by Denise Epstein in interviews with the author.

63. *L'Ennemie*, p.283.

64. *L'Ennemie*, p.307.

65. This is the scene in which the mother's nightdress, still imbued with the odors of a night of lovemaking, is found by the daughter. This scene is found in *L'Ennemie*, p.286, and in *Le Vin de solitude*, p.59.

Notes to Chapter 3

1. Jean Bothorel, *Bernard Grasset, Vie et passions d'un éditeur*, Paris, Grasset, 1989, p.214.

2. Henry Muller, *Trois pas en arrière*, Paris, La Table Ronde, 1952, p.53.

3. *Les Nouvelles littéraires*, January 11, 1930, p.1.

4. Muller, p.53.

5. In his biography of Bernard Grasset, Jean Botherel says that the manuscript was signed "Monsieur Epstein"; Henry Muller maintains that the manuscript carried the name Epstein without either Monsieur or Madame; Françoise Xenakis wrote in *Le Matin* in 1986 that the full name Irène Némirovsky was written on it.

6. Marcel Thiébault, *La Revue de Paris*, February 1930, p.953.

7. "But all readers will be enthralled by a work that very few will believe written by a young woman of 23 years." *Les Nouvelles littéraires*, January 11, 1930, p.1.

8. Bernard Grasset, in *Les Nouvelles littéraires*, December 7, 1929, p.5.

9. André Thérive, *"David Golder* d'Irène Némirovsky." *Le Temps*, January 10, 1930, p.3.

10. See *Les Nouvelles littéraires*, February 8, 1930, p.7.

11. Marcel Prévost, "Reprise," *Gringoire*, March 2, 1930, p.4. We should note that Marcel Prévost was the cousin of Horace de Carbuccia, the publisher who founded *Gringoire* in 1928 and who, as we shall see, played an important role in the career of Irène Némirovsky.

12. D. Decourdemanche in *La Nouvelle Revue Française*, no.197, February 1930.

13. *La Revue de Paris*, February 1930, p.953.

14. *Les Nouvelles littéraires*, January 11, 1930, p.1.

15. *Les Nouvelles littéraires*, January 11, 1930, p.1.

16. See André Thérive, *Le Temps*, January 10, 1930, p.3.

17. Robert Bourget-Pailleron, "La Nouvelle équipe," *La Revue des Deux Mondes*, November 1, 1936, p.94.

18. André Thérive, *Le Temps*, January 10, 1930, p.3.

19. See *Les Nouvelles littéraires*, January 11, 1930, p.1.

20. *Les Nouvelles littéraires*, January 11, 1930, p.1.

21. Gabriel Boissy, "David Golder," *Comœdia*, December 28, 1930, p.1.

22. G. de Pawlowski, "David Golder," *Gringoire*, January 31, 1930, p.3.

23. *Les Nouvelles littéraires*, January 11, 1930, p.1.

24. *Les Nouvelles littéraires*, January 11, 1930, p.1.

25. Nina Gourfinkel, "L'Expérience juive d'Irène Némirovsky," *L'Univers israélite*, February 28, 1930, p.677.

26. *L'Univers israélite*, February 28, 1930, p.678.

27. *Comœdia*, May 23, 1930.

28. Which did not stop the Gestapo from taking Harry Baur for a Jew during the German occupation: The Gestapo arrested him, but then released him after he proved his "Aryan" origins. See André Kaspi, *Les Juifs pendant l'occupation*, Paris, Le Seuil, 1997, p.71.

29. Jean Robin in *Cinémonde*, December 25, 1930, p.933.

30. J. G. Auriol, "David Golder," *La Revue du cinéma*, March 1, 1931. None of the critics could identify the music at the end of the film as a Hebrew chant.

31. *La Cinématographie française*, no.730.

32. For example, *L'Éternel mari*, adapted from Dostoevsky in 1924 and *L'Idiot* from the same author in 1929.

33. *Comœdia*, December 23, 1930.

34. Paul Gregorio, *Comœdia*, December 27, 1930, p.2.

35. Georges Champeaux, *Gringoire*, March 13, 1930, p.9.

36. Gabriel Boissy, *Comœdia*, December 28, 1930, p.9.

37. Letter of December 9, 1930 quoted in *La Cinématographie française*, no.632.

38. *Comœdia*, December 18, 1930.

39. See Claude Gaugeur, "Harry Baur/Sacha Guitry ou la croisée des chemins,"*Cinéma*, no. 305, 1984.

40. *David Golder*, trans. Sylvia Stuart, New York, Horace Livelight, 1930, p.58.

41. *Les Nouvelles littéraires*, January 11, 1930, p.1.

42. *David Golder*, p.51.

43. *David Golder*, p.165.

44. *David Golder*, p.183.

45. *David Golder*, p.223.

46. *David Golder*, p.229.

47. *David Golder*, p.239.

48. *David Golder*, p.240.

49. See for example, *Les Chiens et les loups*, p.93: "We are a greedy race, hungry for so long that reality no longer nourishes us. We require the impossible."

50. *Comœdia*, December 28, 1930, p.1.

51. G. de Pawlowsky, "David Golder," *Gringoire*, January 31, 1930, p.3.

52. *Toute l'édition*, February 23, 1935, p.5.

53. "Mr. Léon Blum is actually more accurately called Karfunkelstein. He is a man with the name *stein* and he comes from Bulgaria." *Gringoire*, April 1, 1938, p.1.

54. *Toute l'édition*, April 8, 1939, p.2.

55. *Gringoire*, March 4, 1938, p.4. In his repeated attacks on Léon Blum, Maxence made much of the anti-Semitic myth of the sexually perverted Jew. See Pierre Birnbaum, p.213.

56. Horace de Carbuccia, *Le Massacre de la Victoire*, Paris, Plon, 1973, p.416.

57. *Candide*, April 7, 1938, quoted by Birnbaum, p.139.

58. *Gringoire*, November 5, 1937, quoted by Birnbaum, p.143. One can read with

interest Birnbaum's analysis of the anti-Semitism of the extreme right-wing, in particular the last part of his book, "L'Héritage de Drumont: l'argent, la perversion et le nomadisme des juifs."

59. *David Golder*, p.223.

60. *L'Univers israélite*, July 5, 1935, p.670.

61. *L'Univers israélite*, July 5, 1935, p.670.

62. *Les Nouvelles littéraires*, June 4, 1939.

63. "Livres de femmes," *Minerva*, July 17, 1930.

64. *Minerva*, July 17, 1930.

65. *Le Bal*, Paris, Grasset, 1930, p.45.

66. *Le Bal*, p.46.

67. *Le Bal*, p.136.

68. *Le Journal de Genève*, August 31, 1930.

69. Paul Reboux, in *Paris-Soir*, August 13, 1930.

70. *Comœdia*, October 1, 1931.

71. *Le Populaire*, November 9, 1930.

72. J. Ernest-Charles, *Le Quotidien*, November 9, 1930.

73. *Le Petit Provençal*, September 16, 1930.

74. *Le Bal*, p.16.

75. *Le Bal*, p.129.

76. *Le Petit Provençal*, September 16, 1930.

77. Marcel Augagneur in *Gringoire*, October 21, 1930, p.4.

78. Long considered lost, the film surfaced in Moscow and now can be found in the Cinémathèque in Toulouse.

79. *Ciné-Miroir*, No. 346, November 20, 1931, p.748. For the actress who played the role of the mother, "Thiele's film will be much gayer than the novel which served as its inspiration. You would not want the author of *Le Chemin du Paradis* to create a sad film, would you?" See "Ce qu'on prépare" in *Cinémonde*, no.315, April 17, 1931, p.254.

80. *Pour vous*, September, 17, 1931, p.8.

81. *Cinémonde*, no.153, September, 1931, p.612.

82. Produced by Wilhelm Thiele, this version used German actors (Lucie Mannheim in the role of Antoinette).

83. Documents on file with the Société des Gens de Lettres de France.

Notes to Chapter 4

1. Virginia Clément, "Relire Irène Némirovsky," *Arts*, November 11, 1952.

2. Irène modestly stated in 1930 (*Les Nouvelles littéraires*, January 11, 1930): "I am not a woman of letters." She also added: "after *David Golder* I would perhaps wait a few years before starting any thing else." These words were obviously belied by her career.

3. See Pierre Abraham and Roland Desné, *Histoire Littéraire de la France*, Paris, Éditions Sociales, 1979, vol.II (1913–1939), p.123.

4. See Benoît Lecoq, "Les Revues," Roger Chartier and Henri-Jean Martin, *Histoire de l'Édition française*, vol. IV, p.353.

5. Quoted by Abraham and Desné, *Histoire littéraire de la France*, pp.124–125.

6. See Alain Vaillant, "L'Ecrivain, la réussite et l'argent," *Histoire de l'édition française*, Paris, Fayard, 1991, Volume 4, p.559. Georges Bernanos, for example obtained almost the double of what his editor (Plon) offered by serializing *La Nouvelle histoire de Mouchette* in *Gringoire*.

7. Having married under the rule of separation of property, Irène had a right to "the free disposition of her revenues" according to her marriage contract.

8. The publishers'magazine *Toute l'édition* regularly asked their writers where they had spent their vacations ; Irène would normally respond Urrugne or Hendaye (see for example *Toute l'édition*, September 7, 1935, p.2.: "I'm true to my friendships, and this year I'm spending my vacation in the Basque country at Urrugne, a few kilometers from the Spanish border not far from the sea.") Other facts regarding Irène's living arrangements and day to day activities come from a transcribed conversation between Cécile Michaud, the nanny employed by the Epstein family, and Denise Epstein.

9. Letter from Michel Epstein to his accountant dated February 21, 1939, property of Denise Epstein.

10. Irène's husband Michel seems to have kept out of her business affairs except when he supported her during the war, typing her manuscripts, and backing her up when she had to ask her publishers for money.

11. On July 28, 1931, Irène signed a contract with the Société Générale du Cinéma, ceding to this organization "the exclusive rights to adapt . . . for the screen . . . a script entitled 'La Symphonie de Paris.'"

12. Jean Bothorel, *Bernard Grasset, Vie et passions d'un éditeur*, Paris, Grasset, 1989, pp.226–297.

13. Letter from J. Vincent to Michel Epstein on November 16, 1934, property of Denise Epstein.

14. Letters from Michel Epstein to Maître Haquin and Maître Maréchal, November 6, 1934.

15. See Emmanuel Haymann, *Albin Michel, le roman d'un éditeur*, p.214.

16. In a letter dated November 15, 1933, Irène asked Albin Michel for permission (which was given) to submit short stories to Carbuccia "whose newspaper has always been extremely accommodating to me."

17. Letter of October 30, 1933.

18. Letter of November 13, 1933.

19. Letter of November 15, 1933.

20. Letter from Irène to Albin Michel on October 27, 1933.

21. Interview with Cécile Michaud.

22. See *Toute l'édition*, March 5, 1938, p.2.

23. Interview with Jeanine Bouissounouse, *Les Nouvelles littéraires*, November 2, 1935, p.3.

24. Letter from Irène to Albin Michel, December 30, 1934.

25. Letter from Albin Michel to Irène, January 6, 1936.

26. Letter from Albin Michel to Irène, January 12, 1936.

27. For example, in an October 19, 1935 letter to her editor, Albin Michel, she suggested that they do with *Le Vin de solitude* the same thing they had done with *Films*

Parlés, that is to send autographed copies to a number of bookstores.

28. "The Popular Front government had predicted (among other things!) that if the bourgeoisie no longer bought books, the latter would find numerous enthusiasts among the working classes, and we would thus be compensated for the loss, but these predictions are far from coming to pass!" Letter from Albin Michel to Irène, January 12, 1936.

29. Letters from Albin Michel to Irène, January 12, 1936, and January 20, 1938.

30. *Toute l'édition*, May 25, 1935, p.4.

31. *Toute l'édition*, December 1, 1939, p.15.

32. Interview with Cécile Michaud.

33. Pierre Milza, "L'Ultra Droite des années trente." Michel Winock, ed., *Histoire de l'extrème droite en France*, Paris, Éditions du Seuil, 1994, p.168.

34. For Colonel de la Roque, immigration had to be tied to "the strict needs of production." *Le Flambeau*, October 1, 1933, quoted by Milza, p.167.

35. Dominique Borne and Henri Dubief, *La Crise des années 30*, Paris, Éditions du Seuil, 1989, p.254.

36. Letter from Irène to Chardonne, December 21, 1932.

37. Jacques Chardonne, *L'Amour du prochain*, Paris, Grasset, 1932, p.20.

38. Chardonne, *L'Amour du prochain*, pp.238, 202.

39. Jacques Chardonne, *Chronique privée de l'an 1940*, Paris, Stock, 1940, p.120.

40. Jacques Chardonne, *Le Ciel de Nieflheim*, quoted by François Duffay, *Le Voyage d'automne*, Paris, Plon, 2000, p.182.

41. These would have been "Film parlé," which appeared in 1931, and "La Comédie bourgeoise," which appeared in 1932. Both would be picked by Morand for *Films parlés*.

42. In 1922 Morand had written "La Nuit nordique," a brief account of a romantic escapade in Finland, featuring a character with the same first name (Aïno) and the same personality as the chief figure of a short story by Irène entitled "Les Fumées de vin" that he had chosen for *Films parlés*.

43. Paul Morand, *France la doulce*, Paris, Gallimard, 1934, p.10.

44. *France la doulce*, p.58.

45. *France la doulce*, p.48.

46. *France la doulce*, p.22.

47. *France la doulce*, p.11.

48. *France la doulce*, p.218. In Germany the book appeared in 1936 with the title *Le Camp de concentration du Bon Dieu*.

49. Ginette Guitard-Auviste, *Paul Morand 1888–1976, légende et vérités*, Paris, Balland, 1994, p.219.

50. These notes from Irène's small notebook are undated, but were probably written in 1938 for they follow closely on a commentary dated December, 1937. Note that Trotsky lived in exile in France from 1933 to 1935.

51. *Toute l'Édition*, November 29, 1935, p.4.

52. Jeanine Delpech in *Les Nouvelles littéraires*, June 4, 1938.

53. René Lalou in *Les Nouvelles littéraires*, April 8, 1939.

54. A law was enacted in November 1938 whose objectives were to reinforce

government control of aliens, modifying the decree of August 10, 1927 on French nationality. For example, newly naturalized citizens could vote only after a waiting period of five years, aliens could be expelled more easily, and newly acquired French nationality could be forfeited.

55. *Je suis partout*, April 15, 1938.

56. *Les Pavés de Paris*, November 4, 1938. See Marrus and Paxton, p.45.

57. Copy of a letter from André Chaumeix to Monsieur le Garde des Sceaux, dated November 30, 1938.

58. Letter from Jean Vignaud, dated September 1, 1939.

Notes to Chapter 5

1. Jean-Pierre Maxence in *Gringoire*, June 10, 1938, p.6.

2. Oscar Wilde, *The Picture of Dorian Gray*, London: Penguin Books, 1985, p.44.

3. Radio interview with Marie-Jeanne Viel, no date.

4. For Jean Zyromski, see Pascal Ory, *La France allemande*, Paris, Éditions du Seuil, p.203. *Silbermann* was published by Jacques de Lacretelle in 1922.

5. *Gringoire*, March 8, 1935, p.4.

6. *Gringoire*, March 22, 1935.

7. *Les Nouvelles littéraires*, March 9, 1935.

8. *Le Figaro*, March 19, 1935, p.6.

9. *Dimanche et autres nouvelles*, Paris, Stock, 2000.

10. The Kra edition was illustrated by André Petroff and had the title *Les Mouches d'automne ou la femme d'autrefois*. The Grasset edition, without illustrations, came out on February 27, 1932 but has the copyright date of 1931.

11. *Les Mouches d'automne*, Paris, Grasset, 1931, pp.148–149.

12. Maurice Bazy in *Les Nouvelles littéraires*, February 27, 1932.

13. *Gringoire*, May 13, 1932.

14. Letter from Michel to André Sabatier, August 9, 1942.

15. *L'Affaire Courilof*, Paris, Grasset, 1933, p.21.

16. *L'Affaire Courilof*, p.125.

17. *L'Affaire Courilof*, p.152

18. *L'Affaire Courilof*, p.249.

19. *L'Affaire Courilof*, p.252.

20. *Les Nouvelles littéraires*, November 2, 1935.

21. Radio interview with Marie-Jeanne Viel, which is undated, but can be situated in 1934 or 1935 owing to a reference to *Le Pion sur l'échiquier*.

22. Reader's report by Robert de la Vaissière sent to Albin Michel.

23. Radio interview with Marie-Jeanne Viel.

24. For example "Ida" in *Films parlés*; Ginette in "Les Rivages heureux," *Gringoire*, November 2, 1934, pp.9,10.

25. For example, the mother in "Jour d'été," *La Revue des deux mondes*, April 1, 1935, vol. 26, pp.618–634; Alice in "Épilogue," *Gringoire*, May 28, 1937, p.12.

26. "Confidence" in *La Revue des deux mondes*, vol. 47, October 15, 1938, pp.886–904.

27. Quoted by Pierre Langers, *Toute l'édition*, July 4, 1936, p.4.

28. *Jézabel*, Paris, Albin Michel, 1935, p.54.

29. *La Proie*, Paris, Albin Michel, 1938, p.91.

30. René Lalou *"Le Pion sur l'échiquier ou les vertiges de la solitude."* *Noir et blanc*, June 7, 1934.

31. Pierre Loewel in *L'Ordre*, June 18, 1934, p.2.

32. Henri de Régnier, "La Vie littéraire." *Le Figaro*, May 23, 1936, p.6.

33. Quoted by Pierre Langers, *Toute l'édition*, July 4, 1936, p.4.

34. *Films parlés*, pp.149, 150.

35. *La Proie*, p.217.

36. *La Proie*, p.247.

37. *La Proie*, p.282.

38. Henri de Régnier, "La Vie littéraire." *Le Figaro*, November 2, 1935, p.7.

39. See Élisabeth Gille, *Le Mirador*, Paris, Presses de la Renaissance, 1992, mainly pp.166–170; see also statements made by Denise Epstein in the article by Jean-Claude Daven, "Souvenez-vous d'Irène Némirovsky," *La Tribune de Lausanne*, April 14, 1957. These sentiments were reiterated in several interviews of the author with Irène Némirovsky's two daughters between 1996 and 1998.

40. *Le Vin de solitude*, p.13.

41. *Le Vin de solitude*, p.81.

42. *Le vin de solitude*, p.83.

43. *Le Vin de solitude*, p.85.

44. *Le Vin de solitude*, p.27.

45. *Le Vin de solitude*, p.110.

46. *Le Vin de solitude*, p.112.

47. *Le Vin de solitude*, p.118.

48. *Le Vin de solitude*, p.226.

49. *Le Vin de solitude*, pp.286–287.

50. *Le Vin de solitude*, pp.310–311.

51. *La Petite République*, June 9, 1898, article quoted by Michel Winock, *Nationalisme, antisémitisme et fascisme en France*, Paris, Éditions du Seuil, p.202.

52. *La France juive*, t.1, p.9. Quoted by Winock, p.129.

53. Georges Mauco, *Les Étrangers en France: leur rôle dans l'activité économique*, Paris, 1932, p.134.

54. Jean-Pierre Maxence, *Gringoire*, October 25, 1935, p.4. The chronicler in *La Revue des Deux Mondes* (October 15, 1935) speaks of "businessmen who have come from the Orient."

55. *Vient de paraître*, October 12, 1935, p.7.

56. René Lalou, *Les Nouvelles littéraires*, April 8, 1939.

57. *Deux*, Paris, Albin Michel, 1939, p.16.

58. These figures were provided by Albin Michel. We should add that *Les Chiens et les loups*, published in 1940 after the defeat of the French, sold 17,016 copies.

59. "Un déjeuner un septembre," *La Revue de Paris*, May 1933, pp.38–55.

60. "Un Jour d'été," *La Revue des Deux Mondes*, April 1, 1935, vol.26, pp.618–634.

61. "Les Liens du sang." *La Revue des Deux Mondes*, Vol.32, March 15, 1936, pp.415–433 (part one); vol.32, April 2, 1936, pp.604–627 (part two).

62. Note included in *Deux* by the editor, Albin Michel.

63. "I wanted above all to bring to life a man and a woman I knew," note included in *Deux* by Albin Michel.

64. *Deux*, p.173.

65. *Deux*, p.202.

66. *Deux*, p.214.

67. "One should tell young girls that love and marriage are two different things that do not go together. They would choose first . . . they would love first and marry afterwards." Léon Blum, *Du Mariage*, Paris, Albin Michel, 1937, p.41.

68. Marius Richard in *Toute l'édition*, April 22, 1939, p.8.

69. See Jean-Pierre Maxence in *Gringoire*, March 23, 1939, p.6.

70. Tape provided by the Institut National de l'Audiovisuel, catalogue number INA 2787.

Notes to Chapter 6

1. Baptismal certificate signed by P. A. Schiano of the archdiocese of Paris.

2. Vladimir Ghika, a descendent of Romanian royalty, was born in 1873 and came to France at the age of five. He converted to Roman Catholicism and was ordained a priest in 1923 in Paris, where his brother was the Romanian ambassador. In 1927, he moved to Villejuif, a working-class suburb, where he lived in an unheated shack and devoted his life to helping the poor. In 1931 Ghika was named a protonotary apostolic by the Pope and assumed the title Monsignor. He returned to Romania in 1940, where he opposed the pro-Nazi regime of Antonescu and, after the war, the Communist regime of Ceaucescu. He was imprisoned by the Communists in 1952, and died in 1954. Irène received at least two letters from Ghika after her conversion. The first of these was postmarked Bucharest in March 1942, and the second letter, which Michel received after Irène's deportation, was postmarked September 1942. For more on Ghika, see James Likoudis, "Monseigneur Ghika, 'Prince and Martyr,'" *Lay Witness*, January-February 1996.

3. These details do not appear in the baptism certificate issued by the Catholic Archdiocese of Paris, but are confirmed in a letter from Monsignor Ghika to Irène in March 1942, as well as a letter from a friend of Father Bréchard dated July 24, 1941.

4. "I remember that I said to her 'But what caused you to change religions like that?'—'One never knows what the future will bring.'"

5. It should be noted that the French law of June 2, 1941, with regard to the status of Jews, made provision for non-Jewish status for any person who would have converted to another religion recognized by the state before June 25, 1940. This provision, however, only applied to individuals for whom at least three grandparents were not "of the Jewish race." But, as shall be seen, Irène would never try to gain advantage from her adherence to the Catholic faith to avoid the restrictive measures leveled against Jews.

6. Letter of Marie Sautanet to Irène dated July 24, 1941, personal collection of Denise Epstein.

7. The title refers to the ports of the Ottoman Empire in which European countries, including France, installed agencies from the sixteenth to the nineteenth centuries. The text, such as it appeared in *Gringoire*, was later transcribed by Denise Epstein, and was finally published by Denoël in 2005 under the title *Le Maître des âmes* (The Master of Souls).

8. *France la doulce*, p.10.

9. *Les Échelles du Levant*, chapter 1. All quotes are taken from the transcribed edition.

10. *Les Échelles du Levant*, chapter 10.

11. *Les Échelles du Levant*, chapter 27.

12. *Les Échelles du Levant*, chapter 3.

13. *Les Échelles du Levant*, chapter 1.

14. *Les Échelles du Levant*, chapter 18.

15. *Les Échelled du Levant*, chapter 9.

16. *Les Échelles du Levant*, chapter 11.

17. *Les Échelles du Levant*, chapter 28.

18. *Les Échelles du Levant*, chapter 26.

19. *Les Échelles du Levant*, chapter 24.

20. *Les Échelles du Levant*, chapter 10.

21. *Les Échelles du Levant*, chapter 34.

22. *Les Échelles du Levant*, chapter 28.

23. "Le Spectateur," *Gringoire*, December 7, 1939, p.8.

24. "Monsieur Rose," *Candide*, August 28, 1940, p.4.

25. Letter of July 24, 1941.

26. The published version of *Suite française* does not contain this chapter and makes of Philippe Péricand a jaded priest who is assigned to supervise young boys.

27. The expression comes from a book published in 1938 by Count A. de Puységur, *Les maquereaux légitimes: du coursier des croisades au bidet de Rebecca.* See Pierre Birnbaum, pp.215–236.

28. "Fraternité," *Gringoire*, February 8, 1937, p.8.

29. Survey by Joseph von Maulle in *Toute l'édition*, September 3, 1938.

30. *Toute l'édition*, December 1, 1939, p.15.

31. Letter from Robert Esménard, September 13, 1940.

32. Remarks in Irène's writers notebook.

33. *Gringoire*, April 25, 1940, p.10.

34. *Les Chiens et les loups*, pp.222,223.

35. *Les Chiens et les loups*, p.181.

36. *Les Chiens et les loups*, p.224.

37. *Les Chiens et les loups*, pp.226–227.

38. *Les Chiens et les loups*, p.236.

39. *Les Chiens et les loups*, p.168.

40. *Les Chiens et les loups*, pp.112–113.

41. *Les Chiens et les loups*, p.106.

42. *Les Chiens et les loups*, p.127.

43. *Les Chiens et les loups*, p.128.

44. *Les Chiens et les loups,* pp.136–137.

45. *Les Chiens et les loups,* p.197.

46. *Les Chiens et les loups,* p.52.

47. The fictitious situation that Irène describes had its basis in reality. Foreigners were increasingly watched and thrown out of the country. In 1939, a number of them were brought to camps in cattle cars and then interned, a fact that made one German Jewish refugee write that "France, for whom most of us had formed a deep attachment . . . suddenly showed us a totally different face, a grimace we met with horror." Heinz Pol, quoted by Marrus and Paxton, p.66.

48. *Les Chiens et les loups,* p.165, our italics.

49. *Les Chiens et les loups,* p.143.

50. *Les Chiens et les loups,* p.151.

51. *Les Chiens et les loups,* p.152.

52. *Les Chiens et les loups,* pp.241–242.

53. *Les Chiens et les loups,* p.243. Irène uses the term "concentration camp" here for the first time. In fact in September 1939, 15,000 German and Austrian refugees, including many Jews, were interned in what the Interior Minister Sarraut called "concentration camps." See Marrus and Paxton, p.65.

54. *Les Chiens et les loups,* p.243.

55. *Les Chiens et les loups,* p.244.

56. *Les Chiens et les loups,* p.249.

57. Letter from Albin Michel, August 28, 1939.

Notes to Chapter 7

1. Letter written by Michel Epstein to his brother Paul on January 23, 1942, personal property of Denise Epstein. I am indebted to Jean Laudet of Issy-L'Évêque (now deceased) for information on the village.

2. Letter to Madeleine Cabour of December 22, 1940.

3. Letter of August 28, 1939.

4. See Henri Amouroux, *La Grande histoire des Français sous l'occupation,* Volume I, Paris: Laffont, 1997, p.95. In July 1939, before the signing of the German-Soviet pact, 45% of the Frenchmen interviewed in and IFOP survey believed there would be a war in 1939, and 76% approved France's entry into the war if Dantzig were to be taken by the Germans.

5. Quoted by Marrus and Paxton, p.64.

6. In a letter of October 12, 1938, Albin Michel had responded to a request by the Italian publisher Genio (who was considering having some of Irène's works translated into Italian) that Irène was "Jewish," but that he had no other information on her "origins."

7. Letter of August 28, 1939.

8. Amouroux, Volume I, p.121.

9. André Kaspi, *Les Juifs pendant l'occupation,* p.93.

10. Robert Debré, *L'Honneur de vivre,* quoted par Kaspi, p.95. Debré stayed in Paris despite these warnings from Chiappe.

11. Letter of July 12, 1940.

12. Letter of December 22, 1940.

13. On October 9 Michel wrote a letter supporting Auguste Barre's candidacy for the Prix Cognacq, established in 1920 to reward large families.

14. I owe a debt to Mademoiselle Marinette Lacombre of Issy-L'Évêque, who knew Irène Némirovsky and who was kind enough to recount her memories to me in May 1996.

15. Amouroux, Vol. 1, p.825.

16. Irène had most likely met René Doumic, director of the prestigious *Revue des Deux Mondes*, in 1935 when the review first published one of her short stories, titled "Jour d'été" (A Summer Day).

17. Letter of September 13, 1940.

18. *Journal officiel*, October 18, 1940, p.5324.

19. Letter of October 16, 1940.

20. "Denken oft und gerne an die schönen Stunden von Issy-L'Évêque zurück." Handwritten note in the personal collection of Denise Epstein.

21. "Kamaraden! Wir haben längere Zeit mit der Familie Epstein zusammengelebt und Sie als eine sehr anständige und zuvorkommende Familie kennengelernt. Wir bitten Euch daher, sie dementsprechend zu behandeln. Heil Hitler! Hammberger, Feldw. 23599A." Document quoted by Michel Epstein in a letter to Sabatier dated July 26, 1942.

22. See Marrus and Paxton, p.65.

23. This biography had been published in Moscow in 1934.

24. Letter to Madeleine Cabour of April 9, 1941.

25. Letter to Madeleine Cabour of March 27, 1941.

26. See Kaspi, pp.212–213.

27. See Gérard Loiseaux, *La Littérature de la défaite et de la collaboration*, Paris, Fayard, 1995, p.71.

28. Loiseaux, pp.72–73.

29. Pascal Fouché, *L'Édition française sous l'occupation*, Volume I, p.292.

30. Fouché, Volume 1, p.307.

31. Fouché, Volume 1, p.319.

32. Letter from Robert Esménard of October 27, 1941.

33. Fouché, Volume 1, p.31.

34. Letter of December 31, 1939.

35. Letter of December 13, 1940.

36. Letter to Mademoiselle Le Fur (Robert Esménard's secretary), August 9, 1940.

37. Letter of September 25, 1940.

38. Letter of September 17, 1940.

39. Letter of September 25, 1940.

40. See Haymann, p 228.

41. Letter of October 3, 1940.

42. Letter of Robert Esménard of March 7, 1941.

43. Letter of March 29, 1941.

44. Letter of May 10, 1941.

45. Letter of July 27, 1940.

46. Typed letter, undated.

47. Letter of July 27, 1940.

48. Letter of October 11, 1940.

49. Law of October 3, 1940, published in the *Journal official*, October 18, 1940, p.5323.

50. Letter of October 14, 1940.

51. Letter of October 17, 1940.

52. Letter of October 22, 1940.

53. The actual wording is as follows: "The access and exercise of liberal professions . . . are permitted to Jews unless rules for the civil service limits their number to a certain proportion."

54. Letter of Irène Némirovsky to Georges Robert dated October 24, 1940, on file at the Société des Gens de Lettres de France, Némirovsky file.

55. Letter from Georges Robert to Irène Némirovsky dated November 6, 1940.

56. Letter to Fernard Brouty, November 8, 1940.

57. Letter of October 13, 1940.

58. Letter to Jean Vignaud, November 16, 1940.

59. Letter from Jean Vignaud, December 2, 1940.

60. See Pascal Ory, *Les Collaborateurs 1940–1945*, p.74.

61. His attitude during the occupation earned him a condemnation of five years of hard labor after the war, but he was subsequently acquitted. Henri Béraud, his anti-Semitic columnist, was sentenced to death. See Pascal Fouché, *L'édition française sous l'occupation*, Vol. 2, p.256.

62. Undated letter to Horace de Carbuccia.

63. There is, for example, a payment receipt for 6000F from the Éditions de France, dated February 15, 1941 and sent to Irène at her Paris address.

64. Kaspi, p.110.

65. "L'Inconnu," *Gringoire*, August 8, 1941.

66. See Emmanuel Heymann, *Albin Michel, le roman d'un éditeur*, pp.236–240.

67. In a letter dated December 11, 1940, Sabatier refers to the end of a tour of duty in the "ports of the Levant," a term referring to the French Naval Division of the Levant, stationed in Beyrouth at the time of the defeat of 1940.

68. He stayed with Albin Michel until 1964; see Heymann, pp.213–214.

69. Letter dated December 13, 1940.

70. Letter dated December 16, 1940.

71. In a letter dated March 7, 1941.

72. In a letter to Sabatier dated May 17, 1942.

73. "Destinées," *Gringoire*, December 7, 1940, p.4.

74. "Destinées," *Gringoire*, December 7, 1940, p.4.

75. See Amouroux, Volume I, p.77.

76. *Les Feux de l'automne*, p.72.

77. *Les Feux de l'automne*, p.72.

78. *Les Feux de l'automne*, p.134.

79. *Les Feux de l'automne,* p.239.

80. *Les Feux de l'automne,* p.103.

81. Hence Monseigneur Gerlier said in 1940: "France has reaped the destructiveness of its own mistakes; it is forgotten or scorned its traditions of moral life and family values, and this has weakened the country." Quoted by Amouroux, Volume I, p.663.

82. *Les Biens de ce monde,* Paris, Albin Michel, 1947, p.28.

83. *Les Bien de ce monde,* p.253.

84. The manuscript for the second volume, titled *Dolce,* existed in a handwritten version. It was practically unreadable.

85. *Suite française* (trans. Sandra Smith, New York, Alfred A. Knopf, 2006), p.143.

86. *Suite française,* p.150.

87. *Suite française,* p.164.

88. This chapter does not appear in the published edition.

89. *Suite française,* pp.165–166.

90. For example, the shoemaker Lacombre is called "Lacombe" in the novel.

91. *Suite française,* p.265.

92. *La Vie de Tchékhov,* Albin Michel, 1946, p.137.

93. *La Vie de Tchékhov,* p.135.

94. *La Vie de Tchékhov,* p.160.

95. *La Vie de Tchékhov,* p.79.

96. Letter to Sabatier, December 21, 1941.

97. "La Jeunesse de Tchekhov," *Les Œuvres Libres,* May 1940, pp.5–48.

Notes to Chapter 8

1. Chapter 21 of *Dolce. Suite française,* pp.324–329.

2. "I am happy that you still think of my husband," wrote one of the wives to Michel. "To date I have always had good news of him. He is on the eastern front" (Es hat mich sehr gefreut, dass sie noch an meiner Mann denken . . . Bis heute habe ich von ihn noch gute Nachrichten. Er befindet sich augenblicklich im Ostern). Handwritten letter, dated August, 1941, personal collection of Denise Epstein.

3. See Kaspi, *Les Juifs pendant l'occupation,* pp.212–214.

4. The French citizenship of Irène's daughters is attested to in an official document of the subprefect of Autun, dated September 3, 1942, containing a list of all Jews registered in the Saône-et-Loire department. The list is made up of fourteen Jews of whom only three have French citizenship, while the others are "Algerian" (the Crémieux decree giving French nationality to Algerian Jews having been revoked).

5. For more on this sad subject see Marrus and Paxton, pp.263–270.

6. These details of the family's finances appear in Michel Epstein's tax returns (document in the personal collection of Denise Epstein).

7. Copy of a letter to Mademoiselle Julie Dumont, in care of Madame Loctin, personal collection of Denise Epstein.

8. Letter of June 23, 1941 to M. Bergeret, personal collection of Denise Epstein.

9. Quoted by Kaspi, p.106.

10. As is attested in her will of July 29, 1953, personal collection of Denise Epstein.

11. Letter from W. I. Pahlen Heyberg, August 6, 1941, personal collection of Denise Epstein; letter from Irène Némirovsky, August 9, 1941.

12. Letter to Madeleine Cabour, September 9, 1941.

13. Letter from Michel Epstein to the subprefect of Autun, September 2, 1941, personal collection of Denise Epstein.

14. Letter to André Sabatier, October 14, 1941.

15. Letter from Michel Epstein to Paul Epstein, January 23, 1942, personal collection of Denise Epstein.

16. In a letter written by Irène to her daughter, Denise, on May 21, 1942 (personal collection of Denise Epstein), Irène mentions receiving a mattress and an armchair that were in the Paris apartment.

17. Letter from Irène to Monsieur Bergeret on September 27, 1941, personal collection of Denise Epstein.

18. Letter from Robert Esménard, October 27, 1941.

19. Letter of October 30, 1941.

20. Letter of October 4, 1941.

21. Letter of October 10, 1941.

22. Letter to Sabatier, May 17, 1942.

23. These details are found in letters written by Irène to her daughter, Denise, in May, 1942. Personal collection of Denise Epstein.

24. Letter of October 30, 1941.

25. "I paid 3000F for 15 'moules' of wood . . . " wrote Irène to Julie Dumot on June 22, 1941. A moule is an old metric unit of measure. The exact equivalent varied among French countryside regions; 15 moules is about 25 steres.

26. Letter to Sabatier, November 20, 1941.

27. Letter from Horace de Carbuccia, March 17, 1942.

28. Jean-Jacques Bernard, *Le Camp de la mort lente*, Paris, Albin Michel, 1944, p.32.

29. Kaspi, p.217.

30. See Pierre Birnbaum, *Un mythe politique: la "République juive,"* p.173.

31. Letter from Joseph Caillaux, December 16, 1941. Personal collection of Denise Epstein. This note is the only evidence there is of a relationship between Caillaux and Irène.

32. "Ich bin in Russland geboren, aber nie war ich Sovietangehörige . . . Ich bin katolisch, meine Eltern waren aber Juden." This letter is in the personal collection of Denise Epstein.

33. "Mein neues buch wird bald veröffentlicht sein."

34. "Die Deutsche Behörde in Paris haben meinem Verlager erlaubt meine Bücher wieder herauszugeben."

35. Letter of December 11, 1941.

36. Letter of March 23, 1942.

37. Letter of May 4, 1942.

38. Benoit's participation in the committee of "friendship" between French and

German authors approved by the Reich would earn him a year in prison after the war; he was released, however, for lack of proof of his collaboration.

39. Heymann, p.240.

40. Letter from Esménard, March 7, 1941.

41. Letter from Michel to the tax collector of the 7th arrondissement of Paris, April 10, 1942, personal collection of Denise Epstein.

42. Ibid.

43. They were entitled to a 25% reduction "because of the absence of heat for the apartment" on a rent of 10,000F a year, as is attested in a letter from Lucien Pastoureau, attorney, to Michel on August 25, 1942, personal collection of Denise Epstein. Paris rents in 1942 were not high.

44. Letter from Michel to Paul Epstein, January 23, 1942, personal collection of Denise Epstein.

45. Letter from Denise to her mother, April 12, 1942, personal collection of Denise Epstein.

46. Letter to Sabatier, June 1, 1942.

47. See Henri Amoureux, *La Grande histoire des Français sous l'occupation*, Volume III, Paris, Laffont, 1998, pp.155–164.

48. This is based on the census of September 3, 1942; it can be possible, however, that other Jews existed who did not identify themselves as such.

49. Letter to Sabatier, May 17, 1942.

50. Letter, July 10, 1942, personal collection of Denise Epstein.

51. Letter, July 11, 1942. Our emphasis.

52. *Le Progrès de Côte d'Or*, nos.194 and 195 (Monday, July 13 and Tuesday, July 14, 1942), p.1.

53. Ibid., p.2.

Notes to Chapter 9

1. Telegram, July 13, 1942.

2. A document drawn up by François Jeaux, mayor of Issy-L'Évêque, on March 26, 1945, confirms these details: "NEMOROVSKY Irène Irma, woman of letters . . . was arrested and deported by the French police on the day of July 13, 1942."

3. These details were told to Denise Epstein in an undated letter from Madame Ravaud, retired school mistress from Issy-L'Évêque. Personal collection of Denise Epstein.

4. Letter from Michel Epstein to Sabatier, July 14, 1942.

5. The case of this bilingual author, who enjoyed an immense popularity with the English and American public prior to the First World War, is bizarre. Dimnet wrote to Michel on September 25, 1942, that he would contact Châteaubriant, but later he appeared totally ignorant of Irène's fate, for at the end of the war he wrote the following message to "Mme Némirovsky-Epstein" in care of Albin Michel: "During the occupation I went twenty times to your old address trying to get news of you. Recently I have three times telephoned Albin Michel. I am very concerned about you. This evening I am leaving for New York, address 2 East 17th Street, but I will be back in

November. My regards to M. Epstein. Faithfully yours, Ernest Dimnet." (Postcard dated June 17, 1945.)

6. See Kaspi, p.256, 257.

7. Camp regulations in Pithiviers, June 14, 1941.

8. Postcard, July 15, 1942.

9. See Amouroux, volume III. pp.189–196, and *Les Camps d'Internement du Loiret: histoire et mémoire*, Centre de Recherche et de Documentation sur les Camps et la Déportation Juive dans le Loiret, undated.

10. Note dated July 18, Sipo-SD of Orléans, Archives of the Centre de Documentation Juive Contemporaine.

11. Letter written in pencil, July 17, 1942.

12. The original list of convoy 6, July 17, 1942, is conserved at the Centre de Documentation Juive Contemporaine.

13. Letter quoted in *Les Camps d'internement: histoire et mémoire*, p.61.

14. File, "Convoy No.6, dated July 17, 1942." Centre de la Documentation Juive Contemporaine.

15. See Kaspi, p.221.

16. See Jeanne Gillot-Voisin, *La Saône-et-Loire sous Hitler*, Mâcon, Fédération des Œuvres Laïques, undated, p.211.

17. Letter from Michel to Sabatier on July 14, 1942.

18. Letter from Jean Giomarc'h to Michel, July 14, 1942.

19. See Ginette Guitard-Auviste, *Paul Morand 1888–1976, légende et vérités*, pp.220–221.

20. Letter from Sabatier, July 16, 1942.

21. Letter from Sabatier, July 15, 1942.

22. Letter from Michel to Sabatier, July 20, 1942.

23. Letter from Sabatier, July 24, 1942.

24. Letter from Michel, July 26, 1942.

25. See Kaspi on this subject, pp.278–283.

26. "My wife has been suffering for many years with a deep chronic asthma; her doctor, Professor Valéry Radot, could attest to this, and an internment in a concentration camp would be fatal," wrote Michel in his letter to Otto Abetz, which we cite *in extenso* further on.

27. Letter, July 28, 1942.

28. Letter from Sabatier to Michel, August 12, 1942.

29. In a sense Michel is right since Irène's name is only on the third "Liste Otto," which appeared in May 1943; however, the second "Liste Otto" did prohibit the circulation of any book written by a Jewish author.

30. Letter of July 27, 1942.

31. Letters of July 28 and 29, 1942.

32. According to documents at the Service International de Recherches de la Croix Rouge, July 23, 1997.

33. Handwritten letter, July 29, 1942.

34. Letter of August 9, 1942.

35. Letter from Sabatier to Michel, August 12, 1942.

36. On the creation of the UGIF see Maurice Moch, "La Tentative de créer un *Judenrat* en France" in *Les Juifs en France dans la seconde guerre mondiale*, Paris, Éditions du Cerf, 1992, pp.39–67; on the activities of the UGIF, see Kaspi, pp.323–352.

37. Letter from André Sabatier, August 12, 1942.

38. Kaspi, p.282. Kaspi reminds us furthermore that in August 1942, the delegate to the Jewish World Congress had warned the British and American governments that extermination of Jews had begun, but this information "was not getting through or getting through very little."

39. The only biographer of Paul Morand to speak of Hélène Morand and her attempts to free Irène is Ginette Guitard-Auviste (*Paul Morand 1888–1976, légende et vérités*). What she says sheds no light on the situation ("[Hélène Morand] will use the influence she has with the occupiers and her ties with Mme Otto Abetz . . . on behalf of numerous Jews. Jean Yonnel, of the Comédie-française will be grateful to her for this; others such as Irène Némirovsky, author of *David Golder*, who died in deportation, were not lucky enough to have her interventions prove useful"). Yonnel, of Romanian extraction, was able to obtain a "certificate of notoriety," which allowed him to keep his position with the Comédie Française (see Ragache and Ragache, p.188).

40. Letter to Maître Pastoureau on August 23, 1942, personal collection of Denise Epstein.

41. Letter from Lucien Pastoureau, August 25, 1942, personal collection of Denise Epstein.

42. Irène's daughter Denise affirmed, in an interview with the author in May 1996, having seen candlesticks belonging to her mother with the concierge of the apartment building after the war.

43. These details appear in an inventory of Jewish property in the Saône-et-Loire ordered by the General Commissioner for Jewish Affairs, August 27, 1942. Original documents (microfilm UGIF no.8) in the archives of the Centre de Documentation Juive Contemporaine.

44. Letter from Michel Epstein, September 15, 1942.

45. Letter from Michel Epstein, September 19, 1942.

46. Letter from André Sabatier, September 23, 1942.

47. Handwritten note card from Michel, September 26, 1942.

48. Letter from Michel to Sabatier, September 29, 1942.

49. Letter from André Sabatier, October 5, 1942.

50. Letter from Michel Epstein, October 8, 1942.

51. Letter from André Sabatier to Michel, October 12, 1942.

52. Statistics quoted by Kaspi, p.283, according to Serge Klarsfeld, *Le Mémorial de la déportation des Juifs de France*.

53. Denise Epstein confirms that they were taken by the French police to a German officer who, finding that Denise resembled his own daughter, let them go.

54. Denise was paid until 1950 when she became 21, and Élisabeth until January 1958 when she too reached the age of 21.

55. Paris, Éditions du Seuil, 1996.

Notes to Conclusion

1. A good first attempt at such analysis appears in an MA thesis by Jeanne Lafon entitled "Irène Némirovsky: un judaïsme ambigu" ("An ambiguous Judaism"), Université de Paris III, 1996.

2. A critical article that touches on anti-Semitism in David Golder—but does not go further than that novel—was written by Alan Astro, "Two Best-Selling French Jewish Women's Novels from 1929," *Symposium*, Winter 1999, pp.241–254.

3. Myriam Anissimov, "Irène Némirovsky, romancière rebelle" ("Rebel novelist"), *Le Matin*, December 24, 1985, p.20.

4. Paul Renard, "Irène Némirovsky, une romancière face à la tragédie" ("A Novelist Faced with Tragedy"), *La Revue littéraire: Roman 20/50*, No. 16, December, 1993, p.169. We have, incidentally, found no evidence that Irène ever knew Brasillach.

5. *Jewish Self-Hatred*, Baltimore, Johns Hopkins University Press, 1986.

6. See Gilman, p.308.

7. *Les Chiens et les loups*, p.248; our emphasis.

8. Jean-Jacques Bernard resisted the efforts of other foreign Jewish prisoners to make him feel his Judaism. "How could we appropriate what had no meaning for us for generations? They could not tear France from us." *Le Camp de la mort lente*, p.71.

9. "Les Conrad français," *Les Nouvelles littéraires*, March 30, 1940.

Bibliography
of Irène Némirovsky's Works

I. Published Works

Novels

Le Malentendu, Paris, Arthème Fayard, 1926, coll. *Les Œuvres Libres*, No. 56, February 1926, p.221–344. Republished by Arthème Fayard, 1930.

L'Enfant génial, Paris, Arthème Fayard, 1927, coll. *Les Œuvres Libres*, No. 70, December 1927, pp.331–375. Republished under the title *Un Enfant prodige* by Gallimard, 1992.

L'Ennemie, Paris, Arthème Fayard, 1928, coll. *Les Œuvres Libres*, No. 85, July 1928.

David Golder, Paris, Grasset, 1929. Many republished editions, the most recent in 1985 by Grasset.

Le Bal, Paris, Grasset, 1930. Republished by Grasset, 1985.

Les Mouches d'automne, Paris, Grasset, 1931. Republished by Grasset, 1988.

L'Affaire Courilof, Paris, Grasset, 1933. Republished by Grasset, 1990.

Le Pion sur l'échiquier, Paris, Albin Michel, 1934.

Le Vin de solitude, Paris, Albin Michel, 1935. Republished by Albin Michel, 1988.

Jézabel, Paris, Albin Michel, 1936. Republished by Éditions J'ai lu, 1969.

La Proie, Paris, Albin Michel, 1938. Republished by Albin Michel, 1992.

Deux, Paris, Albin Michel, 1939.

Les Chiens et les loups, Paris, Albin Michel, 1940. Republished by Albin Michel, 1988.

Les Biens de ce monde, Paris, Albin Michel, 1947.

Les Feux de l'automne, Paris, Albin Michel, 1957.

Suite française, Paris, Denoël, 2004.

Le Maître des âmes, Paris, Denoël, 2005.

Novels (English Translation)

David Golder, translated by Sylvia Stuart. New York, Horace Liveright, 1930.

A Modern Jezebel, translated by Barre Dunbar. New York, H. Holt, 1937.

Suite Française, translated by Sandra Smith. New York, Alfred A. Knopf, 2006.

Biographies

La Vie de Tchekhov, Paris, Albin Michel, 1946. Republished by Albin Michel in 1989. Translated into English as *A Life of Chekhov*, London, Grey Walls Press, 1950.

"La Jeunesse de Tchekhov," in *Les Œuvres Libres*, no. 226, May 1940, pp.5–48.

Short Stories

Films parlés, Paris, Gallimard, 1934, coll. La Renaissance de la Nouvelle.

"Un Déjeuner en septembre," *La Revue de Paris*, vol. 3, May 1, 1933.

"Nativité," *Gringoire*, December 8, 1933

"Dimanche," *La Revue de Paris*, vol. 3, June 1, 1934.

"Écho," *Noir et Blanc*, no. 24, July 22, 1934.

"Les Rivages heureux," *Gringoire*, November 2, 1934.

"Jour d'été," *La Revue des Deux Mondes*, vol 26, April 1, 1935.

"Le Commencement et la fin," *Gringoire*, December 20, 1935.

"Les Liens du sang," *La Revue des Deux Mondes*, vol. 32, March 15, 1936.

"Fraternité," *Gringoire*, le February 5, 1937.

"Épilogue," *Gringoire*, May 28, 1937.

"Espoirs," *Gringoire*, August 19, 1938.

"La Confidence," *La Revue des Deux Mondes*, vol. 47, October 15, 1938.

"La Femme de Don Juan," *Candide*, no. 764, November 2, 1938.

"La Nuit en wagon," *Gringoire*, October 5, 1939.

"Comme de grands enfants," *Marie-Claire*, October 27, 1939.

"Le Spectateur," *Gringoire*, December 7, 1939.

"Aïno," *La Revue des Deux Mondes*, vol. 55, January 1, 1940.

"Le Sortilège," *Gringoire*, February 1, 1940.

"Et je l'aime encore," *Marie-Claire*, February 2, 1940.

"Le Départ pour la fête," *Gringoire*, April 11, 1940.

"Monsieur Rose," *Candide*, August 28, 1940.

"Destinées," *Gringoire*, December 5, 1940, pseudonym Pierre Nerey.

"La Confidente," *Gringoire*, March 20, 1941, pseudonym Pierre Neyret.

"L'Honnête homme," *Gringoire*, May 30, 1941, pseudonym Pierre Nérey.

"L'Inconnu," *Gringoire*, August 8, 1941, "Nouvelle écrite par une jeune femme."

"Les Revenants," *Gringoire*, September 5, 1941, pseudonym Pierre Nérey.

"L'Ogresse," *Gringoire*, October 24, 1941, pseudonym Charles Blancat.

"L'Incendie," *Gringoire*, February 27, 1942, pseudonym Pierre Nerey.

"Les Vierges," *Présent*, July 15, 1942, pseudonym Denise Méraude.

II. Unpublished Works

Novels

Les Échelles du Levant, novel serialized in *Gringoire* beginning 18 May 1940.
Chaleur de sang, unfinished novel.

Short Stories

"La Voleuse"
"La Grande allée"
"L'Ami et la femme"
"Un Beau Mariage"

Works about Irène Némirovsky

Gille, Elisabeth. *Le Mirador.* Paris: Presses de la Renaissance, 1992.